Human Rights Violations

MAGILL'S CHOICE

Human Rights Violations

Volume 2

1961-1979

edited by

Charles F. Bahmueller
Center for Civic Education

Salem Press, Inc.
Pasadena, California   Hackensack, New Jersey

Essays originally appeared in *Great Events from History II: Human
Rights* (1992). New material has been added.

Library of Congress Cataloging-in-Publication Data
Human rights violations / edited by Charles F. Bahmueller.
    p. cm. — (Magill's choice)
Includes bibliographical references and index.
    ISBN 1-58765-089-4 (set : alk. paper) — ISBN 1-58765-090-8 (vol. 1 :
alk. paper) — ISBN 1-58765-091-6 (vol. 2 : alk. paper)— ISBN
1-58765-092-4 (vol. 3 : alk. paper)
    1. Human rights. 2. Civil rights. I. Bahmueller, Charles F. II. Series.
JC571 .H783 2003
323'.044'0904—dc21

                                                                2002015776

First Printing

Table of Contents — Volume 2

Complete List of Contents

Volume 1

Volume 2

Volume 3

Human Rights Violations

Eichmann Is Tried for War Crimes

Category of event: Atrocities and war crimes; accused persons' rights
Time: April-August, 1961
Locale: Jerusalem, Israel

> *Adolf Eichmann, the man most responsible for executing six million Jews in concentration camps during World War II, was captured by Israeli agents in Argentina and tried in Israel*

Principal personages:

ADOLF EICHMANN (1906-1962), the commander of the Reich Security Head Office, in charge of Nazi extermination camps during World War II

ISSER HAREL (1912-   ), the head of the Mossad, the Israeli Central Bureau of Intelligence and Security

ROBERT SERVATIUS (1896-?), Adolf Eichmann's attorney

GIDEON HAUSNER (1915-1990), the attorney general of Israel and prosecuting attorney at the trial of Adolf Eichmann

MOSHE LANDAU (1912-   ), the Israeli Supreme Court justice who presided at the trial of Adolf Eichmann

Summary of Event

Headlights blinded the slightly built, middle-aged man as he began walking the short distance from the bus stop to his rented house in a suburb of Buenos Aires. Suddenly three men grabbed him, forced him into a car, and sped away. The kidnapped man was Adolf Eichmann. As commander of the Reich Security Head Office, he was indirectly responsible for the deaths of several million Jews during World War II. He had been living in Argentina under the name of Ricardo Klement. His sons, however, still used the name Eichmann. His wife had remarried, but her second marriage was to her first husband under his assumed name.

For fifteen years Israeli agents had sought the whereabouts of this most notorious war criminal and were quite sure he was in Tucumán or in Buenos Aires. Early in 1960, when Eichmann's father died, the obituary listed Vera Eichmann as a daughter-in-law, not Vera Klement. The surveillance team watching the Klement house noticed Mrs. Klement's husband bringing her a bouquet of flowers on March 21, 1960, the twenty-fifth anniversary of her original marriage to Adolf Eichmann. This confirmed what their photographs and other information already indicated. The decision was made to arrest Eichmann, without the knowledge of the Argentine government, and to take him to Israel to stand trial. The kidnapping was timed to coincide with an Israeli state visit to Argentina. While the Israeli government delegation was in Buenos Aires, the Israeli Mossad, or Central Bureau of Intelligence and Security, used the Israeli airplane to transport Adolf Eichmann to Israel.

The El Al plane landed in Israel on May 22, 1960. The news of its arrival electrified the world. For many months, the Eichmann trial would be prime-time news around the world. Eichmann was taken to the prison in Ramla under elaborate security precautions. He was allowed to choose his own legal counsel and selected Robert Servatius, an attorney from Cologne, Germany, who had experience in defending other war criminals at the Nuremberg Trials in 1945. Israel paid $30,000 in legal expenses for the accused.

Eichmann gave a fluent and detailed statement that took 3,564 typewritten pages to transcribe. He demonstrated an incredible memory except regarding his actions in the Holocaust. The Israeli investigation of his statement took eight months to complete. Finally, on April 11, 1961, Adolf Eichmann's trial began at Beit HaAm, a large public auditorium in Jerusalem with six hundred foreign correspondents in attendance. The prisoner's dock was enclosed in bulletproof glass. The three judges, two of whom were born and educated in Germany, were all members of the Israeli Supreme Court. The presiding judge, Moshe Landau, read the indictment accusing Eichmann of causing the deaths of millions of Jews between 1939 and 1945. He was the person responsible for the extermination of Jews by the Nazis in their "final solution" to what they saw as "the Jewish problem."

Eichmann's defense attorney offered two preliminary objections: The judges should be disqualified because they had preconceived opinions about the case, and the court had no jurisdiction over Eichmann since he had been kidnapped from Argentina. Servatius further claimed that Israel's Nazi Law had no validity because it had been enacted after the historical events had occurred.

The court spent six days discussing the matter and citing legal precedents, especially from British and American court decisions. The court held that the judges should be fair, but they could not be expected to be neutral. As for Eichmann's kidnapping, the manner in which a defendant was brought within the jurisdiction of a national state had no bearing on the state's competence to try him in a court of law. Finally, the Nuremberg Trials were cited as precedent for the Eichmann trial. Those trials had also involved accusations of acts that had been declared crimes only after their occurrence.

The attorney general of the state of Israel, Gideon Hausner, was the chief prosecuting attorney. In recounting Eichmann's crimes, Hausner cited age-old condemnations of murder, antedating even the Ten Commandments. "Murder is murder," Hausner proclaimed. "And even if one shouts, *'Der Führer befahl, wir befolgen'* ('The Führer has ordered, we obey'), even then, murder is murder, oppression is oppression and robbery is robbery." In his eight-hour introductory address, the attorney general dramatically accused Eichmann:

> When I stand before you, O Judges of Israel, to lead the prosecution of Adolf Eichmann, I do not stand alone. With me here are six million accusers. But they cannot rise to their feet and point their finger at the man in the dock with the cry *"J'accuse"* on their lips. For they are now only ashes—ashes piled high on the hills of Auschwitz and the fields of Treblinka and strewn in the forests of Poland. Their graves are scattered throughout Europe. Their blood cries out, but their voice is stilled. Therefore will I be their spokesman. In their name will I unfold this terrible indictment.

From April until August, there followed an incredible parade of witnesses from all over Europe who recounted Eichmann's role in the crimes of the Nazis. After 114 sessions, the trial ended on August 14, 1961, and the court adjourned for four months. When it reconvened on December 11, Eichmann was found guilty on all fifteen counts and sentenced to death by hanging.

A Protestant clergyman was given the task of ministering to Eichmann's spiritual needs. The clergyman sought to persuade Eichmann to repent. Eichmann's reply was, "I am not pre-pared to discuss the Bible. I do not have the time to waste!" Nevertheless, with the noose literally around his neck just before execution, Adolf Eichmann said, "I have lived be-lieving in God and I die believing in God." The clergyman later com-mented that Eichmann was "the hardest man I ever saw."

Adolf Eichmann listening to testi-mony during his trial in Jerusalem. (Library of Congress)

On May 31, 1962, at midnight, Adolf Eichmann was hanged on the gallows. His body was later cremated. Early in the morning of June 1, a police launch carried his remains beyond the three-mile territorial limit and scattered his ashes into the Mediterranean Sea.

Impact of Event

The arrest, trial, and execution of Adolf Eichmann dramatically demonstrated that there are people in the world determined to bring to justice those responsible for horrible violations of basic human rights. Neither time nor national barriers prevented justice from being meted out to the commander of the Holocaust.

It is significant that world opinion was solidly behind what Israel sought to achieve. West Germany, as well as Britain and the United States, cooperated in the investigation and trial. West Germany had issued an arrest warrant for Eichmann in 1956, but there was no extradition treaty with Israel, and the West German government did not request Eichmann's extradition. Argentina's sovereignty had been violated by the Israelis, and Argentina, of course, protested. The matter was discussed in the United Nations, and Argentina eventually accepted Israel's apology.

Besides bringing an exceptionally notorious war criminal to justice, this trial also demonstrated that no matter how terrible the crime, the accused still possessed certain basic human rights that were inviolate. He did not possess the right to avoid public trial, but his personal safety and decent conditions of incarceration were paramount. Eichmann was not tortured or physically abused, and he was protected from those who would harm him. He had adequate living conditions and food, and the ability to communicate with friends and family. Not only was he given legal counsel of his own choosing, but the Israeli taxpayers paid his legal fees. The Jewish people, whose own human rights had been so viciously violated by Germany during the war, demonstrated that human rights are more significant than raw power. The meticulous care for fairness, judicial process, and systematic gathering of evidence in the trial in Israel contrasted sharply with the Gestapo methods familiar to Adolf Eichmann.

The German people knew all this. There was outrage in Germany when, on November 20, 1961, the *Stuttgarter Zeitung* reported a statement by Eichmann's defense attorney that "every German could have found himself in Eichmann's situation." They knew that this was not true. His crime was that of mass murder, not that of being a German or even a member of Hitler's military command.

Ironically, the Eichmann trial fostered a new understanding and a greater empathy between West Germany and Israel. West German loans, at favorable interest rates, were made to Israel. German investments in Israel increased considerably, and German arms shipments to Israel were made at a time of critical need in Israeli history. During the 1960's, West Germany was one of Israel's chief markets, and exports to West Germany rose sharply during the decade.

The intense worldwide publicity surrounding the trial of Eichmann educated a new generation on the atrocities of the Nazi regime. This was particularly true of the many young Germans who were horrified to learn details of the Holocaust. They had been kept in virtual ignorance of these details and felt a sense of betrayal for the silence surrounding these events. Twenty thousand German youths visited Israel between 1961 and 1967 to help in the work of building the young nation. The "final solution" to those Germans and Israelis was mutual respect and service.

Bibliography

Aharoni, Zvi, and Wilhelm Dietl. *Operation Eichmann: The Truth About the Pursuit, Capture and Trial.* Translated by Helmut Bogler. New York: J. Wiley, 1997. Written by the investigator who tracked and interrogated Eichmann, this is a first-hand account of Eichmann's pursuit and capture.

Arendt, Hannah. *Eichmann in Jerusalem: A Report on the Banality of Evil.* Rev. ed. New York: Penguin, 1994. Revised edition of the classic philosophical exploration of the Eichmann trial and the lesson it teaches about evil.

Dawidowicz, Lucy S. *The War Against the Jews, 1933-1945.* New York: Holt, Rinehart and Winston, 1975. Recounts in detail Hitler's "final solution" and Adolf Eichmann's key role in bringing it about.

Harel, Isser. *The House on Garibaldi Street.* New York: Viking Press, 1975. Isser Harel was the head of the Mossad and made the key decisions involved in the capture of Eichmann. His account is limited to the capture and removal of Eichmann to Israel.

Pearlman, Moshe. *The Capture and Trial of Adolf Eichmann.* New York: Simon & Schuster, 1963. This is a lengthy and full account of the entire Eichmann episode, but most of the book is a detailed account of the trial: the arguments and counterarguments, conclusions, sentence, and final days of Adolf Eichmann.

William H. Burnside

Amnesty International Is Founded

Category of event: Accused persons' rights; international norms; prisoners' rights
Time: May 28, 1961
Locale: London, England

> *Reading of the imprisonment of two Portuguese students who toasted freedom, Peter Benenson was inspired to found Amnesty International, the world's largest human rights organization*

Principal personages:

PETER BENENSON (1921-   ), the wealthy English lawyer who founded Amnesty International

ERIC BAKER (1920-   ), a cofounder of the initial "Appeal for Amnesty 1961" and interim secretary-general after Benenson's forced resignation in 1967

SEÁN MACBRIDE (1904-1988), a chair of Amnesty International's executive committee and recipient of the Nobel Peace Prize

ANTÓNIO DE OLIVEIRA SALAZAR (1889-1970), the longtime military dictator of Portugal

Summary of Event

In the fall of 1960, Peter Benenson read a news item while on a London-bound train. There was nothing unusual about the item; in fact, it was a routine report of a human rights violation. Two Portuguese students had been sentenced to seven years' imprisonment by the military dictatorship of António Salazar for raising their glasses in a toast "to freedom" at a restaurant. Salazar had exercised power since 1932 in Portugal in a manner typical of dictatorships—repressing democracy and human rights. What was unusual was that Benenson, a wealthy and successful English lawyer, decided at that moment that ordinary citizens must find some effective way to raise their collective voices on behalf of these students, and the thousands of others like them who were imprisoned for the peaceful exercise of their human rights.

Benenson, who had already founded "Justice," an organization of British lawyers working on behalf of the Universal Declaration of Human Rights, immediately began discussing his idea with Eric Baker, a prominent British Quaker, and Louis Blom-Cooper, an internationally prominent lawyer.

Through Benenson's friendship with David Astor, editor of the liberal London Sunday newspaper *The Observer*, they were given free space for an "Appeal for Amnesty 1961" on May 28, 1961. The date, Trinity Sunday, was deliberately chosen by Benenson, a Roman Catholic (of Jewish ancestry). To open a newspaper any day of the week, Benenson wrote, is to read of someone imprisoned, tortured, or executed because "his opinions or religion are unacceptable to his government." The article, immediately reprinted in major newspapers around the world, identified eight "Forgotten Prisoners."

Among the eight prisoners was Dr. António Neto, an Angolan poet and one of few Angolan physicians, who later became the first president of Angola. Three religious leaders were also included: the Reverend Ashton Jones, an American imprisoned for his involvement in the Civil Rights movement; Archbishop Josef Beran of Prague, previously imprisoned by the Nazis; and Cardinal Mindszenty, primate of Hungary. The other political activists who peacefully criticized or organized opposition to their governments were Constantin Noica, a Romanian philosopher; Patrick Duncan, a white South African; Tony Abiaticlos, a Greek communist and trade unionist; and Antonio Amat, a Spanish lawyer.

If the "sickening sense of impotence" most readers feel "could be united into common action," Benenson concluded, "something effective could be done." He therefore proposed the creation of a "Threes Network." Each group of human rights activists would adopt three prisoners—one each from the West, the Communist bloc, and the Third World. Their strategy would be to write letters to the prisoners, comfort their families, and harass the governments which imprisoned them. This scheme later evolved into Amnesty's Prisoner of Conscience program. At Benenson's request, British artist Diana Redhouse designed a logo which would become the internationally recognized Amnesty symbol, a candle encircled by barbed wire. She created it as an illustration of the aphorism, "It is better to light one candle than to curse the darkness."

The response was tremendous. Within six months of the "Appeal for Amnesty 1961," Amnesty International emerged as a permanent organization coordinating the Adoption Groups for prisoners of conscience which sprang up throughout Western Europe. (Amnesty defines prisoners of conscience as those detained for their beliefs, color, sex, ethnic origin, language, or religion, who have neither used nor advocated violence.) In addition to demanding the immediate release of all prisoners of conscience, Amnesty's official mandate also included two other points: the prompt and fair trial of all political prisoners and the absolute prohibition of the use of torture or the death penalty.

Although Amnesty was on its way to becoming the 1977 recipient of the Nobel Peace Prize as the world's largest and best-known human rights organization, it nearly collapsed in its early years from internal conflict. A crisis was instigated in 1966 by Benenson, who had long considered it a serious problem that Amnesty was not based in a neutral country. Few in Amnesty shared this concern. Benenson was suspicious that British intelligence and Central Intelligence Agency money had compromised the organization. When a strongly critical Amnesty report on British activities in Aden (Yemen) was delayed, Benenson took it upon himself to release the report. He then asked longtime friend Seán MacBride, chair of Amnesty's executive committee, to authorize and oversee an investigation.

The inquiry, however, led to Benenson's ouster. Apparently without the knowledge of London headquarters, Benenson himself had taken money from the British government for the purpose, he later explained, of aiding the families of Prisoners of Conscience in Rhodesia (now Zimbabwe). This was regarded in MacBride's report as one of the many examples of Benenson's one-person rule, which was characterized by his reliance on personal connections, haphazard organization, and sloppy record keeping. The result, according to MacBride (who earned both the Lenin Peace Prize and the Nobel Peace Prize), was a tendency of Benenson to act through "unilateral initiatives" which resulted in "erratic actions."

Seán MacBride, a chair of Amnesty International's executive committee and recipient of the Nobel Peace Prize. (© The Nobel Foundation)

Benenson's resignation was accepted, and his position of president was abolished. Eric Baker, one of the organizers of the initial "Appeal for Amnesty 1961," acted as interim secretary-general for a year. Baker took the organization from the edge of self-destruction to a stable and professional organizational foundation. Martin Ennals followed up Baker's critical stabilization with twelve years of sustained growth and the crystallization of Amnesty's international reputation for credibility, impartiality, and accuracy. His tenure as secretary-general was highlighted by the organization's attainment of the Nobel Peace Prize in 1977.

The international organizational structure is based in Amnesty's London headquarters, which verifies all information and authorizes all campaigns. London headquarters collects and analyzes information from newspaper accounts, journal articles, governmental bulletins, reports from lawyers and human rights organizations, and prisoners themselves. Fact finding missions by leading experts are also used to investigate and gather evidence. Amnesty notes in every publication its responsibility for the accuracy of all information and states its willingness to correct any errors. Amnesty rigorously maintains ideological neutrality and does not accept money from governments. Perhaps its most well-known and widely used work is *Amnesty International Reports* (published annually), which reviews the human rights record of every country in the world. In it, Amnesty never ranks governments but reviews each country's record, discussing specific individuals about whom Amnesty has verified information.

Amnesty's growth has been remarkable. At the close of its first decade following the "Appeal for Amnesty 1961," Amnesty had generated one thousand Adoption Groups in 28 countries. By the time it received the Nobel Peace Prize in 1977, this had grown to more than 165,000 active members in more than one hundred countries. At its thirtieth birthday celebration on May 28, 1991, Amnesty claimed nearly 700,000 members in 150 countries and more than four thousand Adoption Groups in more than 60 countries. The research department of the international secretariat employed a staff of two hundred people, comprising some thirty nationalities. At that time, Amnesty remained largely based in the constitutional democracies of the West, however, with the United States providing nearly one-third of its membership.

Despite the welcome crumbling of the Berlin Wall and the end of the Cold War at the close of the 1980's, Amnesty noted that two out of three people in the world still lived in the nearly 130 countries of the world that imprisoned unjustly, tortured, or killed their own citizens. Therefore, the work begun in 1961 continued with a thirtieth birthday campaign on behalf of thirty prisoners of conscience whose fate Amnesty pledged to publicize until all were released.

Impact of Event

A new attention to human rights violations by the international community followed in the aftermath of the public exposure of the terrible atrocities committed during World War II, especially those committed in the name of

Nazism. The Nuremberg Trials, the Universal Declaration of Human Rights, and the numerous treaties which followed were all aimed at eroding the state sanctuary of "domestic jurisdiction."

International law traditionally has upheld the inviolability of domestic jurisdiction—a state's exclusive authority over its own people and territory. A state's prerogatives regarding domestic jurisdiction clash with the ideal of a citizen's universal human rights. Because states are recognized as sovereign, the most effective way to breach domestic jurisdiction is through treaty agreements by which the states bind themselves under international law to human rights standards. Enforcement remains problematic.

Because human rights have honorific status, states unfailingly posture as champions of human rights. For example, virtually all states endorse the Universal Declaration of Human Rights. Governments, however, often suppress human rights to stay in power. As Amnesty noted in its twenty-fifth anniversary celebration, this leaves a wide gap between commitment and reality. Because of this hypocrisy, nongovernmental human rights organizations such as Amnesty International have a crucial role to play.

As the most prominent independent, impartial international watchdog for human rights, Amnesty International can embarrass states by spotlighting flagrant violations. Public opinion can be brought to bear and thereby affect the conduct of sovereign states, which may well conclude that holding an individual prisoner is not worth the negative publicity being generated by Amnesty.

The power of states often leads to the conclusion that one person's actions do not matter, but Amnesty International's format provides an opportunity for individuals to make a difference. Amnesty International was organized by the inspiration of one man, Peter Benenson, on the premise that an organization can bring together numbers of such people to create an international citizens' lobby on behalf of human rights. In such an organizational form, it is an effective participant in international politics.

Perhaps the most significant and poignant confirmation of Amnesty's impact is that more than thirty-eight thousand individuals for whom Amnesty has worked from 1961 to 1991 have been released. A released Prisoner of Conscience from the Dominican Republic testified to Amnesty's effectiveness this way:

> When the first two hundred letters came, the guards gave me back my clothes. Then the next two hundred letters came, and the prison director came to see me. When the next pile of letters arrived, the director got in touch with his

superior. The letters kept coming and coming: three thousand of them. The President was informed. The letters still kept arriving, and the President called the prison and told them to let me go.

Bibliography

Clark, Ann Marie. *Diplomacy of Conscience: Amnesty International and Changing Human Rights Norms.* Princeton: Princeton University Press, 2001. Detailed, scholarly history of the organization and its impact on international law. Bibliography.

Drinan, Robert. *Cry of the Oppressed: History and Hope of the Human Rights Revolution.* San Francisco: Harper & Row, 1987. Good general introduction to human rights, including the Nuremberg Trials, United Nations efforts, and American foreign policy. The chapter on nongovernmental human rights organizations focuses on Amnesty. The author was part of an Amnesty mission to Argentina in 1976. Index and bibliography.

Larsen, Egon. *A Flame in Barbed Wire: The Amnesty International Story.* New York: W. W. Norton, 1979. An accessible, anecdotal presentation of the history of Amnesty International, including its origins, torture in various countries, the death penalty debate, the stories of numerous individual prisoners, and evaluations of Amnesty's work. Index, no bibliography, many illustrations.

Power, Jonathan. *Amnesty International: The Human Rights Story.* New York: McGraw-Hill, 1981. Excellent coverage of the founding and development of Amnesty International, including its attainment of the Nobel Peace Prize in 1977. Describes Amnesty's mandate, organizational arrangements, and campaigns on torture, the death penalty, and children. The records of the Soviet Union, the People's Republic of China, Nicaragua, and Guatemala are examined. Controversies are frankly discussed. Many illustrations; no index or bibliography.

_____. *Like Water on Stone: The Story of Amnesty International.* Boston: Northeastern University Press, 2001. A thorough account of the forty-year history of the organization. Chapters examine human rights violations in places such as Guatemala, Nigeria, Argentina, Germany, and China.

Stephenson, Thomas. "Working for Human Rights." *Bulletin of Atomic Scientists* 37 (August/September, 1981): 54-56. Good general description of Amnesty. The author gives an excellent picture of the work of an Adoption Group by explaining his own and its work on behalf of prisoners in Guatemala and Romania.

Youssoufi, Abderrahman. "The Role of Non-Governmental Organizations in the Campaign Against Violations of Human Rights, Apartheid, and Racism." In *Violations of Human Rights.* Paris: UNESCO, 1984. Good back-ground on nongovernmental human rights organizations. The author explains what they are and how they operate. Offers concrete discussions of their activities on behalf of human rights, using Amnesty in illustration. Appendices include the final report of a U.N.-sponsored conference on individual and collective action to stop human rights violations.

Nancy N. Haanstad

Communists Raise the Berlin Wall

Category of event: Civil rights; political freedom; refugee rights
Time: August 13, 1961
Locale: Berlin, East Germany

> *The Berlin Wall, erected to halt the debilitating exodus of East Germans to West Germany and to assert definitively the permanence and legitimacy of the East German regime, in fact attested to the failure of that regime*

Principal personages:
KONRAD ADENAUER (1876-1967), the leader of the Christian Democrats, chancellor of the Federal Republic of Germany (West Germany) from 1949 to 1963
WILLY BRANDT (1913-1992), the mayor of West Berlin from 1957 until 1966, when, with his Social Democratic Party, he entered into a national coalition government
JOHN F. KENNEDY (1917-1963), the president of the United States from 1961 to 1963
NIKITA S. KHRUSHCHEV (1894-1971), the first secretary of the Communist Party from 1953, actual leader of the Soviet Union from 1955 until his dismissal in 1964
WALTER ULBRICHT (1893-1973), the communist leader of the German Democratic Republic (East Germany) from 1949 to 1971

Summary of Event

Berlin became a focal point for East-West tensions after the breakdown of cooperation between the former World War II Allies. As the Western occupying powers, led by the United States, amalgamated their zones of occupation and began the process of organizing an indigenous government for West Germany, the Soviets responded with their blockade of West Berlin from June, 1948, until May, 1949. A strong response by the Americans and the British preserved the liberty of West Berlin, and the Federal Republic of Germany was proclaimed in the western portion of Germany. The Soviets responded by organizing the German Democratic Republic in the eastern sector, which was under their control. The regime was imposed upon the East German popula-

301

tion, whose distaste for the repressiveness and relative material deprivation that characterized it was borne out in desperate uprisings in East Berlin and other cities of East Germany in June, 1953.

Although the Soviets lifted the blockade of Berlin, they continued to exert pressure upon it during the Cold War crisis. The Soviets were concerned by the linkage of a rearmed West Germany to the North Atlantic Treaty Organization in 1955. In 1958, the Soviets applied pressure on Berlin in an effort to obtain a European security agreement that would recognize the status quo in Germany. On November 10, 1958, Soviet leader Nikita Khrushchev announced that the Soviet Union was reconsidering its position on the four-power control of Berlin and might hand over control of East Berlin to the East Germans. On November 27, he called for West Berlin to be transformed into a demilitarized free city and for the two German states to be united in a confederation. He threatened to turn over all Soviet rights to the East German regime if the Western powers had not worked out an agreement within six months.

West Berlin, linked to the West, was both an embarrassing symbol of freedom and prosperity and a breach through which the disaffected people of East Germany could escape to the West. By 1958, approximately 2.3 million East Germans, fifteen percent of the East German population, had fled to the West. The majority of these people were of working age, and their emigration constituted a serious drain on the talent and skill of the German Democratic Republic. Unless the hemorrhage could be stopped, the stability and even viability of the East German regime would be threatened. The Soviet Union was concerned not to lose its control of East Germany, which, in addition to having great military importance, was vital economically to the Soviet Union and to the Eastern Bloc. The economy of East Germany, with a level of technological quality superior to that of the rest of the Soviet bloc, had been structured to provide for the needs of the Soviet Union rather than its own people.

At Geneva meetings of the foreign ministers of the four occupying powers in May and July, 1959, the Soviets repeated their demands that the occupation of West Berlin be ended and the city transformed into a "free city." Rebuffed by the West, the Soviets allowed the East Germans to seize the initiative. This tactic was geared to reinforce the sovereignty of the German Democratic Republic and add a new source of pressure. The Soviet Union's principal concern was to gain definitive recognition of the division of Germany. When the East Germans and the Soviets began harassing communications with the city in August, Willy Brandt, the mayor of West Berlin, vigorously defended the rights of the city's inhabitants. In response to suggestions that West Berlin was untenable as a Western enclave, he prophetically asserted that a free West Berlin was indispensable if hope for freedom was to be nurtured in Eastern Europe.

Following a momentary thaw in relations between the Soviet Union and the United States, capped by the Camp David meeting between Khrushchev and President Dwight D. Eisenhower, a Paris summit in May, 1960, fell apart after the Soviets shot down an American spy plane. Sensing Western irresolution on Berlin, Khrushchev tightened the screws on West Berlin to pressure the West and simultaneously to bolster his client regime. In August, the Soviet sector of the city was temporarily closed to West German citizens. On September 8, the East Germans insisted that West German visitors have visitor permits. On September 13, they announced that they would no longer recognize West German passports as legal documentation for West Berlin visitors. The trade agreement between the two parts of Germany was suspended by the East Germans on January 1, 1961.

An overbearing Khrushchev met the new American president, John F. Kennedy, in Vienna on June 3 and 4, 1961. He threatened to sign a separate peace treaty with East Germany and give it control of Berlin communications if a general peace and an independent status for West Berlin had not been effected within six months. On June 15, Walter Ulbricht, the East German leader, stated that West Berlin would have to stop accepting refugees from the East and cease being a source of propaganda beamed to the East. Kennedy responded in a July 25 "Report to the Nation" that he was determined to support West Berlin. Kennedy discouraged Khrushchev from additional pressure on West Berlin, but his report, by avoiding references to East Berlin, was interpreted as relinquishing any rights there to the Soviet Union. Konrad Adenauer, the chancellor of West Germany, was never overwhelmingly interested in East Berlin and also limited his concerns to maintaining the status of West Berlin.

Unable to pressure West Berlin, Khrushchev decided to take advantage of Western acquiescence to shore up his client state. Births exceeded deaths in East Germany by only eight thousand annually, and 250,000 East Germans were leaving each year. Many of the departing citizens were very difficult to replace. In the seven years before August, 1961, they included five thousand doctors, seventeen thousand teachers, and twenty thousand engineers and technicians. Nineteen thousand refugees crossed over to the West in June, 1961, and more than thirty thousand emigrated in July. In early August, the rush turned into a flood. By August 11, sixteen thousand East Germans had crossed to West Berlin. On August 12, twenty-four hundred crossed, more than had ever done so in a single day.

West Berliners looking across the wall at East Berlin in 1961. (National Archives)

Ulbricht had requested Khrushchev's permission to block off West Berlin in March. Khrushchev had hesitated then, but now he gave his permission. Just after midnight on the morning of August 13, the Berlin Wall, in the form of barbed wire, began to go up, sealing West Berlin off from East Berlin. At 1:00 A.M., the East German press agency announced that the border had been closed. Thirty Soviet and East German divisions stood ready to counter any armed intervention by the West. Brandt demanded immediate diplomatic pressure to protest this violation of the four-power agreements on Berlin, but, to his great disappointment, the response of the West was too slow and too weak to deter the construction of the barrier. Adenauer, who was engaged in an electoral contest against Brandt, was particularly remiss in his tardy and ineffectual reaction. The dispatch of fifteen hundred American reinforcements and the return of General Lucius Clay, the hero of the blockade, bolstered the morale of the West Berliners as did visits by U.S. vice president Lyndon Johnson and President Kennedy. The Berlin Wall, however, continued to grow, as did the death and misery it brought. The Basic Treaty between the Federal Republic and the German Democratic Republic, signed on December 21, 1972, and ratified in June, 1973, again granted West Germans the right to travel to

East Germany and enter East Berlin, but the Berlin Wall was not genuinely open to free access until November 9, 1989.

Impact of Event

Before the construction of the Berlin Wall, people could move fairly freely through both parts of Berlin. East Berliners could visit family and friends in the evening and on weekends in West Berlin. They had access to the Western press and entertainment. Nearly sixty thousand East Berliners daily took trains to work in factories and shops in West Berlin. The Berlin Wall put an end to this as well as to the permanent movement of East Germans to the West.

The Berlin Wall was eventually elaborated into an impenetrable barrier one hundred miles long, encircling all of West Berlin. Escape was relatively easy at first. Some jumped across barbed wire; others climbed out of second story windows of buildings which formed part of the new frontier. Eventually the windows were bricked over and a genuine wall was erected, fortified by 238 watchtowers and 132 gun emplacements. It was set off by an exposed "death strip" and guarded by twenty thousand East German police. On the Friedrichstrasse, Checkpoint Charlie, the only crossing point open to the Allied occupation forces, was permanently guarded on both sides by armored vehicles facing a fifty-yard slalom-like barrier designed to thwart motorized escape attempts.

The Berlin Wall was the brutal product of a regime willing to employ repression and deadly force against its own citizens. From 1961 until the Berlin Wall was opened on November 9, 1989, seventy-seven people were killed trying to escape through it. Another 114 people were killed trying to cross the increasingly deadly fortified border that divided East Germany from the remainder of West Germany. Observers in the West saw the failed escape attempts and witnessed the refugees being dragged back, sometimes wounded, to the East. One young victim, Peter Fechter, was shot by the East German police in August, 1962, and allowed to lie in view of horrified West Berliners as he bled to death. In 1974, Erich Honecker, Ulbricht's successor, in an effort to further intimidate the East German people, made his regime's practice explicit by issuing a shoot-to-kill order.

The Berlin Wall, in the short term, was perhaps a success of sorts. It stopped the flow of East Germans to the West, and it also played a role in the formation of Brandt's policy of *Ostpolitik*, which resulted in the recognition of East Germany by West Germany. Accepted as a legitimate entity, the German Democratic Republic became, along with the Federal Republic, a member of the United Nations in 1973. Brandt feared that, as a result of the Berlin Wall, the two German states and their people would grow progressively estranged. He also believed that the prospect of German reunification in the near future was remote. When he became chancellor in 1969, he presided over an effort to bring the two Germanies together through small steps. He was greatly concerned with lessening the burden on families created by the separation of the Berlin Wall. The Basic Treaty of 1972, however, did not bring an end to the paranoia of the East German regime. In 1980, to discourage excessive contact between its people and Germans from the West, the East German regime increased the visa fee and the daily foreign exchange requirement for visitors to East Germany. This created a formidable impediment for elderly pensioners wishing to visit relatives in East Berlin.

In the long term, the Berlin Wall was a dismal failure. Psychologically, it further damaged the credibility of the East German regime, which was seen as having to wall in its own citizens. When Mikhail Gorbachev, who became president of the Soviet Union in 1985, lifted the threat of violence, the support of the East German regime disappeared. As East Germans in 1989 fled to West Germany through Hungary and Czechoslovakia, the demand for change in the German Democratic Republic became irrepressible. Honecker was forced from office and, on November 9, 1989, in a prelude to German reunification, the Berlin Wall was breached by the new East German government.

Bibliography

Griffith, William E. *The Ostpolitik of the Federal Republic of Germany.* Cambridge, Mass.: MIT Press, 1978. Griffith provides an excellent survey of the development of West German policy toward the East and, in particular, toward East Germany. Griffith provides a very sound and clear analysis of the origins of Brandt's *Ostpolitik,* an explanation of its substance, and a solid short-term evaluation of its results.

Merritt, Richard L., and Anna J. Merritt, eds. *Living with the Wall: West Berlin, 1961-1985.* Durham, N.C.: Duke University Press, 1985. This book provides a collection of articles on the history of the wall and its impact upon the inhabitants of Berlin.

Ross, Corey. *Constructing Socialism at the Grass Roots: The Transformation of East Germany, 1945-1965.* New York: St. Martin's Press, 2000. The author looks at the effects of the East German regime and of the raising of the Berlin Wall at the grassroots level. Bibliography.

_____. *East German Dictatorship.* New York: Oxford University Press, 2002. Collects and analyzes the various scholarly interpretations of the legacy of the East German regime.

Waldenburg, Hermann. *The Berlin Wall Book.* London: Thames and Hudson, 1990. This book provides a pictorial history of the wall.

Whetten, Lawrence L. *Germany East and West: Conflicts, Collaboration, and Confrontation.* New York: New York University Press, 1980. Whetten places the wall in the context of East-West German relations. According to Whetten, because of the wall and the subsequent development of détente, Brandt believed that West Germany had to pursue a different policy toward the East. Brandt hoped that improving relations with the Soviet Union and East Germany would gain acceptance by the East of the status of West Berlin, improve conditions for the East Germans, and preserve the identity of the German nation.

Wyden, Peter. *Wall: The Inside Story of a Divided Berlin.* New York: Simon & Schuster, 1989. A detailed history of the wall from its construction to the year that it was finally breached. The book was completed too early to include the events of November 9, 1989.

Bernard A. Cook

Soviet Jews Resist Oppression

Category of event: Civil rights; racial and ethnic rights; religious freedom
Time: 1963-1970
Locale: Soviet Union

> *The Jewish population of the Soviet Union became more active in demanding that the Soviet state permit religious freedom, respect minority rights, and allow free emigration*

Principal personages:
LEONID ILICH BREZHNEV (1906-1982), the successor to Nikita Khrushchev
HENRY "SCOOP" JACKSON (1912-1983), a U.S. senator with presidential ambitions
NIKITA S. KHRUSHCHEV (1894-1971), the premier and first secretary of the Communist Party of the Soviet Union
RICHARD M. NIXON (1913-1994), the president of the United States (1969-1974)
ANDREI SAKHAROV (1921-1989), a leading Soviet dissident and spokesperson for human rights
JOSEPH STALIN (1879-1953), the dictator of the Soviet Union from 1924 until 1953; a noted anti-Semite

Summary of Event

As the old Russian Empire expanded into Eastern Europe in the eighteenth and nineteenth centuries, increasing numbers of Jews fell under Russian control, with the total at one point reaching five million. Jews were subject to persecution by czarist authorities: They were confined by law to the Pale of Settlement, a strip of territory along Russia's western border; restricted from entering certain trades and professions; made subject to forcible religious conversion; forbidden to write or teach in Yiddish or Hebrew; and, on occasion, made the target of spontaneous or even government-sponsored pogroms (massacres and evictions). The intensity of persecution waxed and waned according to the degree of tolerance and enlightenment of the ruling czar or provincial governor. Despite decades of religious and cultural oppression aimed at their assimilation and "Russification," Jews maintained a rich religious life and vibrant cultural independence, if only in the sanctuaries of their homes and the enforced segregation of their ghetto communities.

After the 1917 revolution and the fall of Czar Nicholas II, the new provisional government repealed most laws discriminating against Jews. The few remaining discriminatory regulations were abolished by the Bolsheviks after they took power in Russia in November, 1917. For a brief period, Jews were able legally to practice their religion in the renamed Soviet Union. After a short spring of emancipation, Jews fell victim to two major forces, one old and one new. First, anti-Semitism in the lands of the old Russian Empire had deep roots among the Orthodox population and with certain national groups. Despite the change in legal status, in everyday life Jews still encountered discrimination, persecution, and at times even lynchings and pogroms. Second, the Bolshevik ideologues in charge of the Soviet state harbored a deep animosity toward organized religion of any kind, and they soon embarked on a general campaign to suppress religious belief which swept up Jews along with Orthodox, Roman Catholics, Protestants, and others. Finally, the Jews presented a special problem to the Soviet authorities, as they formed not simply a religious community but a distinct national group without a specific national territory. During the 1920's an attempt was made to create a Jewish region (Birobidzhan) along the desolate Chinese-Soviet border, but fewer than one hundred thousand Jews chose to relocate.

With Joseph Stalin's ascent to full dictatorial power in 1928, Jews faced a whole new level of persecution and terror. Like millions of other Soviets during the 1930's, the years of Stalin's great purges, Jews were subject to persecution, imprisonment, and execution both as individuals and as Jews, for in addition to being paranoid and cruel, Stalin was a hardened anti-Semite. Soviet policy in general aimed at breaking down Jews' separate sense of religion and culture: Yiddish once again was banned; synagogues, schools, and Talmudic academies were closed; Jewish literary and artistic expression was attacked as anti-Soviet; and under the labor code Jews were forced to work on the Sabbath. The average Jew, for survival's sake, had to maintain an outward appearance of conformity with Stalinism.

Then came the Holocaust, in which Soviet and other Jews were singled out from the general population for "liquidation" by the Nazis. The Holocaust had a great effect on Soviet Jews, as it did on Jews everywhere, by impressing many with the reality that assimilation was no barrier to persecution. Germany's Jews had been among the most assimilated in Europe. The Holocaust gave rise to a new consciousness of Jewish identity, spurred by the fact that not even the Nazi genocide led average Soviet citizens to question anti-Semitism, in part because their leaders suppressed information about the Holocaust.

The State of Israel came into existence in 1948. That had two lasting effects: It stimulated a fierce pride among Jews and raised hopes of escape from persecution by emigration to Israel. It also led to a new round of persecution, as Stalin denounced Zionism as a form of imperialism and accused Jews of being potential traitors. At the time of his death in 1953, Stalin was about to launch a large-scale purge of Jews as a way of distracting the public from his foreign and domestic policy failures.

Nikita Khruschev took power and modified the excesses of Stalinism in the 1950's but failed to attack the sources of anti-Semitism in Soviet society. In 1961, he too began to blame Jews for the failures of the Soviet centrally planned economy. Between 1961 and 1964, official propaganda about "economic crimes" blamed Jews for impeding economic progress. In some areas, such as the Ukraine, Jews were arrested, tried, and often executed in greatly disproportionate numbers. Khruschev's successor, Leonid Brezhnev, also was personally prejudiced against Jews, especially after Israel humiliated the Soviet Union's Arab allies in the 1967 Arab-Israeli war. That conflict created a surge of pride among Soviet Jews, who began to demand that their religious and ethnic rights be respected and that emigration to Israel be permitted. Efforts were made to revive fluency in Yiddish and Hebrew, to start up religious schools, and to reopen synagogues and Talmudic academies. Soviet leaders responded swiftly: Jewish activists and other dissidents were arrested; some were sent to labor camps and others to mental institutions on the ground that their religious belief was evidence of mental disorder. The activism of Soviet dissidents caught the attention of foreign observers and of Jewish communities in Israel and the United States. From 1967 on, Soviet persecution of Jews was subject to increasing criticism from foreign human rights groups, both Jewish and non-Jewish, and to growing pressure from the United States.

In the early 1970's pressure began to build in the United States to tie *détente* with the Soviet Union to the treatment of dissidents, and especially to free emigration for Jews. President Nixon and his national security advisor, Henry Kissinger, at first resisted linkage between human rights, emigration, and *détente*, although they pressured Brezhnev in private. Between 1972 and 1974, however, majority support developed in Congress for the Jackson-Vanik amendment to a trade bill, named for its sponsor Senator Henry "Scoop" Jackson, a man with presidential ambitions and hopes for strong support from the American Jewish community. The amendment linked free Jewish emigration and religious rights to expanded trade with Moscow. A critical moment came on

October 21, 1974, when Andrei Sakharov, a leading Soviet dissident and founder of the Moscow Human Rights Committee, threw his support behind the amendment in an open letter to Jackson and Kissinger. Congress soon passed the amendment, but it quickly backfired: The Soviets proclaimed outrage that their internal policy was being questioned and immediately cut off all Jewish emigration. With the complete collapse of *détente* the following year, Jewish religious rights and especially emigration became hostage to larger currents in Soviet-American relations and remained tied to other issues for the rest of the 1970's and most of the 1980's.

Impact of Event

The impact of rising demands from the Soviet Jewish community for greater respect for religious and minority rights had a profound effect on hundreds of thousands of lives. On the positive side, many Jews discovered or rediscovered a personal cultural and religious identity that had been unknown or forgotten under the influence of Soviet daily life and antireligious education. There was a renaissance of Yiddish and Hebrew literature, an increase in participation in religious ceremonies and observance, and a new sense of community both within the Soviet Union and with respect to the larger Jewish world, most notably in Israel and the United States. On the other hand, this revival provoked a fresh round of persecution which adversely affected thousands. Well-known Jewish dissidents such as Yuri Orlov and Anatol Scharansky were imprisoned for long periods of time but eventually were released and expelled, after the West applied pressure. Less well-known activists, or ordinary people who applied to emigrate to Israel, quickly found that they lost their jobs, their apartments, and often their freedom. In the worst cases, and there were many of these, Jews were sent to prison camps or to mental institutions, away from Western eyes. Even when a trickle of emigration was permitted, the wait for an exit visa could be as long as five to seven years, and then the request might be refused, with no reason given. That situation continued in spite of the fact that the Soviet Union in 1975 signed a comprehensive human rights agreement that was included in the Helsinki Accords on European peace and security.

On a larger plane, the conditions under which Soviet Jews lived were determined by both the Arab-Israeli dispute and also the Cold War, as Arabs lobbied Moscow to curtail emigration and the United States lobbied for an increase. Soviet leaders turned the emigration tap on and off according to the changing stakes of foreign policy, greatly disrupting individual lives and families. By the mid-1980's, however, Jews began to benefit from the enormous changes convulsing Soviet society with the beginnings of *glasnost* and *perestroika* under Mikhail Gorbachev. As the Cold War drew to a close and a severe Soviet need for Western aid and trade became clear, the new Soviet leadership moved away from persecution and toward free Jewish emigration. After 1988, hundreds of thousands of Jews left the Soviet Union, so many that Israel had difficulty housing them. Housing problems placed new pressures on the occupied territories, thereby complicating the Arab-Israeli dispute. Within the Soviet Union there developed more official tolerance for religious belief and practice. By the early 1990's, however, an old pattern started to repeat itself, as the desire of Jews to emigrate was seen by some Soviets as evidence of disloyalty. Incidents of open anti-Semitism increased in number and talk was even heard from *Pamyat*—a reactionary nationalist group opposed to *glasnost* and *perestroika*—of a pogrom against the Jews of Moscow and Leningrad. Although government policy had entered a more liberal phase, Jews still faced the daily reality of deeply rooted anti-Semitism among large segments of the Soviet population.

Bibliography

Amnesty International. *Prisoners of Conscience in the USSR: Their Treatment and Conditions.* London: Author, 1980. A well-documented account of general conditions and individual cases. Photographs and index.

Cohen, Roberta. "The Soviet Union: Human Rights Diplomacy in the Communist Heartland." In *The Diplomacy of Human Rights,* edited by David Newsom. Lanham, Md.: University Press of America, 1986. A useful, short introduction to the problems of outside powers attempting to influence Soviet human rights behavior.

Gitelman, Zvi Y. *A Century of Ambivalence: The Jews of Russia and the Soviet Union 1881 to the Present.* 2d rev. ed. Bloomington: Indiana University Press, 2001. Provides a detailed history of the Soviet Jewish experience with a chapter on events in the 1960's. Illustrated.

Kahan, Arcadius. "Forces for and Against Jewish Identity in the Soviet Union" and "Religion and Soviet Policy." In *Essays in Jewish Social and Economic History,* edited by Roger Weiss. Chicago: University of Chicago Press, 1986. These two articles are interpretive rather than documentary and serve as good complements to the drier presentations of Amnesty International and Joshua Rubenstein.

Levin, Nora. *The Jews in the Soviet Union Since 1917: Paradox of Survival.* New York: New York University Press, 1991. Broad two-volume history of the Jewish people in the Soviet Union. Based largely on primary and secondary sources.

Low, Alfred D. *Soviet Jewry and Soviet Policy.* New York: Columbia University Press, 1990. A good introduction to the history of Jews in the Soviet Union. Particularly useful for its discussion of the interrelationship between anti-Semitism and Marxist-Leninist theory. Select bibliography and index.

Pospielovsky, Dimitry. *The Russian Church Under the Soviet Regime, 1917-1982.* 2 vols. Crestwood, N.Y.: St. Vladimir's Seminary Press, 1984. Important for an understanding of the larger question of the Soviet attitude toward organized religion and of Orthodox attitudes toward Jews.

Rubenstein, Joshua. "Zionists and Democrats" and "Deteute and the Dissidents." In *Soviet Dissidents: Their Struggle for Human Rights.* Boston, Mass.: Beacon Press, 1980. These two articles provide detail on individual cases as well as a general overview of the connections and tensions between Zionists and dissident movements. Full index.

Cathal J. Nolan

Civil War Ravages Chad

Category of event: Atrocities and war crimes; revolutions and rebellions
Time: 1965-1980's
Locale: Chad

> *Intermittent civil war between rival factions in the poverty-stricken Saharan nation of Chad took an awful toll in human lives and suffering*

Principal personages:

FRANÇOIS TOMBALBAYE (1918-1975), the first president of Chad (1960-1975)

FÉLIX MALLOUM (1932-   ), the successor to Tombalbaye, overthrown in 1979

HISSEN HABRÉ (1942-   ), a guerrilla leader who seized power in 1979, was replaced in 1979, and regained the presidency in 1982

GOUKOUNI OUEDDEI (1944-   ), a principal rival of Habré who ruled a provisional government (1979-1982)

Summary of Event

Civil war, political brutality, frequent *coups d'etat,* a hostile physical environment, and endemic poverty have plagued Chad's four million inhabitants since shortly after independence from France in 1960. Like those of many other African nations, Chad's boundaries reflect interimperial rivalries (in this case, between France and Italy) rather than social cohesion, so national politics revolve around competition among the myriad social and ethnic groupings of the three arid, predominantly Arab districts of the north; the seminomadic people of the Sahelian central region; and the people of the relatively more arable, densely populated, ethnically diverse south. Backed by Libya, France, and other countries, rival movements have struggled for national power since 1965.

A large, desolate, landlocked territory, Chad was inhabited mainly by nomads and fugitive slaves when it became a colony separate from French Equatorial Africa in 1920. Because of its agricultural potential, the southern region had enjoyed most of the colonial development efforts, including cotton production and social services such as schools and utilities. The first president, François (later Ngarta) Tombalbaye, a member of the minuscule

French-educated southern elite, assumed leadership of Chad soon after it was declared a republic with its capital at N'Djamena (formerly Fort Lamy) on August 11, 1960.

Independence brought neither liberation nor peace. Virtually from the beginning, Muslim Chadians from the northern and central parts of the country resisted government efforts to settle nomads and force them to pay usurious rates on government "farm loans." Moreover, they demanded a greater say in the southern-dominated government. The regime responded by outlawing opposition parties in March, 1962, and organizing well-controlled elections. Riots against tax collectors and loan officers broke out in eastern and central Chad in November, 1965, marking the beginning of the civil war. These tax revolts were suppressed by the army, only to erupt again nearby. On June 22, 1966, two or three dissident groups met in neighboring western Sudan to form the *Front de Libération Nationale* (Fronilat). Within a year, the rebellion against imposed sedentarization and heavy taxation spread throughout the north. The army was directed to stop demonstrations and disband the opposition. At least 250 strikers and regime opponents were imprisoned for banditry, and some of them died, disappeared, or were tortured in jail. Amid spreading unrest and even mutiny in 1968, Tombalbaye called on France to support his anti-insurgency campaign. French paratroopers engaged directly in fighting against insurgents and their sympathizers from April, 1969, through mid-1971.

In response to Tombalbaye's strong-arm tactics, the rebellion spread not only throughout the central and northern districts but also to the Sara peoples of his native southern region, where his "authenticity" campaign, which required Sara youth to undergo traditional initiation rites, was resented by more educated Sarans. Pockets of resistance therefore appeared in the south. After Muammar al-Qaddafi's rise to leadership in neighboring Libya in 1969, Libyan aid to Fronilat increased, and the movement became more militantly anti-imperialist and pro-Islamic. Eventually, even Tombalbaye's own top military commanders, including General Félix Malloum, turned against the eccentric, ineffectual, and increasingly hated dictator. Several officers were arrested for plotting against the regime.

After a military coup in 1975 in which Tombalbaye was assassinated, the new president, Malloum, released about 175 political detainees from prison and promoted some reforms. The respite from chaos and repression was, however, short-lived. The rebels controlled rural areas of the central and northern regions and gained on N'Djamena. There was discord within Fronilat, an increasingly motley, diverse, and divided collection of warlord armies. A quarrel between the front's two most prominent leaders, Hissen Habré and Goukouni Oueddei, partly over the treatment of a French archaeologist held hostage by the commandos and exacerbated by al-Qaddafi's efforts to control the movement, split Fronilat. While Oueddei became Libya's favorite client, Habré was brought into the Malloum government as prime minister.

The year 1979 saw countrywide anarchy and chaos, with intercommunal violence as well as military confrontations among the guerrilla groups and with the army. A strike by Muslim students in N'Djamena in February touched off a spate of incidents, some of them reported as massacres, between Muslims and non-Muslims. Within days of the student strike, Habré's forces took the capital from Malloum, who retired under French asylum. Lacking power and water, and prey to Habré's pillaging militia, civilians fled N'Djamena. Meanwhile, as rebel forces fought for control of the provinces, the Organization of African Unity (OAU) sponsored a series of talks leading to a short-lived cease-fire agreement that put Goukouni Oueddei at the head of a "transitional government" with Habré as defense minister. Habré's forces and those of other rebel commandos continued the armed struggle, capturing several towns and besieging the capital.

In 1980 and 1981, direct and indirect foreign intervention further complicated the imbroglio. Fighting broke out in March, 1980, and raged continuously for the rest of the year. After the remaining eleven hundred French forces were recalled to Paris, President Oueddei invited Libya to assist his government in defending the positions under its control against Habré's troops. Anxious also to consolidate Libya's claims to the long-disputed Aozou strip on the Libyan-Chadian border, al-Qaddafi willingly complied, dispatching tanks, helicopters, and mortars south across the desert. By December, they had effectively defeated Habré's forces militarily, and in January, 1981, al-Qaddafi declared Libyan unity with Chad. This prompted the formation of an OAU peacekeeping force and, more important, U.S. and French backing for Habré in the form of both arms and diplomacy. The Libyans withdrew in late summer, 1981, their positions ostensibly being handed over to OAU peacekeepers. Habré's forces gradually took control of the country, entering N'Djamena in June, 1982.

For the next four years, Chad was effectively divided between Libyan-backed, Oueddei-led factions that dominated the northern two-thirds of the country and the western-backed Habré government in the south. Sarans and other southerners resisted military occupation by Habrés army, and soon whole neighborhoods and villages were fleeing before the presidential guard's counterinsurgency campaign. After consolidating his positions, Oueddei be-

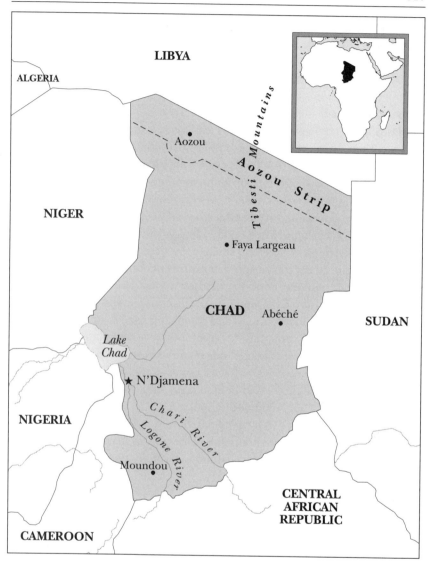

gan penetrating south in late 1983. This occasioned a new French intervention, including three thousand troops and fighter-bombers, to halt any Libyan
advance, allowing Habré armies to reoccupy some fallen towns. Clashes continued, with Libyan and French support, until a falling out between Oueddei

and al-Qaddafi allowed Habré to gain the upper hand in 1986. He gradually conquered the north, and on September 12, 1988, an OAU cease-fire was accepted by all major forces in Chad. The twenty-three year Chadian civil war appeared to be ended, but the country's future was uncertain.

Impact of Event

Throughout the several phases of Chad's civil war, atrocities were committed by all sides. With the number of political, civilian, and combatant deaths numbering in the tens of thousands, staggering infant and child mortality, and the further disastrous effects of drought, famine, and desertification, Chad's rate of population growth was among Africa's lowest. Chadians on the whole were among the most deprived and terrorized people in the world.

The Tombalbaye and Habré regimes in particular, but also other leaders, resorted to execution of rivals and challengers, detention of activists and demonstrators, and heavy military and tax pressure on civilian communities. Dozens of "conspirators" were executed by martial law authorities between 1965 and 1990. Hundreds of students, professionals, civil servants, and peasants were detained at least briefly, and some languished indefinitely without formal charges being brought. The combined forces of climate, unsanitary conditions, and state security methods made disease and death common in detention. All the armies took hostages. For example, in 1983 the Habré and Oueddei forces each claimed to hold at least one thousand captives, an unknown number of whom died or disappeared.

As each region formed its own militias, the strongest men went off to fight, sometimes to die, leaving their families vulnerable to marauding rival armies and a farm economy hard-pressed to function without their labor. Brutal treatment of one clan was likely to provoke retribution, as in April, 1983, when forty villagers in the far south were massacred. Internecine conflict, particularly between Muslims and non-Muslims, helped perpetuate the vicious cycle of violence. Few families remained unscathed.

As in the Sudan, Ethiopia, and other war-ravaged Sahelian countries, more than two decades of widespread conflict also exacerbated an incipient environmental disaster by killing livestock and crops, pillaging grain stores, removing the strongest farmers, polluting or depleting water wells, driving people from their homes, destroying buildings and power stations, and diverting resources from desperately needed development projects. Weakened by the effects of war, the farm economy of central and northern Chad was decimated by the drought of the mid-1980's. Moreover, since the intermediate-rainfall zone in the south was planted mainly in cotton, there was a small domestic food supply. In 1985, approximately one million people, one-fourth of the population, were weakened by famine and in danger of starvation. At least fifty thousand sought refuge in relief camps. With fewer than one hundred paved miles of road amid thousands of miles of desert, and with much less publicity of its plight than Ethiopia had, Chad was in no position to deliver food, medical supplies, and water to the hardest-hit central regions. Well-intentioned humanitarian relief efforts were nowhere near adequate, especially given that the government was bankrupt and continued to be more concerned with state security than with the quality of its citizens' lives.

Some African theorists have argued that in the African context "human rights" might have a different meaning than in the West. In Chad, the human rights conditions from 1965 until at least 1988 were horrible by any criteria. There was no question of freedom of speech, religious communities were at war with one another, martial law was applied by numerous factions, and property rights could not be guaranteed. Beyond these abuses were the terrible loss of and threat to the lives of Chadians, many of whom suffered physical danger and deprivation for years on end.

Bibliography

Burr, Millard. *Africa's Thirty Years War: Libya, Chad, and the Sudan, 1963-1993.* Boulder, Colo.: Westview Press, 1999. Comprehensive history of three decades of war in three African nations.

Mazrui, Ali A., and Michael Tidy. *Nationalism and New States in Africa from About 1935 to the Present.* Nairobi: Heinemann, 1984. Among the many available books on the colonial background and postindependence problems of African states, this one is useful not only for its fairly thorough review of nationalist, interethnic, and political struggles throughout the continent but also for its section on the civil war in Chad. This is currently one of the few studies of Africa to have such a section.

Nolutshungu, Sam C. *Limits of Anarchy: Intervention and State Formation in Chad.* Charlottesville: University Press of Virginia, 1996. Examines the consequences of foreign intervention in Chad during its thirty years of civil war.

Thompson, Virginia, and Richard Adloff. *The Emerging States of French Equatorial Africa.* Stanford, Calif.: Stanford University Press, 1960. A detailed account of political and economic developments in the four territories of French Equatorial Africa, including a fifty-page chapter on conditions in "Tchad" during the colonial period. Conflicts prior to independence laid the groundwork for civil war.

Whiteman, Kaye. *Chad.* London: Minority Rights Group, 1988. A brief but densely written, information-packed primer on the conundrum of Chadian politics. This study details the events, groups, and leaders that tore Chad apart during the twenty-five years after independence in one of the most embroiled, complex, and violent postcolonial conflicts. Particular attention is paid to civil and political rights and human suffering.

Sheila Carapico

China's Cultural Revolution Starts Wave of Repression

Category of event: Civil rights; political freedom; revolutions and rebellions
Time: 1966-1976
Locale: People's Republic of China

Mao Zedong's ideology motivated millions of Chinese youths to revolt against the bureaucracy, which in turn helped Mao to regain political prominence at the cost of thousands of lives

Principal personages:

MAO ZEDONG (1893-1976), one of the founders of the Chinese Communist Party (CCP), instrumental in the overthrow of Chiang Kai-shek and the Nationalists (1949)

LIN BIAO (1908-1971), Mao's handpicked minister of defense and the de facto head of the People's Liberation Army, the key promoter of Maoist policies and propaganda

JIANG QING (1914-1991), Mao's third wife and a member of the Gang of Four

YAO WENYUAN (1930-   ), a member of the Gang of Four

WANG HONGWEN (1936-1992), a member of the Gang of Four

ZHANG CHUNQIAO (1917-1991), a member of the Gang of Four

DENG XIAOPING (1904-1997), the dominant figure in Chinese politics after Mao's death and the demise of the Gang of Four in 1976

Summary of Event

In 1966, in an effort to restore the revolutionary spirit to the Chinese people and to prevent China's departure from socialism, Mao Zedong motivated millions of Chinese youths to challenge authority and capitalist tendencies— "to make revolution." He called for the masses to challenge authority by removing reactionary elements from Chinese society. These vague objectives only invited abuse, and, as in Mao's Great Leap Forward debacle of 1958, the initial ideological euphoria soon gave way to the reality of mass chaos and societal disarray.

After the Great Leap failure, Mao had found himself on the outside of the political power structure. He would find a new power base not in the traditional political arena but in the ranks of the visionary youth—soon dubbed "Red Guards." These militants, mostly young teens, violently disbarred many authority figures and ushered in a state of chaos, the first stage of the Great Proletarian Cultural Revolution, Mao's direct attack on the very party he helped to found.

Most historical accounts identify the Wu Han case as the beginning of the Cultural Revolution, when in reality this case only set the stage. Although Wu's play *The Dismissal of Hai Rui from Office* (1961) ostensibly depicted Ming politics, it clearly reflected the errors of the contemporary Chinese Communist Party (CCP) cabinet, and, by inference, of Mao himself. Wu's character of the "average official" did not "dare to oppose anything even though he knew it was bad," and his monarch was "self-opinionated and unreceptive to criticism." Subsequently, Mao and his allies began a campaign against antisocialist literature and any antisocialist "poisonous weeds" found in the Chinese cultural garden. Mao had criticized the Ministry of Culture in Beijing for its fascination with ancient history and suggested that the ministry be renamed "the Ministry of Foreign Mummies," "the Ministry of Talents and Beauties," or "the Ministry of Emperors, Kings, Generals, and Ministers." The Maoist People's Liberation Army (PLA) vowed to help "destroy blind faith in Chinese and foreign classical literature." Lin Biao, Mao's rising star and military leader, asserted that "if the proletariat does not occupy the positions in literature and art, the bourgeoisie certainly will. This struggle is inevitable."

The arts struggle interested Mao because it was a plausible pretext for revolution. Mao and his confidants soon signaled an attack on the "four old" elements within society—old customs, old habits, old culture, and old thinking. Unabashedly, Mao expected every communist Chinese to be a revolutionary. Those who were uneducated or inexperienced could be taught and shown the personal value of revolution. China's youth, who had been called on to lead lives of restraint and obedience, readily absorbed lessons of violence. While combating his own political ostracism, Mao publicized legitimate weaknesses in the communist central committee and planned a radical avenue back to political potency. He would rise on the backs of millions of youths who would follow his visionary teachings, canonize his homilies, and attack authorities at every turn. Mao was fulfilling his public promise made in 1958, when the committee had seriously questioned the Great Leap Forward policies, then only a few months old. Mao had informed his obstinate colleagues that he could "go to the countryside to lead the peasants to overthrow the government." He threatened, "If those of you in the Liberation Army won't follow me, then I will go and find a Red Army, and organize another Liberation Army." History substantiated the fears of the acquiescing CCP cabinet, for in 1927, a much younger Mao had predicted that "In a very short time . . . several hundred million peasants will rise like a mighty storm, like a hurricane, a force so swift and violent that no power, however great, will be able to hold it back." Two decades had been a very short time for the world's most durable civilization to wait, but Mao's bold 1958 threat would be realized in just eight years.

Mao's vague tirade against "reactionary" elements was permission enough for the Red Guards to wreak violence on nearly 10 percent of the Chinese population (bureaucrats, those with foreign connections, and unpopular professors were particularly targeted). Suicides (after Red Guard harassment), public humiliations (for example, the cutting of girls' long hair, the forcing of public retractions, and the wearing of dunce caps), and murders became commonplace.

Following Mao's pyrrhic victory via the Red Guards (1966-1968) came the second of the revolution's three stages, dominated not by the Red Guards but rather by the PLA—the stabilizing force between the Red Guards and the Chinese workers. By August of 1968, Mao had organized the Worker-Peasant Mao Zedong Propaganda Teams to disband the Red Guards, which by then were plagued with factional fighting and anarchy. By 1969, Mao had halted the excesses of the revolutionaries by sending them all home or to the fields to work with the peasants. With the assistance of his wife, Jiang Qing, and her associates, Mao launched the Campaign to Purify Class Ranks (1967-1969). Liu Shaoqi and Deng Xiaoping had already been removed from the highest ranks of the CCP, paving the way for its restructuring.

After a period of intense calculated transition and the suspicious death of Lin Biao (1971), the final stage of the revolution ensued, led by Jiang Qing and her associates, collectively dubbed the "Gang of Four." The Four became the dominant political force, having assumed investiture duties, and by 1974 they were also solidly in charge of economics. This oligarchy was short-lived, however, and the Gang of Four's rule abruptly ended with the death of Mao in 1976. The Chinese masses blamed the four for manipulating the aging Mao into starting the misguided revolution and subsequently usurping the dying leader's power. The trial and conviction of the Gang of Four brought an ugly end to an uglier era, but at least there was closure.

Although the secrecy of Chinese communism discredited any definitive explanation of the revolution's causes, two factors loomed large: Mao's radical revolutionary vision and his political aspirations. His revolution was based on ideological incentives, a scheme that would fail not only economically but also diplomatically. Perhaps worst of all, the Cultural Revolution would invoke more humanitarian needs than it could solve. As it had in the 1958-1960 disaster, Mao's ideology paled in the face of pragmatic policies. Volunteerism supplanted planning. In the span of just eight years (1958-1966), Mao instituted such radical measures to protect and propagate his anticapitalist ideology that more than fifty million people would die because of his disregard for social, demographic, and economic realities. His guiding principle was that the quickest route to full communism was revolution. Mao sincerely believed that the Chinese Communist Party (CCP) should be preoccupied with creating a new kind of individual, one committed more to the country than to personal gain. China, Mao thought, needed to be totally self-sufficient, not like the capitalist countries, which would ultimately be swallowed up by communism when their colonial exploitation ceased to be profitable.

Besides the political and social chaos that ensued during "the ten bad years" (1966-1976), a generation of teens later referred to by their fellow Chinese as the "lost generation" would lose as many years of education. At least twenty thousand others lost their lives because of Mao's ill-conceived revolution. Mao's visionary ideology, underlying both the Great Proletarian Cultural Revolution and the Great Leap Forward, lacked any sense of realism.

Impact of Event

The political motivation for the revolution seemed straightforward. Mao and his wife most likely felt disregarded; real political power had obviously shifted to others. A study of the Cultural Revolution is, in large part, a study of Mao's rise in power and popularity and most certainly his fall from political prominence in the early 1960's. As a revolutionary with an ardent belief in involving the masses in revolution, Mao had the singular ability to motivate the Chinese to action. The legendary Long March of 1934 had made him a folk hero, a national symbol for constructive change—a legitimate avenue to reform. Only someone of Mao's stature could reemerge to national prominence after a mistake as grandiose and costly as the Great Leap Forward.

Slogans and scars would survive past the early 1960's, and it would take the Cultural Revolution to put Mao back at the political helm. Even then, the economic scars would persist for at least another generation. Between 1958 and 1965, famine and near-famine touched all of China. Demographic data confirmed that starvation and malnutrition claimed the lives of between twenty and thirty million Chinese between 1959 and 1962. Obviously, Mao's plan to revive the economy had failed. What at first appeared to be an acceptable retreat, a possible prelude to progress, became a glaring economic leap in the wrong direction. Mao was still chairman of the CCP in 1960 but could not pre-

Lin Biao, minister of defense and chief propagandist under Mao Zedong. (Library of Congress)

vent its senior members, led by Liu Shaoqi and Deng Xiaoping, from reversing most of his policies. While his political opponents took aggressive steps to alleviate the food shortage, Mao found himself relegated to the role of a revered ancestor; consultations with Mao were only polite gestures. Thus, the Cultural Revolution was a golden political opportunity, or so it seemed.

After Mao's death in 1976, the most common Chinese reassessment of their great statesman found him responsible for twenty years of misguided policies. Inherent within his system was "the fundamental policy to guide the peasants to accelerate socialist construction, complete the building of socialism ahead of time, and carry out the gradual transition to communism." These boasts were not only visionary but looked at the human condition through clouded ideological glasses. The conditions of life and basically all human rights of the peasants were being ignored. Deng Xiaoping was rehabilitated in 1977 and quickly invoked pragmatic policies. The "Four Modernizations" campaign was launched, emphasizing science and technology, industry, agriculture, and the military.

For Mao, the achievement of full communism justified the certain loss of some lives and the possible loss of millions. At the outset of the Cultural Revolution, the Soviets had long since effaced Joseph Stalin for such faulty logic (later, even the Lenin colossi disappeared). By 1958, Mao asserted that the interests and needs of the Chinese masses could be met only in the context of Maoist, not Marxist-Leninist, socialism. One of the main charges against the Gang of Four was their idealism. They cogently argued for a strict adherence to the communist principles of Marx, Lenin, and Stalin and a plan for world communism, yet they would risk any and all of the gains of the revolution. After the revolution, China was left without any strong belief system. While China looked to the West for modernization assistance, materialism, freedom, capitalism, individualism, and other Western values entered an already vacillating Chinese society.

Bibliography
Hayhoe, Ruth, ed. *Contemporary Chinese Education*. Armonk, N.Y.: M. E. Sharpe, 1984. These six essays give insight into the radical Cultural Revolution system of education and contrast it with the later reformist model of Deng Xiaoping.
Heng, Liang, and Judith Shapiro. *Son of the Revolution*. New York: Vintage Books, 1984. A look at the Cultural Revolution by ex-Red Guards.
Jin, Qiu. *The Culture of Power: The Lin Biao Incident in the Cultural Revolution*. Stanford, Calif.: Stanford University Press, 1999. Fascinating account of the career and mysterious death of Lin Biao in the midst of the Cultural Revolution. Indexed, and includes bibliography.
MacFarquhar, Roderick, Timothy Cheek, and Eugene Wu, eds. *The Secret Speeches of Chairman Mao: From the Hundred Flowers to the Great Leap*. Cambridge, Mass.: Harvard University Press, 1989. An important contribu-

tion of primary sources prefacing Mao's actions during the Cultural Revolution.

Ogden, Suzanne. *Global Studies: China.* 4th ed. Guilford, Conn.: The Dushkin Publishing Group, 1991. A concise account of the Great Leap Forward, with interesting details, that relies almost entirely on primary sources. The section on the People's Republic of China includes twenty-seven articles from leading journals.

Pye, Lucian W. *China: An Introduction.* 4th ed. New York: HarperCollins, 1991. This text places the modern political crises of China in historical and cultural context. Pye poignantly chronicles the Great Leap Forward with nuggets of Maoist quotations. The last three chapters serve as good overviews of the aftermath of the Great Leap Forward, covering "The Leadership of Deng Xiaoping," "China's Bold Effort at Reforms Under Deng Xiaoping," and "China's Future Domestically and Internationally."

Spence, Jonathan D. *The Search for Modern China.* New York: W. W. Norton, 1990. An excellent account of China's history that chronicles the key events that have factored significantly in the state of affairs in China. Spence also includes resourceful footnotes, complemented by an extensive topical bibliography.

Warsaw, Steven. *China Emerges: A Concise History of China from Its Origin to the Present.* 7th ed. Berkeley, Calif.: Diablo Press, 1990. The chapter on "Communism in China" serves as a useful outline of Mao's rise and fall from power. The last two chapters provide a useful outline of the various factors giving rise to open criticism of the CCP. The eleven indexes are filled with both primary sources and research data.

Yan, Jiaqi, and Gao Gao. *Turbulent Decade: A History of the Cultural Revolution.* Edited and translated by D. W. Y. Kwok. Honolulu: University of Hawaii Press, 1996. Based on memoirs and primary sources, the authors provide a readable, comprehensive examination of the Cultural Revolution. Incorporates several useful research tools, such as glossary, bibliography and guide to further reading.

Zang, Xiaowei. *Children of the Cultural Revolution: Family Life and Political Behavior in Mao's China.* Boulder, Colo.: Westview Press, 2000. Sociological study, based on personal interviews, of the impact of the cultural revolution on Chinese youth.

Jerry A. Pattengale

Greek Coup Leads to Military Dictatorship

Category of event: Civil rights; political freedom; revolutions and rebellions
Time: April 21, 1967
Locale: Athens, Greece

> *Colonel George Papadopoulos led a right-wing military coup against the government of Panayiotis Kanellopoulos and established a dictatorship that limited political and civil liberties*

Principal personages:

GEORGE PAPADOPOULOS (1919-1999), the right-wing military leader of the coup

CONSTANTINE II (1940-   ), the king of Greece from 1964 to 1967, sympathetic to the conservatives

PANAYIOTIS KANELLOPOULOS (1902-1986), the prime minister of Greece at the time of the coup, a leader of the conservative National Radical Union

GEORGE PAPANDREOU (1888-1968), the leader of the left-of-center Center Union, the most popular party at the time of the coup

ANDREAS PAPANDREOU (1919-1996), the son of George, also led the Center Union and was popular at the time of the coup

Summary of Event

The history of Greece in the twentieth century is one of turmoil and political struggle. Divided by regionalism, ideology, and economic class, the country has endured war and revolution, occupation and dictatorship. During World War II, Germany, Italy, and Bulgaria conquered and divided the country among themselves. Guerrilla resisters, most of whom opposed both the king and the occupiers and many of whom were communists, believed that they had earned the right to rule the country. After the war, however, the Western-sponsored monarch, George II, returned to the throne. A long civil war, lasting from 1944 until 1949, ensued. The civil war became a struggle between communist forces, backed only half-heartedly by Moscow, and the monarchist supporters, backed whole-heartedly by Washington. Republican noncommunists made their peace with the king.

After King George II died in 1947, his brother King Paul reigned until 1964 and was succeeded by his ineffectual son, King Constantine. In the meantime, Greece, one of the poorest countries in Europe, underwent an economic and political revival with help from the United States and Western Europe. Constitutional government and popular institutions were restored and strengthened, although the United States Department of State preferred and favored the conservative parties to those of the left and center. Washington particularly distrusted George Papandreou, the leader of the popular Center Union, even though he had been one of the first republican leaders to announce support for the monarchy during the war.

In the 1960's, Greek politics once again became chaotic. The slow pace of modernization and gradually rising standard of living produced struggles between town and countryside, the capital and the provinces, and rich and poor. The left, which included labor unions, Marxists, anarchists, and intellectuals, challenged the conservative elements of Greek society—the monarchy, the right-wing politicians, and the church. The right, for its part, incessantly proclaimed the danger of communism, even though by then such danger had largely disappeared.

In 1963, the National Radical Union, a conservative party led by Panayiotis Kanellopoulos and Constantine Karamanlis and backed by Washington, surrendered power after eight years in office. George Papandreou's Center Union took over. Papandreou's son, Andreas, an American-educated economist and flamboyant politician, played a major role in the new government. In 1964, a new election returned George Papandreou with an even larger mandate.

The one policy upon which left and right agreed was the claim for irredenta and the insurance of national homogeneity. Greeks wanted the lands of southern Albania and the island of Cyprus incorporated into their territory. Furthermore, although Greece in the 1960's became more and more democratic in fact as well as in law, one area of significant oppression remained—the right to choose national identity. Greeks traditionally claimed that Albanian and Slavic speakers in the north whose forefathers had belonged to the Greek Orthodox confession were Albanophonic and Slavophonic Greeks, not Albanians or South Slavs. Using a carrot-and-stick policy, the authorities encouraged and pressured inhabitants in the north to "acknowledge" their Greek nationality and to adopt Greek ways, including the use of the Greek language.

The Cyprus question was of greatest concern to the Greeks. The island of Cyprus, while mostly Greek, nevertheless had a minority of 15 to 20 percent

Muslim Turks. Furthermore, although Turkey was the traditional enemy of Greece, both countries now belonged to the North Atlantic Treaty Organization (NATO). Greece also hoped to associate with the European Common Market, and for this reason the Greek governments, whether the National Radical Union or the Center Union was in control, did not push for the incorporation of Cyprus into Greece, but were content to leave it as a separate Greek state.

Not content with this solution, the left-wing military circle *Aspida* (the shield), with the encouragement of Andreas Papandreou, aided and supported those on the island who favored union with Greece. Right-wing military officers disliked George Papandreou's military policies, particularly those governing promotions and appointments within the armed forces. Their fear of *Aspida*'s strength led to further conflicts. Papandreou tried to remove his minister of defense, who supported the right, and assume the post himself. Against custom, King Constantine intervened and prevented the change. In July, 1965, Papandreou protested by resigning. Constantine further confused issues by refusing to grant him a new mandate, even though the Center Union still retained its large majority in parliament.

This "July Crisis" led to a weakening of the Center Union, as renegade members broke with Papandreou in order to preserve their own positions. In the fall, the king appointed a prime minister from the ranks of the right, but he lasted only a few weeks. Indeed, in the period from July, 1965, to April, 1967, five prime ministers served in Greece, but none could muster sufficient force to govern effectively.

In the meantime, Center Union leadership fell to Andreas Papandreou, who began to assume power once held by his aging father. His youth and vigor as well as his nationalism made him a popular figure. Greeks viewed the American-educated Papandreou as a national version of the recently martyred and popular John F. Kennedy.

In the fall of 1966, a trial began of a group of *Aspida* officers charged with treason for their involvement with the Cypriot union movement. The government sought to try Andreas Papandreou as well, but he enjoyed parliamentary immunity. Guilty verdicts against the officers and rumors concerning the arrest of the popular Papandreou led to demonstrations and some outbreaks of violence. The king, desperately seeking a more stable government, consulted with all leading politicians at the end of March. After failing to come up with a solution, Prime Minister Panayiotis Kanellopoulos dissolved parliament and called for new elections in May. With parliament dissolved, the government could arrest Andreas Papandreou, but fear of violence as well as the possibility

Andreas Papandreou was educated in the United States and had an American wife.
(Library of Congress)

of intervention from the right led the elder Papandreou and Kanellopoulos to
agree to extend parliamentary immunity during the campaign. The military
right-wing acted anyway. They had already choreographed a move against
the expected popular demonstration which would come with the arrest of
Andreas Papandreou. To legitimize their coup, they claimed that Papandreou
was involved in a communist conspiracy and that the existing politicians could
not govern. On the morning of April 21, 1967, coup leaders—mostly colonels,
not generals—drove their armored vehicles into Athens. There they arrested
the leading politicians and pressured the king into acknowledging their deed.

Later in the day, Constantine issued a decree suspending the civil liberty provisions of the constitution. Colonel George Papadopoulos soon emerged from the background to become the chief leader of the coup and assumed the premiership.

Impact of Event

Despite some infractions against constitutional and democratic government in the years preceding the coup, the Greek monarchy could be classified as a government generally adhering to modern standards of jurisprudence and civil and political liberties. In contrast, the South American term *junta* soon caught on as descriptive of the coup and as carrying a connotation of contempt. Immediately following the coup, the colonels arrested leading politicians who opposed them, but over the next few months released the most prominent. The *junta* also arrested opposition military officers and forced those who refused to cooperate to resign. This enabled the colonels to move themselves and their friends into the higher ranks, one of the chief goals of the takeover. The *junta* also carried out a purge of the civil and educational establishments, forcing out opponents and replacing the higher ranks with retired military officers. They appointed commissioners in every college, university, and institute and assigned them the tasks of checking curricula and uncovering "subversive" individuals and ideas. The colonels introduced a new constitution that severely limited political and civil liberties. Even the church was purged. The new government dissolved trade unions, even those with right-wing leanings, and appropriated their assets. The new leaders also closed dozens of other organizations which they found distasteful. They forbade gatherings of more than five even in private homes.

The *junta* extended its regulations into the daily lives of the Greek people. They forbade long hair on men and short skirts on women. Church attendance became compulsory. Censors banned hundreds of books and the playing of the works of the leftist composer and poet Mikis Theodorakis, one of the country's most prominent international figures. Newspapers found themselves under strict censorship as well, mitigated only by a limited freedom for foreign journalists, whose papers were still sold in Greece and who could be quoted to an extent by the Greek press. The government closed many newspapers and arrested journalists or hounded them into exile.

The colonels treated offenses against the martial law regime with draconian rigor. One well-known diplomat was imprisoned for having a group larger than five in his home. Many ordinary citizens as well as prominent opponents of the regime were detained without fair trial and subjected to torture and abuse. Papadopoulos attempted to give his government a populist appearance, but despite some superficial acts, such as the forgiving of some peasant indebtedness, the masses of Greeks fared no better than they had in the past, and with regard to civil liberties were far worse off.

Active and passive resistance to the *junta* expanded both inside the country and abroad, but this opposition, even with foreign support, could not oust the colonels. The king tried to organize a countercoup at the end of 1967, but the colonels foiled it and drove him from the country. In the fall of 1973, some of the dictator's own associates removed him from power, although the *junta* remained intact. Eight months later, in July, 1974, the military leaders resigned and democratic government was restored. The main catalyst for the change in 1974 was the Cyprus issue, over which the Turks and Greeks were in open conflict. When Turkey invaded the island and the *junta* could not respond effectively, the government resigned within a few days. Ironically, that same issue, Cyprus, had played a major role in sparking the coup of 1967.

Bibliography

Andrews, Kevin. *Greece in the Dark: 1967-1974.* Amsterdam: Adolf M. Hakkert, 1980. A narrative accounting the crimes and violations of human rights by the colonels' regime. Contains interviews, statements, and documents, some in the original Greek with English translation. Documentation, no bibliography or index.

Becket, James. *Barbarism in Greece: A Young American Lawyer's Inquiry into the Use of Torture in Contemporary Greece, with Case Histories and Documents.* New York: Walker, 1970. A collection of case histories, documents, and statements about the violations of human rights by the *junta.* Appendices contain lists of resistance movements and of persons killed and tortured.

Closs, Richard. *A Concise History of Greece.* New York: Cambridge University Press, 2002. 2d ed. Written for a general audience, this volume provides an accessible introduction to the history of modern Greece. Illustrated, includes tables, chronology and guide to further reading.

Danopoulos, Constantine P. *Warriors and Politicians in Modern Greece.* Chapel Hill, N.C.: Documentary Publications, 1984. A narrative and analysis of the Greek military before and after the coup. Excellent bibliography. Illustrations, documentation, and index.

Kaloudis, George S. *Modern Greek Democracy: The End of a Long Journey?* Lanham, Md.: University Press of America, 2000. Includes a chapter on Greece under the dictatorship of 1967-1974.

Kourvetaris, George A. *Studies on Modern Greek Society and Politics.* Boulder,

Colo.: East European Monographs, 1999. Includes a chapter on the 1967 military coup and the role of the military in Greek politics. Bibliography.

Papandreou, Margaret. *Nightmare in Athens.* Englewood Cliffs, N.J.: Prentice-Hall, 1970. A personal account of the coup and of the succeeding events, by the American-born wife of Andreas Papandreou. The author describes the effects of the coup on her family and friends and gives some background from Papandreou's perspective. Castigates Washington for unfairly supporting conservative governments in Greece. Valuable as a primary source. Contains a list of the fates of some persons mentioned in the text. Index, no bibliography.

Theodorakis, Mikis. *Journal of Resistance.* Translated by Graham Webb. New York: Coward, McCann & Geoghegan, 1973. A diary written by the prominent Greek composer, poet, and author of the years he spent in prison under the colonels. Contains some of his poetry and polemics against the *junta.* Translated from French. Contains a chronology and glossary. No index or bibliography.

Woodhouse, C. M. *The Rise and Fall of the Greek Colonels.* London: Granada, 1985. A well-researched, authoritative account of the *junta*'s regime by a leading scholar of modern Greek history. Although the author is generally unsympathetic to the colonels, his work maintains the highest standard of scholarship and was written long enough after the events to provide perspective. The best single work on the subject. Illustrations, references, bibliography, and index.

Frederick B. Chary

Biafra's Secession Triggers Nigerian Civil War

Category of event: Accused persons' rights; indigenous peoples' rights; political freedom
Time: May 30, 1967-January 15, 1970
Locale: Eastern Region, Nigeria

> *The secession of Biafra and the Nigerian civil war posed a human rights dilemma for the Nigerian and other governments*

Principal personages:
YAKUBU GOWON (1934-   ), the Nigerian head of state
CHUKWUEMEKA ODUMEGWU OJUKWU (1933-   ), leader of the secessionist Ibo Eastern Region
OLUSEGUN OBASANJO (1937-   ), a military leader who facilitated the surrender of Biafrans and later became Nigerian head of state
PHILIP EFFIONG, replaced Ojukwu in the final days of the Biafran fighting and ordered the cease-fire of the Biafran armed forces

Summary of Event

On May 30, 1967, the Eastern Region of Nigeria, populated by more than nine million Ibo ethnic Nigerians, declared itself the sovereign state of the Republic of Biafra. Lieutenant Colonel Chukwuemeka Odumegwu Ojukwu charged that continuous violations of Ibo human rights by other Nigerians, particularly the Hausa ethnic group in the Northern Region, dictated the need for a separate Ibo state. The federal government of Nigeria vowed to prevent the dismantling of the Nigerian state. A civil war ensued that lasted more than two years.

In 1960, when Nigeria gained its independence, its major ethnic and religious groups competed for political control of the new state. The dominant and populous Northern, Muslim Hausa and the Eastern, Christian Ibo formed an uneasy alliance that effectively excluded the Western Yoruba from power. The new government, however, was unable to rule without recurring challenges to its legitimacy.

Following widespread allegations that the 1963 census and the elections of

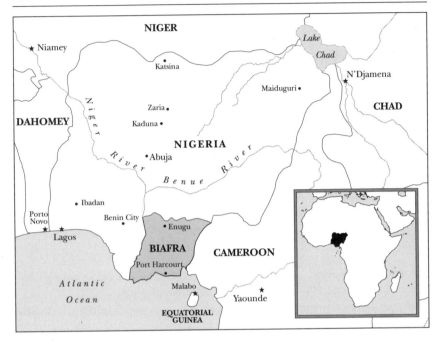

1964 and 1965 were corrupt, Nigerians experienced outbursts of political unrest. Some Western political leaders were imprisoned by the federal government, allegedly for initiating a Western secession movement. In January, 1966, young Ibo army officers revolted and murdered the minister of finance, the prime minister, and other ranking Northerners. The Ibo officers insisted that their revolt was an anticorruption, profederation coup attempt and not an ethnically based action to advance the power of Ibos. Most Northern Hausa rejected this claim, however, because no Ibos had been murdered during the coup attempt. Moreover, the murdered prime minister was viewed as one of the federal government's anticorruption stalwarts.

Lieutenant Colonel Yakubu Gowon, a Northern officer from a small Christian ethnic group, organized government troops to respond to the revolt. Major General J. T. U. Aguiyi Ironsi also responded, and a few days after the coup, Ironsi assumed political power as supreme commander and Nigeria's head of state. Ironsi attempted to replace Nigeria's federal system with a unitary national government. In protest, many Nigerians rioted and used the opportunity to attack Ibos, who were given no government police or military protection. Many Ibos were beaten and killed in three days of rioting. A few weeks later, in late July, 1966, Ironsi was overthrown and murdered by military officers who, observers say, opposed altering the structures of the federal state of Nigeria. Gowon replaced Ironsi.

Gowon attempted to win support of Nigeria's disparate ethnic groups by reinstating the federal system while accommodating some of the demands of the West and the East. Gowon freed a popular political prisoner from the West, Chief Awolowo, and removed northern federal troops from the Eastern Region when Ibo Governor Ojukwu demanded their removal. Ojukwu, however, refused to recognize Gowon as Nigeria's executive authority, illustrating the Ibo's discontent with their lot in Nigerian politics.

On September 29, 1966, Nigerians once again attacked Ibos, slaughtering tens of thousands. The Ibo responded in the East by slaughtering Hausa and Fulani. It was estimated at this time that about one million Ibos fled Nigeria or returned to the Eastern Region for safety. Many of these Ibo were forced to live in refugee camps, and in the ensuing civil war many died from malnutrition and other health-related causes.

In March, 1967, Ibo Governor Ojukwu retained all taxes collected in the Eastern Region. Gowon warned Ojukwu not to attempt any secessionist effort. Western Region officials also began to talk of seceding, and Gowon tried to placate them by removing some federal troops from the West. Some observers have suggested that this effort to ease tensions was interpreted as a sign of weakness.

On May 27, 1967, Ojukwu and a number of Ibo chiefs declared the Eastern Region independent of Nigerian authority. In response, Gowon issued a decree to restructure the existing regions into twelve districts, including five in the East, which would allow non-Ibos in the East to exercise some political influence. On May 30, 1967, Ojukwu announced the secession of the East and declared that region the Republic of Biafra.

Gowon initiated an economic boycott of the East and began a military campaign against Ojukwu and his Biafran army. The French assisted Biafra militarily, and the civil war raged. Food in the East was in short supply. International Biafran relief committees formed and demanded the right to send food and health supplies to the isolated Ibo. Nigeria's federal government opposed relief efforts, arguing that the civil war would end more quickly if the economic boycott were allowed to continue without disruption, forcing the Ibo to surrender. Through the boycott, the federal government hoped to prevent arms, food, and medical supplies from reaching Biafra and to prevent petroleum from being exported by the Biafrans. This would prevent them from earning international foreign currency with which to purchase supplies.

Ojukwu and the Biafrans appealed to the international community for help on the principle of self-determination, argued that the Christian Ibo were victims of religious persecution by Northern Muslim zealots, and charged that the Nigerian federal government was pursuing a policy of genocide against the Ibo through military and economic warfare. Biafrans argued that Nigeria's recent history demonstrated that there was no hope of peaceful co-existence among the contending ethnic and religious groups.

The Biafrans made available to leading Western media officials detailed, well-argued political position papers and photographs of starving Biafrans. Biafran officials claimed that five thousand Ibos a day were dying from malnutrition and that the federal government's air attacks were killing thousands of civilians. The Nigerian federal government obstructed efforts by international aid organizations, such as the International Red Cross, and newly initiated organizations of Western cultural artists seeking to help relieve the famine in Biafra. Reluctantly, Gowon finally agreed to permit a land corridor through which supplies could pass. The Biafrans, however, demanded air relief.

Despite pressures from Western governments for a negotiated settlement, the Nigerian federal government delayed negotiations of a ceasefire, hoping that Biafra would be forced to sue for peace, thus preventing a negotiated compromise that would undermine Nigeria's central government. The federal government also argued against any foreign assistance to Biafra on the grounds that under the rules of the Organization of African Unity (OAU), no foreign power could aid efforts to redraw the boundaries of an African state. Member countries of the OAU, however, were divided in their support of the federal government and the Biafrans. The federal government of Nigeria accused the leaders of the new Biafran state of creating a civil war and a great human tragedy to advance their own careers. Gowon repeatedly pledged to protect the physical security of Biafrans if they would relent in their secessionist efforts.

After two and a half years of fighting, with thousands of federal soldiers who had been killed, millions of Ibos who had suffered and died, and millions more Ibos who were displaced from their homes, the federal government inflicted a major military loss on the Ibo. In January, 1970, with food and ammunition low, the Biafrans were militarily defeated when Colonel Olusegun Obasanjo captured the important town of Owerri. Shortly thereafter, Ojukwu and his family fled to the Ivory Coast. On January 13, 1970, Lieutenant Colonel Philip Effiong, who replaced Ojukwu as the major Biafran authority, surrendered to the federal government. Biafran decision-making bodies were dissolved, and the Ibo waited anxiously for the next actions of the federal government.

Impact of Event

Immediately, the federal government found itself responsible for distributing the much-needed aid that international donors pledged to provide. Nigeria's government would not allow distribution of food and medicine by any international agency that had aided Biafra during the civil war. While the federal government handled thousands of tons of food a week, it could not meet the needs of the Biafrans immediately after the cease-fire.

The fears of massacres and retaliation against Ibos that had provided some of the motivation for support of Biafra never materialized. Gowon enforced a national policy of reconciliation, and observers marveled at the speed and ease with which Ibos were reabsorbed into government and private Nigerian life. Some Ibos who had served in low-level federal government positions and fled to the East seeking safety now returned to their former posts with the federal government. Many leaders of the secessionist movement, however, were not reabsorbed. The ability to reabsorb the Ibo as an ethnic group has been attributed by some observers to the economic boom Nigeria experienced from oil price increases in the early 1970's. These increases provided expanding revenues from which it was possible to distribute resources to Nigerians of many ethnic backgrounds. Although economic discrimination did not fuel Nigeria's ethnic strife in the 1970's, Nigeria's civil war had entrenched military rule; a return to democratic civilian government would elude Nigerians for years. The civil rights that accompany democratic civilian government also eluded Nigerians for years. Union strikes were banned, political movements that the government designated as appealing to secessionist impulses were outlawed, journalists worried about censorship, and academics were restrained from criticizing the government freely. When the oil boom collapsed in the mid-1980's, Nigerians faced economic dilemmas as well.

In the years following the Biafran secession, Nigerians have had to cope with many of the problems that plagued other late-industrializing states. There has not been, however, any repeat of the atrocities and ethnic conflict on the scale of the 1960's. By the 1990's, Nigeria was struggling with issues of democratization and development, not with extraordinary human rights violations motivated by ethnic rivalry.

Bibliography

Ayittey, George B. N. *Africa in Chaos*. New York: St. Martin's Press, 1999. The author provides a scholarly analysis of the social, political and economic troubles that plague the African continent, including Nigeria's collapse.

Draper, Michael I., and Frederick Forsyth. *Shadows: Airlift and Airwar in Biafra and Nigeria 1967-1970.* Hikoki, 2001. Account of the challenges facing the Biafran air force during the three-year civil war. Draper was briefly involved in the airlift during 1968.

Kirk-Greene, Anthony H. M., and Douglas Rimmer. *Nigeria Since 1970.* New York: Africana, 1981. Covers the time period from the aftermath of the Nigerian civil war to the election of Nigeria's first, short-lived, post-civil-war democratic government in 1979. The authors examine the 1970's as a decade of expanding oil profits for Nigeria and explore the alternative schemes for development and democratization. Separate chapters discuss agriculture, petroleum, industrialization, infrastructure, public finance, external trade, and development planning.

Osaghae, Eghosa E. *Crippled Giant: Nigeria Since Independence.* Bloomington: Indiana University Press, 1998. Scholarly, political history of Nigeria. Illustrated.

Stremlau, John. *The International Politics of the Nigerian Civil War, 1967-1970.* Princeton, N.J.: Princeton University Press, 1977. Stremlau offers a richly researched study of the foreign policies of the Nigerian federal government, the Biafrans, and other countries and international organizations that became involved in the Nigerian civil war.

Eve N. Sandberg

Brezhnev Doctrine Bans Independent Behavior by Soviet Satellites

Category of event: Political freedom; revolutions and rebellions
Time: 1968-1989
Locale: Moscow, Soviet Union

> *Under the Brezhnev Doctrine, the Soviet Union exercised the right of direct intervention to restore order anywhere among its satellites that it deemed socialism to be threatened*

Principal personages:

LEONID ILICH BREZHNEV (1906-1982), the general secretary of the Communist Party and the leader of the Soviet Union

MIKHAIL GORBACHEV (1931-   ), the president of the Soviet Union who renounced the Brezhnev Doctrine in 1989

NIKITA S. KHRUSHCHEV (1894-1971), the first secretary of the Communist Party and premier of the Soviet Union who formulated the policy of the Brezhnev Doctrine

ALEXANDER DUBČEK (1921-1992), the first secretary of the Czechoslovak Communist Party who oversaw the liberalization of the "Prague Spring" in 1968

IMRE NAGY (1896-1958), the Hungarian communist premier who led the revolt against the Soviet Union in 1956

TITO (1892-1980), the Yugoslav communist leader who helped to separate his country from the Soviet empire in 1948

Summary of Event

As a victorious Ally and in direct violation of the provisions of the Atlantic Charter (1941) against territorial aggrandizement at the expense of the enemy, after World War II the Soviet Union came to inherit an empire larger than the old Romanov, Hohenzollern, and Habsburg empires combined. This diverse, multinational new empire consisted of an expanded Soviet Union plus numerous satellite states surrounding its Eurasian frontiers, and it reflected the Soviet Union's status as an emerging superpower in the vacuum left by the total defeat of the Axis by the Allied Powers. The founding of this communist empire through the victories and subsequent occupation by the

341

counterattacking Red Army after the Battle of Stalingrad (1942-1943) also marked a beginning of the post-World War II Cold War between the Soviet Union and its Western allies.

The Brezhnev Doctrine was a policy evolved by the Soviet Union for the maintenance of its empire against the right and forces of national self-determination. Under this coercive and punitive program, the Soviet Union assumed the right to intervene directly anywhere in its sphere—from East Germany, Hungary, and Czechoslovakia to Afghanistan—where it deemed "socialism" to be threatened. It was specifically enunciated by Leonid Brezhnev in his "Speech to the Fifth Congress of the Polish United Workers Party" in Warsaw on November 12, 1968, in connection with the Soviet-Warsaw Pact invasion of Czechoslovakia on August 20-21, 1968, to suppress the moves toward greater independence during the so-called Prague Spring. The policy's foundations actually were laid in the late 1940's.

With the split of Yugoslavia under Josip Broz Tito from the Soviet empire in 1948 and the success of the communists in China in 1949, new centers of communism in addition to Moscow began to arise in Belgrade, Beijing, and elsewhere, threatening Soviet hegemony. World communism was becoming polycentric and multinational with the appearance of Titoism, Maoism, and other forms. Nationalism began to express itself through communism as well as affecting the nature of communism.

Events in Eastern Europe mirrored these changes in the Soviet empire and communist ideology. In the early 1950's, continued repression and deteriorating economic conditions led to worker unrest in Poland and East Germany, culminating in a Soviet military intervention to put down strikes in East Germany in 1953. This invasion to suppress German worker and national aspirations was the first application of the Soviet policy later to be dubbed the Brezhnev Doctrine. In 1956, Nikita Khrushchev similarly ordered the Soviet army to crush the Hungarian uprising under Imre Nagy. The Hungarian situation was seen as much more severe than the earlier ones in Poland and East Germany. After initially trying to reform communism in Hungary, the revolutionaries had quickly moved toward discarding it and adopting national independence. Consequently, the Soviet reaction also was much more severe, earning Khrushchev, the real author of the Brezhnev Doctrine, the nickname "the butcher of Budapest."

Thereafter, East Germany and Hungary stood as clear examples to the peoples of the Soviet empire dreaming of national rights and freedoms. During the 1960's and 1970's, any moves toward the realization of these dreams had to be carried out carefully so as not to bring down the full force of Soviet power.

Leonid Brezhnev laid out his doctrine in a speech in Warsaw on November 12, 1968. (Library of Congress)

Over the next two decades, for example, Romania slowly moved toward greater independence, Hungary gradually established a more Western national economy, and Albania broke away from the Soviet empire under Chinese sponsorship. As part of this process, liberalization came to Czechoslovakia under Alexander Dubček in 1968. Brezhnev and the Soviet leadership watched these events closely and periodically issued warnings to the Czech leadership. Once again, when the situation deteriorated too far for the Soviet Union, it declared socialism in danger in Czechoslovakia and interfered, with the Brezhnev Doctrine as its justification.

The invasion of Czechoslovakia demonstrated the Soviet Union's commitment to maintaining its hegemony, and internationally this event had significant negative ramifications for the Soviet Union. For example, the process of Soviet-American détente was set back at least five years, the Soviet-Yugoslav rapprochement was halted, and the Soviet Union generally lost prestige abroad. Despite these consequences, the policy was not abandoned, and late in 1979 the Soviet Union intervened again, this time in Afghanistan to prop up and finally to replace a faltering communist regime. This intervention precipitated prolonged Western-supported resistance and a civil war which became the Soviet Union's Vietnam.

The Brezhnev Doctrine not only put pressure on the various satellites to remain loyal and to conform to the Soviet ideology but also was used to intimidate the subject nationalities of the Soviet Union. The message was clear: If the Soviet leadership was willing to use whatever force was necessary in East Berlin, Budapest, Prague, or Kabul, it certainly would not hesitate to do so in Vilnius, Kiev, Yerevan, or Tashkent to stifle any national aspirations or disorders. The Soviet "socialist peace" was maintained until 1985 and the coming of Mikhail Gorbachev.

Enforcement of the Brezhnev Doctrine, especially in the case of the costly war in Afghanistan, contributed greatly to the decline of the Soviet economy. Gorbachev inherited this economy, which was on the verge of collapse. Like the Russian empire before it, the Soviet Union was not only economically bankrupt but ideologically bankrupt as well. Gorbachev's eventual response was sweeping reform, and the more democratic era of *glasnost* (openness) and *perestroika* (restructuring) was initiated. With this liberalization of the Soviet system came the demise of the Brezhnev Doctrine.

From the time of the founding of the opposition Solidarity trade union at the Lenin Shipyard in Gdansk in 1980, Poland was in danger of running afoul of the Brezhnev Doctrine. The Soviet Union did not respond as in the past, in part because of the sorry state of the Soviet economy and the war in Afghanistan and in part because of the instability of top leadership after the death of Brezhnev. Under Gorbachev, the Soviet Union withdrew from Afghanistan in 1989, and with Poland and Yugoslavia leading the way, Eastern Europe also began to liberalize.

In the waning weeks of 1989, Gorbachev indicated on several occasions, such as during an official visit to Finland, that the Soviet Union would no longer intervene in the internal affairs of its satellites and, thereby, that the Brezhnev Doctrine was dead. Thereafter, Poland and the other Central and Eastern European satellites quickly asserted their national independence from the disintegrating Soviet empire. Following their lead, other republics and peoples in the Soviet Union began to assert their national rights and identities.

The Brezhnev Doctrine, as it became known in the West, was never proclaimed publicly as such by the Soviet Union, which even denied that such a policy existed. From its real inception under Khrushchev through its practice and justification by Brezhnev to its passing under Gorbachev, it was a major foundation for the centralized control exercised from Moscow throughout the Soviet domains.

Impact of Event

For four decades, the Brezhnev Doctrine helped to restrict severely the human rights of the Eurasian peoples under Soviet domination. For example, in forcing the adherence of Hungarian, Polish, or Lithuanian Catholics, Jews, Volga Germans, and Crimean Tatars to the Soviet state and its Stalinist ideology, the Soviet Union deprived these peoples of rights of national self-determination; they tried to destroy their national cultures, aspirations, and identities and replace them with artificial and alien Soviet substitutes. The Brezhnev Doctrine was nothing more than a brutal policy of Stalinist imperialism and totalitarian control.

In these years, Soviet power rested largely on the use of force, force which the Soviet Union readily exercised to control its satellites and to bully its own citizens into submission. Partially under the auspices of the Brezhnev Doctrine, the Soviet Union tried in vain to substitute material progress and hollow superpower prestige for national and individual freedoms. It succeeded only in stifling real leadership and productivity, initiative, and creativity.

While somewhat dampened perhaps, the fires of nationalism were not so easily extinguished. In 1989, once the oppression of communism began to lift through Gorbachev's reforms and abandonment of the Brezhnev Doctrine, the blossoms of national rights quickly began to bloom again. One by one, Soviet satellites moved toward national self-determination and took on its challenges. Civil war persisted in Afghanistan, but without foreign involvement, indicating that the country would find its own solutions to its problems. Germany was reunited, and Poland, Czechoslovakia, and Hungary moved rapidly toward democracy. Romania, Bulgaria, and Mongolia moved more slowly, but all took steps toward independent and more democratic futures.

The abandonment of the Brezhnev Doctrine was part of a general Soviet pullback internationally. Consequently, settlements to problems became more readily achievable in areas of former Soviet involvement from the Middle East, where the curtailment of Soviet aid to Syria, Libya, and the Palestine Liberation Organization brought a regional peace agreement closer, to southern Africa, where Soviet moderation brought an end to the Angolan civil war and a greater willingness of the African National Congress to cooperate with reform efforts in the Republic of South Africa, and to Central America, where the new Soviet stance helped force the Sandinista government to grant free elections and left Cuba effectively isolated. Even in tiny Albania, the Soviet moves contributed to the breakdown of Stalinist isolationism and to democratic changes.

On the other hand, in the Soviet Union itself, the resultant resurgence of nationalism, inspired in part by events and changes in Central and Eastern Europe, brought major problems. It also speeded the drastic political and economic restructuring by fostering democratization and the transition to a free market system as well as the national realignment of the Soviet Union. The Brezhnev Doctrine was a major impediment to human rights and progress in the Soviet empire and ultimately was symptomatic of its political, economic, social, and ideological weaknesses. Its renunciation contributed substantially to a dynamic for momentous change in the Soviet Union and elsewhere by ending the Cold War and encouraging international cooperation.

Bibliography

Dawisha, Karen. *Eastern Europe, Gorbachev, and Reform: The Great Challenge.* 2d ed. Cambridge, England: Cambridge University Press, 1990. A contemporary evaluation of the era of *glasnost* and *perestroika.* Offers an understanding of the reasons for and consequences of the Soviet renunciation of the Brezhnev Doctrine by Gorbachev.

Dawisha, Karen, and Bruce Parrott, eds. *Conflict, Cleavage, and Change in Central Asia and the Caucasus.* New York: Cambridge University Press, 1997. A scholarly examination of the impact of democracy on former Soviet states.

Gati, Charles. *The Bloc That Failed: Soviet-East European Relations in Transition.* Bloomington: Indiana University Press, 1990. A good study of contemporary Soviet-European relations. Deals with the formulation and impact of the Brezhnev Doctrine as well as the current outcomes of its abandonment by the Soviet Union under Gorbachev. A factual and well-written account.

Gorbachev, Mikahil S. *Gorbachev.* New York: Columbia University Press, 1999. Translated by George Shriver. This collection of essays reflecting on the political history of the Soviet Union is mainly useful for the perspective it provides on its author, the former president of the Soviet Union.

Hamsik, Dusan. *Writers Against Rulers.* New York: Random House, 1971. A detailed discussion of the coming of the Prague Spring by a leading Czech intellectual and participant. Chapter 8 deals specifically with the Soviet-Warsaw Pact intervention, the Czech reaction to it, and the Brezhnev Doctrine. Written from the Czech point of view.

Hutchings, Robert L. *Soviet-East European Relations: Consolidation and Conflict 1968-1980.* Madison: University of Wisconsin Press, 1983. A concise history of post-1968 Soviet-East European relations, stressing the impact of the Brezhnev Doctrine on foreign policy. Internal as well as external factors shaping the policy are examined. Includes a good bibliography.

Nogee, Joseph L., and Robert H. Donaldson. *Soviet Foreign Policy Since World War II.* 3d ed. New York: Pergamon Press, 1988. A standard history of contemporary Soviet foreign policy. Puts the emergence of the Brezhnev Doctrine in the broader perspective of post-World War II Soviet international relations. Chapter 7 concerns the events surrounding the formation and executions of the policy.

Staar, Richard F. *USSR Foreign Policies After Détente.* Stanford, Calif.: Hoover Institution Press, 1987. Social-science analysis of Soviet foreign policy and its making in the years since Khrushchev and Brezhnev. The impact of the Brezhnev Doctrine, its deterioration, and its reversal are aptly discussed in a wider context. Somewhat dated but still very good for the basics of policy making.

Stokes, Gale, ed. *From Stalinism to Pluralism: A Documentary History of Eastern Europe Since 1945.* New York: Oxford University Press, 1991. These edited primary sources put the Brezhnev Doctrine into the broader historical perspective of post-World War II Eastern Europe. Part 2 concerns the formulation of the policy and contains the actual speech by Brezhnev of November 12, 1968, enunciating it.

Volkogonov, Dmitri. *Autopsy for an Empire: The Seven Leaders Who Built the Soviet Regime.* New York: Free Press, 1998. Edited and translated by Harold Shukman. The author, a prominent historian and former Soviet general, with access to formerly secret files, provides a sweeping history of Soviet leaders including Khrushchev, Brezhnev, and Gorbachev. Indexed.

Dennis Rienhartz

Proclamation of Teheran Sets Human Rights Goals

Category of event: International norms
Time: May 13, 1968
Locale: Teheran, Iran

The International Conference on Human Rights adopted the Proclamation of Teheran, setting priorities for the future human rights work of the United Nations

Principal personages:

PRINCESS ASHRAF PAHLAVI (1919-   ), the elected president of the conference, wife of the ruling shah of Iran

MARC SCHREIBER (1915-   ), the director of the United Nations' Division of Human Rights; executive secretary of the conference

U THANT (1909-1974), the secretary-general of the United Nations who presented the opening address to the conference

C. K. DAPHTARY (1893-?), the representative of India and chair of the drafting committee

Summary of Event

In December, 1963, the United Nations General Assembly proclaimed 1968 as the International Year for Human Rights. In connection with this celebration, the International Conference on Human Rights met in Teheran, Iran, from April 22 through May 13, 1968. The meeting was seen as an occasion for detached stocktaking and long-term planning, as Secretary-General U Thant put it in his address to the conference, in an environment of recently renewed international human rights activity.

The adoption of the Universal Declaration of Human Rights in December, 1948, was followed by more than a decade of little progress in U.N. human rights activity. Like most other issues in international relations, human rights became subordinated to Cold War rivalry. Each bloc focused its attention on violations in the other and raised issues of human rights primarily as a matter of ideological struggle. In such an environment, even the further development of international human rights norms became problematic. For example, drafting of the international human rights covenant, which attempted to

348

give binding legal force to the rights proclaimed in the Universal Declaration, was largely complete by 1953. Nevertheless, the covenant was tabled because of insuperable ideological rivalry over the status of economic and social rights.

By the mid-1960's, however, the political context began to change. A large part of the explanation lies in the one area of human rights in which the United Nations had been active, that of self-determination and decolonization. In 1945, when the United Nations was founded, most of Africa and Asia were Western colonial possessions. That situation began to change with the independence of Indonesia and India in 1947. The process of decolonization took off dramatically, with the active support of the United Nations, in the late 1950's and early 1960's. By 1970, more than 99 percent of the world's people lived in independent states.

The Afro-Asian bloc became the largest voting bloc in the United Nations during the 1960's. These countries, which had suffered under colonial rule, had a special interest in reviving the issue of human rights. They also found a sympathetic hearing from at least some Western European and Latin American countries. There was thus a renewed flurry of activity, beginning in 1960, when the General Assembly adopted resolution 1514, the Declaration on the Granting of Independence to Colonial Countries and Peoples. In 1961, the Nonaligned Movement (NAM) first met on a formal basis, in an attempt to organize the political power of what became known as the Third World.

The political subordination of colonialism was usually associated with pervasive discrimination against indigenous people of color. Therefore, it is not surprising that racial discrimination was another high-priority item for the new states of Africa and Asia. In 1963, the General Assembly adopted a Declaration on the Elimination of All Forms of Racial Discrimination, and in 1965 it completed work on the International Convention on the Elimination of All Forms of Racial Discrimination.

The momentum generated by these new initiatives on self-determination and racial discrimination spread into the general human rights work of the United Nations. In 1966, the International Human Rights Covenants were finally completed. The Teheran Conference reflected this reinvigoration of international human rights activity.

The Teheran Conference was the largest intergovernmental human rights conference ever held. Eighty-four states participated, along with representatives or observers from fifty-seven nongovernmental organizations, seven other U.N. bodies and specialized agencies, and four regional organizations. In addition to the Proclamation of Teheran, a statement of human rights priorities for the international community, the conference adopted twenty-six substantive resolutions on a great variety of human rights issues.

The operative paragraphs of the Proclamation of Teheran begin by stressing the importance of states fulfilling their human rights obligations as laid out in the Universal Declaration of Human Rights. The goal of human rights activity should be "the achievement by each individual of the maximum freedom and dignity." In pursuit of this goal, freedoms of expression, information, conscience, and religion, as well as the right to participate in political, economic, cultural, and social life, are proclaimed to be particularly important.

The proclamation also gives specific attention to apartheid and racial discrimination; self-determination; international cooperation to avoid aggression and war; the widening gap between rich and poor countries; the special importance of economic, social, and cultural rights and economic and social development; illiteracy; women's rights; the rights of families and children; the rights and contributions of youth; scientific and technical developments; and disarmament. It concludes by urging "all peoples and governments to dedicate themselves to the principles enshrined in the Universal Declaration of Human Rights and to redouble their efforts to provide for all human beings a life consonant with freedom and dignity and conducive to physical, mental, social and spiritual welfare."

The fact that the Proclamation of Teheran covers so much ground in just a few pages suggests its extreme generality. For the most part, each topic receives only a short paragraph that reiterates general and often-expressed principles and aspirations. There is little that is innovative, but the special priorities of the conference and the proclamation do reflect changes in the makeup of the international community in the twenty years after the Universal Declaration of Human Rights.

Much the same is true of the resolutions of the conference, most of which are short and very general. In addition to the topics covered in the proclamation, the conference adopted resolutions on human rights in Israeli-occupied territory, Nazism and racial intolerance, opponents of racist regimes, nondiscrimination in employment, model rules of procedure for human rights bodies, cooperation with the United Nations High Commission for Refugees, rights of detainees, family planning, legal aid, human rights education, an International Year for Action to Combat Racism and Racial Discrimination, publicity for the Universal Declaration of Human Rights, and sporting boycotts of South Africa.

Article 4 of the proclamation noted that considerable progress had been made in the elaboration of international human rights standards but that much remained to be done in the area of implementing these rights. Likewise,

Secretary-General U Thant, in his opening address to the conference, noted that it "must find new means of carrying out the continuing struggle for the recognition and enjoyment of human rights." In this endeavor, however, the International Conference on Human Rights achieved little or nothing. It made no suggestions for new international institutions or procedures to implement internationally recognized human rights. In fact, the conference did not even vote on, let alone adopt, draft resolutions by Haiti and the Ivory Coast suggesting the creation of an international human rights court.

Impact of Event

The lack of both substantive and procedural innovation in the products of the International Conference on Human Rights might suggest that it was of ephemeral importance. Nevertheless, it (along with the completion of the International Human Rights Covenants in the fall of 1966) marks an important turning point in international action on behalf of human rights.

By the mid-1960's, there was a growing recognition that if the United Nations was to continue to contribute significantly in the field of human rights, it would have to move into new areas of activity. Through 1966, the principal human rights work of the United Nations was focused on creating international norms, supplemented by efforts to publicize and promote these norms. The United Nations simply did not have the power to require states to implement internationally recognized human rights.

If there was to be major progress in international action on behalf of human rights after 1966, it would have to come primarily in the area of implementing, or monitoring the implementation of, these standards. In the late 1960's, the United Nations did launch a number of new initiatives that attempted to monitor national human rights performance. In 1967, the Commission on Human Rights was given the authority to discuss human rights violations in particular countries. In 1968, a special committee of investigation was created to consider human rights in the territories occupied by Israel after its war with its Arab neighbors in 1967. In the same year, the Security Council imposed a mandatory blockade on the white minority regime in South Rhodesia. The 1965 racial discrimination convention, which was the first international human rights procedure that required states to submit mandatory periodic reports on implementation, came into force in 1969. In 1970, Economic and Social Council Resolution 1503 authorized the Commission on Human Rights to conduct confidential investigations of communications (complaints) that suggested "a consistent pattern of gross and reliably attested violations of human rights and fundamental freedoms."

None of these new initiatives appears to have been directly influenced by the International Conference on Human Rights. They do, however, reflect the human rights concerns of the new Third World majority in the United Nations. As the place at which these concerns were first given international prominence, the Teheran Conference almost certainly had some indirect influence.

The other major objective of the conference was to emphasize economic, social, and cultural rights and the linkage between human rights and economic and social development. This was an attempt to redress a serious imbalance in past U.N. work. Efforts to redress the imbalance began in the early 1960's. They were given a significant boost by the International Conference on Human Rights and the Proclamation of Teheran. Paragraph 13 of the proclamation states: "The achievement of lasting progress in the implementation of human rights is dependent upon sound and effective national and international policies of economic and social development." Critics have contended that in the 1970's, the U.N. majority, rather than establish a balance between civil and political rights and economic, social, and cultural rights, in fact attempted to subordinate civil and political rights to the pursuit of economic development and struggles for a new international economic order. Whatever the validity of such claims, it is clear that the Teheran Conference was a significant event in the rising prominence of economic, social, and cultural rights in international human rights discussions. This was probably the most important contribution of the International Conference on Human Rights. Issues of race and colonialism had already been placed at the center of international human rights agendas prior to the conference. After, and partly as a result of, the International Conference on Human Rights, economic, social, and cultural rights also had prominent places on the U.N. human rights agenda.

The International Conference on Human Rights was an important event in the genesis of the human rights policies and priorities of the United Nations in the 1970's. It effectively marked the close of the period of norm creation and Western domination of the human rights work of the United Nations and the opening of a new phase that would be politically dominated by the Third World, with the support of the Soviet bloc. Much of the human rights work of the United Nations in the 1970's reflected the priorities of the Proclamation of Teheran and the political processes that shaped it.

Bibliography

Development, Human Rights, and the Rule of Law. Oxford, England: Pergamon Press, 1982. This is a report of a conference held in The Hague, April 27-

May 1, 1981, convened by the International Commission of Jurists. Although the link between human rights and development was a central theme at Teheran, little was done until the early 1980's. This book, and the conference that it records, were important first steps toward concrete action on this central objective of the Teheran Conference.

Final Act of the International Conference on Human Rights. New York: United Nations, 1968. The Final Act includes a brief review of the organization and operation of the conference along with the texts of the Proclamation of Teheran and the resolutions adopted by the conference.

Firestone, Bernard J. *The United Nations Under U Thant, 1961-1971.* Lanham, Md.: Scarecrow Press, 2001. This scholarly text provides a concise account of U Thant's administration as U.N. secretary-general. Bibliography.

Moskowitz, Moses. *International Concern with Human Rights.* Dobbs Ferry, N.Y.: Oceana, 1974. A good general introduction to the evolution of international action on behalf of human rights. Provides a useful discussion of the context in which the Teheran Conference took place.

Van Dyke, Vernon. "Self-Determination and Minority Rights." In *Human Rights, the U.S. and World Community.* New York: Oxford University Press, 1970. A useful contemporary overview of self-determination, which was both a central theme at the Teheran Conference and one of the principal political factors that led up to it.

Jack Donnelly

Soviets Invade Czechoslovakia

Category of event: Political freedom; revolutions and rebellions
Time: August 21, 1968
Locale: Czechoslovakia

> Soviet and Warsaw Pact forces entered Czechoslovakia to suppress the independence movement popularly known as the "Prague Spring"

Principal personages:

ALEXANDER DUBČEK (1921-1992), the first secretary of the Czechoslovakian Communist Party and the architect of the Prague Spring reforms

LEONID ILICH BREZHNEV (1906-1982), the general secretary of the Soviet Communist Party and leader of the Soviet Union from 1964 to 1982

ANTONIN NOVOTNY (1904-1975), the president of Czechoslovakia from 1957 to 1968

LUDVIK SVOBODA (1895-1979), the president of Czechoslovakia from 1968 to 1975, whose popularity was tied to his support for the Prague Spring reforms

Summary of Event

In 1963, Czechoslovakia began to emerge from the severe political and cultural repression imposed by the Czechoslovakian Communist Party in the early 1950's. The moderation of restrictions corresponded with an economic upswing that created an atmosphere of confidence and optimism in the government of Antonin Novotny, who was also chair of the Czechoslovakian Communist Party. Novotny believed the time had come to appease Czechoslovakian intellectuals, who had complained for years about government censorship. A more permissive policy was introduced that allowed cultural exchanges with the West and the publication of essays that questioned the Soviet Union's domination of Czechoslovakia. In 1967, Novotny, under pressure from Soviet leader Leonid Brezhnev, reestablished censorship. By that time, however, Czechoslovakia had gained international recognition for its writers, film making, and theater. In response to renewed censorship, the Czechoslovakian Writer's Union, on June 27, 1967, issued a vigorous protest.

The position taken by the writer's union in 1967 came at a time when some leaders within the Czechoslovakian Communist Party were disillusioned with President Novotny's economic policies and his unwillingness to show greater independence from Moscow. Opposition to Novotny was acute in Slovakia, where the president's policies were viewed as heavily favoring the Czech majority. Although the Slovak Communist Party had remained loyal to the government in Prague, in 1967 the leader of the Slovak Party, Alexander Dubček, openly criticized Novotny for failing to address the country's economic and political problems effectively.

Dubček's assault on Novotny seemed to galvanize those who were dissatisfied with the president's performance. Novotny received little help from Brezhnev, who resented the fact that the Czech president had remained loyal to the previous Soviet leader, Nikita Khrushchev. In the autumn of 1967, it was apparent that Novotny was finished. There was surprise, however, when the Czechoslovakian Communist Party announced in January, 1968, that Dubček would succeed Novotny as first secretary of the Party. Dubček was not well known outside the Slovakian bureaucracy; moreover, he was a notoriously poor speaker with a benign personality. There is some reason to think, as William Shawcross noted in his 1970 biography of Dubček, that Brezhnev may have intervened on his behalf.

Early in 1968, Dubček began to discuss a "new model" for socialist Czechoslovakia, one that would bring communists and noncommunists together. The Communist Party would retain its leading role, but it would permit the full range of freedoms associated with a democratic society. Aided by dissident Party members who agreed with him, Dubček incorporated his ideas into what became known as the "Action Program." The Action Program was published on April 9, 1968, and quickly gained the attention of Soviet authorities in Moscow. The program called for personal freedoms, significant political reform, a new constitution for the Slovak peoples, and economic liberalization.

Over the next three months, Dubček's reforms came under increasingly heavy attack from Moscow. The Soviet press criticized Dubček for trying to undermine the unity of the Warsaw Pact countries. The Czechs had become, according to Moscow, apologists for the bourgeois system. In Czechoslovakia itself, there was widespread support for Dubček's Action Program.

Three times between May and August, Dubček and other Czechoslovakian Communist Party leaders were called to meetings with Soviet officials, including Brezhnev. At each of these gatherings, the most important of which was held at Bratislava on July 30, Dubček insisted that he had no intention of destroying communist unity. He remained convinced that communism and political freedom were completely compatible. That, he contended, was what

Karl Marx and Friedrich Engels had believed. Brezhnev, however, made it clear that he had no interest in allowing the Prague Spring to set an example for other Eastern European communist regimes.

When the Bratislava conference ended, a tepid statement, the Bratislava Declaration, was released in which both sides agreed to carry on mutually advantageous relations. In early August, a succession of Eastern European leaders visited Prague to warn of possible Soviet intervention. Dubček and recently selected Czechoslovakian president Ludvik Svoboda seemed unconvinced that Brezhnev would unleash Soviet power against the popular reforms.

The warnings of Soviet intervention became fact on the night of August 20. Soviet planes and equipment began to arrive at Prague's Ruzzone airport. At dawn, tanks rolled toward the center of the capital. By the next night, some three hundred thousand troops from East Germany, Poland, Hungary, Bulgaria, and the Soviet Union had crossed the Czechoslovakian border. There was no significant armed opposition. Dubček asked the residents of Prague to go to their workplaces as usual. At first, the citizens of Prague tried to convince the invading soldiers to turn back, and, when that tactic failed, they turned to passive resistance. They refused to provide troops with food and water, they removed street signs and house numbers, they published clandestine newspapers, and they displayed huge pictures of Dubček and President Svoboda.

The events of August stunned the Western world. There were expressions of support for Czechoslovakia from many countries, including the United States, but no help was forthcoming. The United States, at the time heavily involved in Southeast Asia, condemned the Soviet intervention while saying that it intended to abide by the terms of the Yalta agreement. The Yalta accord, signed at the conclusion of World War II, had, in effect, given Moscow dominion over Eastern Europe.

Shortly after the intervention began, Dubček and several other Czech officials were arrested and taken to Moscow. Several days later, President Svoboda also was summoned to the Soviet capital. Svoboda and Dubček realized that they would have to compromise in order to preserve even a small amount of the independence Czechoslovakia had claimed. They returned to Prague subdued and talking of a needed accommodation with the Soviet Union. There were some who felt betrayed by Dubček and Svoboda, but the reality was that the Czech leaders had no choice. By early September, the situation in Czechoslovakia was much as it had been prior to the publication of the Action Program, and the occupying forces had begun to withdraw. Dubček continued to hope that some portion of the April reforms could be preserved, but, in fact, the Prague Spring had come to an end.

Impact of Event

The Soviet intervention caught world leaders by surprise, especially in the West. The Cold War, which had appeared to be winding down in the mid-1960's, was not quite finished after all. Soviet leaders were not ready to relinquish Moscow's stranglehold over Eastern Europe. Western officials, who had been encouraged by the Nuclear Test Ban Treaty of 1963 and by the seeming insouciance of Leonid Brezhnev, were now required once again to condemn the actions of the Soviet Union. It was clearly a setback for those in the West who had hoped for continuing progress toward détente.

For those in Eastern Europe who sought greater independence from Moscow and greater political freedom, the intervention was even more crushing. National communist leaders understood that the Kremlin would not allow them to chart their own course. Some of them, particularly Romanian president Nicolae Ceausescu, openly upbraided the Soviet leadership, but all had received Moscow's clear message.

In Czechoslovakia, the disappointment was acute. Within a year of the intervention, Soviet officials had forced local Communist Party leaders to re-impose restrictions on political and cultural freedom. Dubček was gradually removed from a position of power in the Party until, in June, 1970, he was expelled from the Party. Those most negatively affected by the Soviet action were the artists, writers, and intellectuals who had enjoyed a brief period when they could express their ideas as they wished. The end of the Prague Spring meant the stifling of what had been a major cultural renaissance in the mid-1960's. Still, Czechoslovakia's intellectual community did not surrender easily. In January, 1969, Jan Palach, a university philosophy student, inspired a violent demonstration by burning himself to death as a protest against censorship. Many writers, particularly Václav Havel, maintained a stream of protests. Dubček, while under surveillance, continued to offer his opposition. Lesser-known intellectuals who lacked international support were dismissed from their academic and cultural posts or sent to prison.

Although the Prague Spring had been repressed, the ideas that inspired it lived on. When Soviet president Mikhail Gorbachev introduced his policies of *glasnost* (openness) and *perestroika* (restructuring) in 1985, the spirit of the Prague Spring was revived throughout Eastern Europe. In Czechoslovakia, all the reforms promised in the Action Program were restored. Dubček returned to political prominence in 1989 and was chosen to lead the Czechoslovakian parliament. In December, 1989, the parliament selected Václav Havel to be president of the country. After more than twenty years, Czech reformers had eased the effects, if not the memory, of the Soviet invasion in August, 1968.

Bibliography

Czerwinski, E. J., and Jaroslav Pielkalkiewicz, eds. *The Soviet Invasion of Czechoslovakia: Its Effects on Eastern Europe.* New York: Praeger, 1972. Accounts, many of them firsthand, of the reaction to the invasion in each Eastern European country. E. Bennett Warnstrom's chapter on Romania is naïve, particularly his gushing praise for President Ceausescu.

Golan, Galia. *The Czechoslovak Reform Movement.* Cambridge, England: Cambridge University Press, 1971. Golan is an expert on Czechoslovakian affairs, and this book can be read with great profit by students and the general public. Highly recommended. Index and bibliography.

Kusin, Vladimir V. *Political Grouping in the Czechoslovak Reform Movement.* New York: Columbia University Press, 1972. This is an account of the creation of reform political organizations from the post-World War II era through 1968. It is essential background information for understanding the Prague Spring. Recommended for serious students. Bibliography and index.

Navratil, Jaromir, et al., eds. *The Prague Spring 1968: A National Security Archive Documents Reader.* New York: Central European University Press, 1998. The editors have compiled 140 documents relating to the invasion of 1968. Includes chronology and glossary.

Schwartz, Harry. *Prague's 200 Days.* New York: Praeger, 1969. Schwartz takes a close look at the first two hundred days of 1968 in Czechoslovakia. A readable, and generally reliable, account. The chapters dealing with the invasion itself and the reaction of the Czech people are especially compelling. Index.

Skilling, H. Gordon. *Czechoslovakia's Interrupted Revolution.* Princeton, N.J.: Princeton University Press, 1976. Skilling's work provides excellent information on all aspects of the Prague Spring. There are superb insights into Dubček's behavior during 1968 and an excellent discussion of relevant scholarship on the events of 1968 published in the early 1970's. Bibliography and index.

Skoug, Kenneth N. *Czechoslovakia's Lost Fight for Freedom, 1967-1969: An American Embassy Perspective.* Westport, Conn.: Praeger, 1999. The author, a diplomat who lived in Czechoslovakia from 1967-1969, recounts the events of the invasion. Indexed with bibliography.

Williams, Kieran. *The Prague Spring and Its Aftermath: Czechoslovak Politics, 1968-1970.* New York: Cambridge University Press, 1997. Using recently declassified documents, the author examines the events of the Prague Spring. Includes select bibliography.

Ronald K. Huch

Statute of Limitations Is Ruled Not Applicable to War Crimes

Category of event: Atrocities and war crimes; international norms
Time: November 26, 1968
Locale: United Nations, New York City

The United Nations General Assembly ratified the Convention on the Non-Applicability of Statutory Limitations to War Crimes and Crimes Against Humanity

Principal personages:

U THANT (1909-1974), the secretary-general of the United Nations (1962-1971)

LUDWIG ERHARD (1897-1977), the West German chancellor from 1963 to 1966

KURT WALDHEIM (1918-   ), the Austrian diplomat who served as secretary-general of the United Nations (1971-1981)

Summary of Event

War crimes tribunals have been used throughout history to compel states to follow existing laws of warfare. The war crimes tribunals in Nuremberg and Tokyo and the 1949 Geneva Conventions were examples of international efforts to expand the scope of international law after World War II. The tremendous suffering of both combatants and civilians during the war clearly aroused international interest in protecting human rights. Statements of the Allied leaders at Yalta and Potsdam clearly indicated that the Allied Powers intended to pursue individuals responsible for war crimes and crimes against humanity. In its preamble, the United Nations Charter stated that the protection of fundamental human rights and justice were fundamental goals of the organization. The barbarous actions of Germany in its persecution of European Jews were an indication that rules of state and individual conduct in war had to be strengthened.

Unable to establish an international criminal court of justice after the war, the United Nations gave states jurisdiction to prosecute in municipal courts individuals charged with war crimes. The 1949 Geneva Convention for the

U Thant (left), secretary-general of the United Nations at the time the General Assembly ratified the Convention on the Non-Applicability of Statutory Limitations to War Crimes and Crimes Against Humanity. (Library of Congress)

Protection of Civilian Persons in Time of War required each signatory to search for persons alleged to have committed, or to have ordered to be committed, war crimes, and to bring such persons, regardless of their nationality, before its own courts. The origins of the 1968 U.N. convention can be found in the efforts of the Polish delegation to the U.N. Commission on Human Rights. The Polish delegation introduced resolutions that drew attention to the debate in the Federal Republic of Germany (West Germany) over the applicability of statutes of limitations for persons accused of war crimes.

In 1965, the West German Bundestag passed a resolution that excluded the period from May, 1945, to December, 1949, from statute-of-limitations protections for all persons accused of serious crimes. The 1965 resolution extended the period in which persons accused of crimes could be prosecuted by the German government. The Polish delegation expressed concern that under German law, all legal proceedings against accused war criminals would be stopped in December, 1969. This was troubling to many states in 1965 because it was estimated that although sixty-one hundred individuals had been convicted in West German courts for Nazi war crimes since 1945, as many as eighteen thousand individuals suspected of war crimes remained at large.

To many member states of the United Nations, the application of statute-of-limitations protection to accused war criminals appeared to contradict the intent of the 1946 genocide convention. The General Assembly declared in a 1946 resolution that genocide is always a crime under international law. The efforts of the Polish delegation led the Commission on Human Rights to ask U.N. secretary-general U Thant to begin examining laws that would hinder the prosecution of accused war criminals. The report of the secretary-general and the efforts of the Economic and Social Council culminated in a draft proposal of the convention on the nonapplicability of statutory limitations to war crimes and crimes against humanity in 1968.

The convention adopted the definition of war crimes established during the military tribunal at Nuremberg in 1946 and affirmed in the Geneva Conventions of 1949. The Nuremberg Principles adopted by the General Assembly stated that "any person who commits an act which constitutes a crime under international law is responsible therefor and liable to punishment." Article 6 of the Charter of the International Military Tribunal at Nuremberg had previously defined war crimes as violations of the laws or customs of war. Such violations included murder, ill treatment, or deportation to slave labor of civilian populations in occupied territory; murder or ill treatment of prisoners of war; killing of hostages; plunder of public or private property; wanton destruction of cities, towns, or villages; or devastation not justified by military necessity.

Although some United Nations members expressed reservations about incorporating the Nuremberg Principles into the 1968 convention, attempts to alter the definition of war crimes were strongly opposed by many members of the General Assembly. Article 1 of the convention also included the United Nations definitions of crimes against humanity defined in the Nuremberg Charter. The United Nations had accepted these definitions in the 1946 genocide convention. The only addition to the category of crimes against humanity was the addition of the United Nations resolution condemning apartheid, the policy of racial discrimination by the government of South Africa.

While there was general agreement that statutory limitations clauses existing in municipal law should not shield individuals from prosecution, a number of states strongly objected to provisions of the U.N. draft proposal. The four-year debate in the United Nations over the wording of the convention symbolized the tremendous differences in opinion a number of states had concerning the eleven articles of the convention. One of the most fundamental issues surrounding the convention was whether the exemption of statutory limitations to war criminals already existed in international law.

The United Kingdom and the United States took the position that the nonapplicability of statutes of limitations for war criminals already existed in international law. The Soviet Union and its allies rejected this position and lobbied to strike any language from the convention that would have established that existing international law had addressed this issue. As the debate over the convention continued, many in the West began to characterize the convention as an attempt by Eastern European states and the Soviet Union to embarrass the Federal Republic of Germany by insinuating that it had not vigorously pursued individuals linked to atrocities during World War II.

The Convention on Non-Applicability of Statutory Limitations to War Crimes and Crimes Against Humanity was adopted by the General Assembly in 1968 with more opposing votes than any previous human rights convention: fifty-eight states approved its adoption, seven opposed, and thirty-six abstained. Israel, Czechoslovakia, Poland, and the Soviet Union were some of the states that supported the convention. The United States, the United Kingdom, and South Africa voted against the convention. Argentina, Bolivia, Brazil, Uruguay, and Venezuela were among the states that abstained from voting.

Impact of Event

The 1968 convention was important in the history of international law because, for the first time, an international convention clearly stated that crimes against humanity by individuals had no statute of limitations. The 1968 convention's treatment of the issue of retroactivity has been criticized because it failed to address the rights of individuals accused of war crimes and crimes against humanity. The United States opposed the convention because of concerns about what it saw as political rather than legal objectives in not clearly addressing how the convention would address existing laws of various states.

The convention's effect on international human rights is difficult to assess because of the nature of the offenses that the convention addresses. While it is a fundamental tenet of criminal law that a defendant is entitled to full protection under the laws of the state, critics of the convention have questioned whether individuals accused of crimes during war were provided the same rights as persons accused of other types of crime. The convention's main provisions required all states party to the convention to eliminate all legal statutes that provide statutory limitations protection to individuals accused of war crimes, crimes against humanity during peacetime, or acts related to the policy of apartheid.

Many have also expressed disappointment with international efforts to bring to justice individuals responsible for crimes against humanity. The provisions of the genocide convention have been used only two times in the postwar period. The inability to define genocide clearly has led to obstacles when national courts have attempted to punish individuals accused of international crimes. An example of this difficulty was the trial and execution of Marcias Nguema, the former leader of Equatorial Guinea. After murdering a number of individuals, he was overthrown and found guilty of genocide in 1979. A later report by the International Commission of Jurists found that although mass murder was clearly proven, Marcias was wrongly convicted of genocide because there was no compelling evidence to prove intentional destruction of racial, ethnic, or religious groups.

The absence of an international tribunal to prosecute war criminals after World War II made it possible for many to avoid prosecution by finding sanctuary in other countries. The number of individuals who actually have been put on trial for crimes against humanity did not significantly change after the adoption of the 1968 convention. The various resolutions adopted by the United Nations and the attention given to the apprehension and punishment of war criminals found in the 1968 convention has not been matched by U.N. actions to seek out individuals responsible for war crimes. Information about many of the individuals accused of Nazi war crimes has come from private citizens interested in bringing the accused to justice. The most prominent of these citizens was Simon Wiesenthal, who was instrumental in Israel's apprehension, trial, and execution of one of the principal planners of the persecution of European Jews, Adolf Eichmann. Kurt Waldheim, the secretary-general of the United Nations from 1971 through 1981, has himself been accused of Nazi collaboration during World War II. Many of the states that objected to the language of the original resolution have refused to become signatories to the 1968 convention. Because universal acceptance of the convention has not occurred, the effect of this convention on national and international law since 1968 has been limited.

Bibliography

Clausnitzer, Martin. "The Statute of Limitations for Murder in the Federal Republic of Germany." *International and Comparative Law Quarterly* 29 (April-July, 1980): 473-479. Examines the debate in Germany over the thirty-year limitation for murder in Germany and its effect on Nazi war criminals still at large. Includes notations.

Falk, Richard, Gabriel Kolko, and Robert Jay Lifton, eds. *Crimes of War.* New York: Random House, 1971. A collection of essays and documents that examine the legal framework of various laws of war. Index.

Green, Leslie C. "Human Rights and the Law of Armed Conflict." In *Essays on the Modern Law of War.* Dobbs Ferry, N.Y.: Transnational Publishers, 1984. A very readable account of the historical development of laws of warfare. Although it does not specifically address the 1968 resolution, it is a valuable introduction to the subject of human rights and warfare.

"Human Rights-Actions of the Third Committee." *U.N. Monthly Chronicle* 5 (November, 1968). A brief account of the debate in the Social, Humanitarian, and Cultural Committee over the draft convention on the non-applicability of statutory limitations on war crimes. Includes text of the resolution and individual countries' votes on the convention.

Kuper, Leo. *The Prevention of Genocide.* New Haven, Conn.: Yale University Press, 1985. An examination of the United Nations and its implementation of the 1948 genocide convention. Includes notations, appendices, bibliography, and index.

Miller, Robert H. "The Convention on the Non-Applicability of Statutory Limitations to War Crimes and Crimes Against Humanity." *American Journal of International Law* 65, no. 3 (1971): 467-501. An excellent treatment of the subject written by a former United Nations official. One of the best sources on the origins of and United Nations debate over the 1968 convention. Includes notations.

Ryan, James Daniel. *The United Nations Under Kurt Waldheim, 1972-1981.* Lanham, Md.: Scarecrow Press, 2001. The author recounts Waldheim's achievements as U.N. secretary-general. Includes chronology, bibliography, and index.

Tolley, Howard, Jr. *The U.N. Commission on Human Rights.* Boulder, Colo.: Westview Press, 1986. A comprehensive history of the United Nations Commission on Human Rights and its impact on international politics after World War II. Includes notations, tables, illustrations, appendices, bibliography, and index.

United Nations Department of Public Information. *The United Nations and Human Rights.* New York: United Nations, 1984. An account of United Nations efforts to encourage the protection of human rights. Includes appendix and index.

Lawrence Clark III

Brazil Begins Era of Intense Repression

Category of event: Civil rights; political freedom
Time: December 13, 1968
Locale: Brasilia, Brazil

> *The suspension of the congress and the promulgation of Institutional Act Number Five signaled the tightening of control over Brazilian citizens by the military government*

Principal personages:

ARTUR DA COSTA E SILVA (1902-1969), the president of Brazil from 1967 to 1969

EMÍLIO GARRASTAZÚ MÉDICI (1905-1985), the head of the Brazilian intelligence service under Costa e Silva and president of Brazil from 1969 to 1974

HUMBERTO DE ALENCAR CASTELO BRANCO (1900-1967), the first military president of Brazil following the 1964 coup

ANTONIO DELFIM NETO (1928-   ), the minister of finance under Costa e Silva and Médici

Summary of Event

Industrial growth in Brazil, already significant in the 1930's and accelerating after World War II, changed the nature of politics in that country. As urban workers became an important voting group, politicians courted their support. The nationalist, populist tone of such politicians became troubling after the Cuban revolution of 1959. The Brazilian military, steeped in anticommunist ideology, watched warily as João Goulart, president of Brazil from 1961 to 1964, appeared to lean ever more dangerously toward the left.

The Brazilian economy suffered under Goulart's administration. Foreign businesses, fearing nationalization, either invested more cautiously or pulled out completely. Inflation soared, and prices nearly doubled in 1963. Workers organized strikes to protest the erosion of their purchasing power. Peasants in the rural areas of the northeast clamored for land reform. Even the lower ranks of the military talked about forming unions to promote their interests.

Political ferment among the lower classes came to an abrupt end on April 1, 1964, when the military deposed João Goulart. The president fled into exile in Uruguay and was replaced by General Humberto de Alencar Castelo Branco. During Castelo Branco's administration, a new constitution was written, political parties were abolished and replaced by a government party and an opposition party, and attempts were made to stabilize the economy in order to attract investment and resume growth. Many of the stabilization policies, while bringing inflation under control, also eroded workers' salaries. At the same time, however, they gave middle- and upper-class Brazilians hope that the uncertainty of progress during the Goulart years was gone. As investments increased, better jobs were indeed created for those with higher levels of education. Meanwhile, the military silenced opposition to its regime, by force when necessary.

When Castelo Branco passed the presidency to General Artur da Costa e Silva in 1967, Brazilians believed that the new president would ease the country back to democracy. Costa e Silva appeared less rigid than his predecessor, giving many Brazilians confidence to voice their opposition to military dictatorship. As vocal opposition grew, a "hard-line" faction within the military became convinced that the country was not yet ready to see the resumption of direct citizen participation in government. Those who argued that the military should take a stronger hold on power pointed to the violence of student demonstrations and the emergence of an urban guerrilla movement in 1968 as evidence that chaos would replace repression. Many believed economic growth would come only in a context of law and order.

By early 1968, more and more Brazilians were protesting visibly against the military government. Workers went on strike for higher pay. Students sponsored large protest rallies in Brazil's major cities, sometimes with tragic results. On March 28, 1968, police fired into a group of protesters, killing a young secondary school student. The outpouring of support for the students, manifested in the huge turnout for the dead student's funeral and memorial mass, strengthened the resolve of those hard-liners who believed that such demonstrations should not be allowed.

At the same time, discontent surfaced in the national congress as well. One congressman in particular, Márcio Moreira Alves, made several speeches urging Brazilians to show that they did not support the violence and repression. He even suggested in jest that Brazilian women keep sexual favors from military men until police brutality ended. This enraged many in the military, who called for the suspension of Moreira Alves's congressional immunity so that he could be expelled from the congress and tried for crimes against the regime. On December 12, 1968, a congress in which the majority of the members belonged to the official government party voted to refuse to suspend their colleague's immunity. At that point, the president realized that he needed to act.

On the evening of December 13, 1968, Institutional Act Number Five was passed. The congress was dissolved indefinitely, strict censorship was instituted, and *habeas corpus* was suspended. Instead of returning the country to democracy, the Costa e Silva administration had succumbed to the pressure of the hard-liners. The military was determined to maintain its control of the country as long as necessary to destroy what it perceived as the destabilizing opposition.

Dissent, albeit illegal and pushed underground, grew during the first months of 1969. Clandestine political parties of the left, including the Brazilian communist party, trained guerrillas for urban and rural warfare against the regime. The army and the police diligently sought out these groups, imprisoning and torturing members of those they uncovered. The forces of the right and of the left polarized. Guerrillas robbed banks to fund their training programs while death squads eliminated leftist suspects.

On August 28, 1969, President Costa e Silva suffered a debilitating stroke that left him partially paralyzed. It quickly became apparent that he was not capable of conducting the affairs related to his office. In the debate over how to proceed with the presidential succession, the hard-liners prevailed. The constitutional succession procedure by which the civilian vice president, Pedro Aleixo, would become chief executive was not acceptable to the hard-line faction because Aleixo had opposed the severe curtailing of civil and political rights in late 1968. Instead, the hard-liners selected a new military president to replace the ailing general. This man, Emílio Garrastazú Médici, had been chief of the intelligence service under Costa e Silva and commander of the Third Army in the south of Brazil. Convinced that it was his military duty to keep the country from falling into chaos, Médici accepted the appointment.

In the days following Costa e Silva's stroke, but before Médici assumed office, one of the guerrilla factions carried out a startling action as a means of getting attention and as a source of pressure for the release of political prisoners. On September 4, 1969, guerrillas kidnapped Charles Burke Elbrick, United States ambassador to Brazil. Their demands for radio time and for the release of prisoners were met, and Ambassador Elbrick was released on September 7. In the following months, guerrillas would kidnap other important foreign officials. The government usually gave in to most of their demands.

The Médici government combined intense repression with a determination to accelerate the economic growth begun under Costa e Silva. Antonio

Delfim Neto, minister of finance in the Costa e Silva administration, was kept on by General Médici. He presided over a period of remarkable economic growth that was dubbed the "Brazilian Economic Miracle." Between 1968 and 1973, Brazil's gross national product (GNP) grew at an annual rate of around 10 percent. The miracle came at great cost to the Brazilian poor. Real wages dropped precipitously, while the ban on protests and strikes meant that demonstrating discontent could be very dangerous. While the majority of the workers suffered, managers did rather well. Many in the middle and upper classes strongly supported the military policy. Brazil, during the miracle years, became the eighth industrial power in the Western world.

The economic boom, however, proved ephemeral. With the increase in oil prices after 1973, the bill for Brazilian industry grew astonishingly. Highly reliant on oil imports, the military administrations sought alternative fuel sources at the same time that they increased exploration for oil off their large coast and in the interior of the country. As inflation climbed once again, the large blue-collar workforce felt the pinch. By the late 1970's, protests and strikes had resurfaced. This time, however, the military met popular criticism with a promise to open up the political system. Saddled with a huge foreign debt that had skyrocketed during the 1970's, Brazilians faced a difficult economic future. The military was blamed for the financial mess. By 1985, protests culminated in demands for the free election of a civilian president. That year, however, a congress controlled by the government party once again selected Brazil's president. This time, popular opinion was so strongly against the regime that the congress selected the opposition party's candidate. Only in 1989 would Brazilian citizens finally elect their president.

Impact of Event

The dissolution of the congress in December, 1968, marked the inauguration of the worst period of repression during the military regime that spanned the period from 1964 to 1985. Strict censorship of the media was enforced, and criticism of the government became grounds for arrest. The fear that "subversive" elements would take advantage of an open political system in order to promote Marxist revolution caused the generals to become overly suspicious of their fellow citizens. Those believed to sympathize with the left were arrested and sometimes tortured. Prisoners were often held without being charged. Universities were purged, and many professors lost their jobs. Fear spread among those who had earlier believed that they could pressure the government to demonstrate concern for the Brazilian poor.

The intensification of guerrilla activity following Costa e Silva's stroke was met by increasingly harsh repression. Many Brazilian students and intellectuals fled into exile rather than risk imprisonment. When guerrillas arranged the release of political prisoners in exchange for their kidnap victims, those prisoners had to agree to perpetual exile from Brazil. Exiled Brazilians, while abroad, published information about the excesses of the military regime, but within Brazil, silence continued to be enforced.

The state coupled its censorship concerning human rights abuses with a program designed to increase the patriotism of Brazilian citizens. Students at all levels, from primary school through the university, were required to take a civics course every semester they attended classes. These courses, taught by individuals who had been certified by the state, denounced the dangers of communism in the region and were meant to inspire support for the regime. During the early 1970's, in their struggle against "subversion" in the hemisphere, Brazilians provided logistical and financial support to highly repressive military coups in Bolivia, Uruguay, Chile, and Argentina. A massive public relations campaign was also mounted, to convince Brazilians that their country was on the way to international greatness. Grandiose projects such as the construction of the trans-Amazon highway signaled Brazil's entry into the developed world at the same time that they often destroyed important elements of Brazil's past, in this case a delicate environmental balance as well as a fragile and rapidly declining Indian population.

The developmental thrust of finance minister Delfim Neto meant continued need for low working-class salaries. Real wages dropped. Strikes were banned, so that discontented workers had no recourse for venting their frustrations and pressuring for salary hikes. Despite impressive economic performance, some members of the Brazilian elite also grumbled. Their complaint was against the state's use of violence against their sons and daughters who participated in protest movements.

Widespread opposition to the military dictatorship surfaced only after the economic miracle soured. Repression, some believed, might be the necessary price to pay for long-term national benefits. A break in the economic boom, however, removed this justification for violence, and the military began to be called to task even by its supporters. The oil shocks of 1973 and 1979 would mark a new era of widespread discontent with the military and would eventually lead Brazil back to a tenuous rule of law.

Bibliography

Dassin, Joan, ed. *Torture in Brazil.* New York: Vintage Books, 1986. Based on records kept by the Brazilian military and clandestinely photocopied by a group of lawyers and clergy, this work documents the routine use of torture against political prisoners during the military years. An excellent introduction to the period is provided by the editor.

Dulles, John W. F. *President Castello Branco: Brazilian Reformer.* College Station: Texas A&M University Press, 1980. The most thorough English-language study of the first presidential administration after the 1964 coup. The author admires Castelo Branco and was given access to his papers to produce this biography. Bibliography and index.

Fausto, Boris. *A Concise History of Brazil.* New York: Cambridge University Press, 1999. Richly detailed history of the country. Illustrated, indexed, and includes bibliography.

Hagopian, Frances. *Traditional Politics and Regime Change in Brazil.* New York: Cambridge University Press, 1996. A scholarly account of the political transformations of Brazil. Includes glossary and index.

Marighella, Carlos. *For the Liberation of Brazil.* London: Penguin Books, 1971. Written by the most important Brazilian guerrilla fighter of the late 1960's, this work provides the view of the left. Includes Marighella's "Handbook of Urban Guerrilla Warfare," explaining how to participate in the struggle against the dictatorship.

Moreira Alves, Márcio. *A Grain of Mustard Seed: The Awakening of the Brazilian Revolution.* Garden City, N.Y.: Doubleday Anchor Press, 1973. Written by the Brazilian congressman whose speeches against the regime brought about the dissolution of the congress, this is a personal view of the 1964 revolution and of the role of Christians in opposition to the state. Provides a firsthand account of the repression along with strong criticism of the military regime.

Skidmore, Thomas E. *Brazil: Five Centuries of Change.* New York: Oxford University Press, 1999. Authoritative volume recounting the history of Brazil.

_____. *The Politics of Military Rule in Brazil, 1964-85.* New York: Oxford University Press, 1988. The best and most comprehensive account of the military years, organized around the individual presidential administrations. Especially good at explaining the transitions among the generals and the importance of the nation's economic performance. Good footnotes and index, but no separate bibliography.

Joan E. Meznar

National Guardsmen Kill Four Students at Kent State

Category of event: Atrocities and war crimes; peace movements and
organizations; political freedom
Time: May 4, 1970
Locale: Kent State University, Kent, Ohio

> *Ohio National Guards called in to restore order following antiwar protests of the*
> *campus of Kent State unexpectedly opened fire on students, killing four and*
> *wounding nine others*

Principal personages:

RICHARD M. NIXON (1913-1994), the president of the United States (1969-
1974)

JAMES A. RHODES (1909-2001), the governor of Ohio who ordered the Ohio
National Guard to the Kent State campus

ROBERT I. WHITE (1908-1990), the president of Kent State University at the
time of the shootings

SYLVESTER DEL CORSO, the adjutant general of the Ohio National Guard

ROBERT CANTERBURY, the senior officer in command of the Ohio National
Guard at Kent State in May, 1970

JOHN MITCHELL (1913-1988), the attorney general of the United States at the
beginning of the Nixon administration

Summary of Event

The shooting at Kent State University left in its wake a complex controversy
which may never be fully resolved, even though some of the facts are simple
and relatively undisputed. On May 4, after dispersing a peaceful rally on the
commons of the Kent State campus, the Ohio National Guard unexpectedly
opened fired on students. Four were killed and nine others were wounded,
some seriously.

No one was convicted of any crime associated with the incident, and no satisfactory explanation was ever given as to why the Guard opened fire. Many
theories have been put forward, all of which have some bearing on the appro-
priateness of the Guard's actions. Like the Kennedy assassination, the incident

was photographed and filmed from several angles and was also recorded on audio tape. The accumulated evidence refutes some theories, but fundamental questions remain unanswered.

Growing opposition to the war had resulted in massive demonstrations nationwide in 1969. The government eventually responded to public pressure, and the war appeared to be winding down. Public opinion on the United States' involvement in the war in Vietnam was still divided in early 1970, and public resentment of the protest movement, which was strongest on college campuses, was high. Shortly before the Kent State shootings, President Nixon had made public statements which were highly critical of those who opposed his Vietnam policy.

On Thursday, April 30, President Nixon announced that U.S. forces had invaded Cambodian territory to search out and destroy enemy bases. The announcement triggered huge demonstrations on college campuses across the country the following day. At Kent State, campus unrest coincided with the first warm night of the season (Friday, May 1) and the arrival of an out-of-town motorcycle gang. Rioting occurred in the streets downtown, and some property was damaged. On Saturday, the protests continued, and the University's Reserve Officer Training Corps (ROTC) building was burned down. This incident precipitated the calling of the Ohio National Guard to Kent.

A peaceful demonstration the following day (Sunday, May 3) was dispersed by the Guard, who used tear gas against the students. Several students were beaten and some were bayoneted by Guards, although no fatalities resulted. The confrontation on Monday began with the dispersal of the students on the commons and ended forty minutes later with a thirteen-second sustained volley in which at least sixty-seven rounds were fired.

Officials claimed at the time that the retreating Guards had fired in self-defense while being attacked by hundreds of students who had charged to within three or four yards of the Guard's position. Eyewitness accounts and analyses of films and photographs showed that this was not the case. The nearest shooting victim was sixty feet from the Guards who did most of the shooting. A photograph taken just an instant after the Guard opened fire clearly shows the victim standing with his middle finger upraised in an obscene gesture, for which he was shot twice (according to the Guard who shot him) and seriously wounded. The majority of the dead and wounded students were standing one hundred or more yards away. At least one of the fatally wounded students had not participated in the demonstration, and one was an ROTC student.

According to many observers and participants, the focus of the students'

President Richard Nixon's April 30, 1970, announcement that U.S. forces had invaded Cambodia triggered antiwar demonstrations on college campuses across the country the very next day. (White House Historical Society)

anger at the Monday rally was actually the presence of the Guard itself, not the Cambodian invasion that had initially triggered the demonstrations. The students were outraged over the use of tear gas, the beatings, and the bayoneting that had taken place the previous evening. Furthermore, students believed that their noon rally was legal and that the Guard was violating their constitutional rights to freedom of speech and freedom of assembly. Brigadier General Robert Canterbury, the senior officer in charge of the Guards, believed that the assembly was illegal and that he had the authority to disperse it. Governor

James Rhodes, however, did not actually sign the martial law decree banning assemblies until May 5, and he then declared it retroactive to April 30. A federal court later ruled that the demonstration was illegal.

Because of the highly charged emotional atmosphere on campus, Guards were subjected to extreme verbal abuse by students after dispersing the rally on the commons. Military experts testified later that tactical orders issued during the confrontation had placed the Guards in an unnecessarily vulnerable position. Some rocks were thrown at them, and some of the tear gas canisters they fired into the crowd were thrown back. Moreover, they had just come from riot duty in Cleveland, where they had been shot at while trying to contain violence during a truckers' strike. They had neither eaten properly nor had much sleep during the several days preceding the incident.

A Justice Department study, parts of which were disclosed by the *Akron Beacon Journal,* found that the shootings were unnecessary and urged the filing of criminal charges against the Guards. The President's Commission on Campus Unrest (the Scranton Commission) also concluded that the shootings were "unnecessary, unwarranted, and inexcusable."

Despite the fact that two federal investigations found the Ohio National Guard to be at fault, public opinion in Ohio ran strongly against any form of punishment for soldiers who had participated in the shootings. A special state grand jury convened by Governor Rhodes exonerated the Guards but indicted twenty-five other individuals, most of whom were students, for various offenses before the shootings. The judge in that proceeding had refused to admit testimony given earlier by Sylvester Del Corso, adjutant general of the Ohio National Guard, in the Justice Department investigation. In that testimony, in response to questions, General Del Corso stated no less than sixteen times that the Guard had no reason to use lethal force.

Substantial evidence indicates that the Nixon administration attempted to obstruct investigation of the case and prosecution of the Guards, apparently for political reasons. It was later disclosed that the Nixon administration had authorized a covert policy of taking illegal measures against antiwar and civil rights groups. In 1971, Attorney General John Mitchell officially closed the case. The Watergate scandal of 1973 weakened Nixon's control of the Justice Department, and Elliot Richardson, who succeeded John Mitchell as Attorney General, reopened the Kent State case. The reopening of the case in 1973 was at least partially prompted by a 1971 report by Peter Davies, in which Davies alleged that several Guards had decided in advance of the shooting to "punish" the students. Photographs lend plausibility to the Davies theory, but none of the Guards was ever questioned on the point.

In March of 1974, a federal grand jury indicted eight Guards on charges that they violated Section 242 of the United States Code, depriving the rights of the students to due process by summarily executing them. In November, a federal judge dismissed the charges, saying that prosecutors had failed to prove their case beyond a reasonable doubt. After a three-month-long civil trial in 1975, a jury decided not to award damages to victims and survivors, but that decision was set aside in 1977. The victims settled out of court shortly after the beginning of the second civil trial in 1979. The out-of-court settlement included a statement of regret signed by the defendants. Some of the victims regarded the statement as an apology, but the defendants and their lawyers disagreed.

Impact of Event

A Gallup poll published in *Newsweek* a few weeks after the incident at Kent State showed that fifty-eight percent of the American public thought that the shootings were justifiable and that the Guard was not at fault. This may reflect the success of early efforts by officials to manage the news and to portray the demonstrators as a violent mob. The Scranton Commission, which inter-viewed many Kent State students as part of its investigation, reported that many parents had supported the shootings, even to the point of hypothetically condoning the shooting of their own children if the children had participated in the demonstrations.

In a public statement made the day before the shootings, Governor Rhodes had characterized the protesters as "the worst type of people that we harbor in America. . . . I think that we're up against the strongest, well-trained, militant revolutionary group that has ever been assembled in America. . . . We are going to eradicate the problem, we're not going to treat the symptoms."

The governor's statement, in retrospect, seems out of line in reference to the comparatively staid student body of Kent State. Even though Kent State had been a fairly conservative campus, however, its students were substan-tially radicalized by the shootings, as demonstrated by their subsequent public statements and writings.

The search for a "larger meaning" to the tragedy has proved inconclusive for most of those who were involved. Some believe that it marked the begin-ning of the end for the war in Southeast Asia. In this view, the event marked a climax of repressive tendencies in the government and so appalled the public that it generated a strong momentum for change. To others, this view not only is erroneous but also represents a kind of romantic idealism. For the idealists, the gunfire brought an end to the belief that one could stand up to one's government in dissent and ultimately prevail against injustice. In support of this interpretation, they cite the virtual end to campus protest that followed. Still others claim that the decline of campus protests is more properly associated with the end of the draft in 1973. This perspective sees student protest as a matter of self-interest that became unnecessary when the Selective Service stopped conscripting students.

At the very least, the shootings marked a rare historical case in which American soldiers killed American civilians engaged in protest of government policy. The shootings also touched off an unprecedented student strike, which shut down more than two hundred colleges and universities nationwide and disrupted classes in hundreds more. Although the strike was also partially in response to shootings at Jackson State University, in which two students were killed on May 12, the Jackson State incident never resulted in the same degree of controversy and litigation. Many observers have since pointed out that the Jackson State students were African American and the victims at Kent State were white. Thus, the Kent State incident indirectly may have shed light into another dark corner of American life.

Bibliography

Gordon, William A. *Four Dead in Ohio: Was There a Conspiracy at Kent State?* Laguna Hills, Calif.: North Ridge Books, 1995. Well-researched and documented account of the cover-ups that followed the tragedy at Kent State.

_____. *The Fourth of May: Killings and Coverups at Kent State.* Buffalo, N.Y.: Prometheus Books, 1990. Good photo section, extensive source notes, chronology, and annotated bibliography. A very even-handed treatment of the event, the participants, and the subsequent coverage.

Hensley, Thomas R. *Kent State and May 4th: A Social Science Perspective.* 2d ed. Dubuque, Iowa: Kendall/Hunt, 2000. The author presents and analyzes social science research conducted upon the May 4 incident at Kent State.

Kelner, Joseph, and James Munves. *The Kent State Coverup.* New York: Harper & Row, 1980. Kelner represented the plaintiffs in the court case demanding damages. Includes a detailed chronology, May 1 through May 4, and itemized details of charges and litigants. Appendix includes pertinent information about the Ohio National Guard and logs of the legal proceedings.

Reeves, Richard. *President Nixon: Alone in the White House.* New York: Simon and Schuster, 2001. A definitive, authoritative biography of this most intriguing president. Highly recommended.

L. B. Shriver

Canada Invokes War Measures Act Against Quebec Separatists

Category of event: Civil rights; political freedom; racial and ethnic rights
Time: October 16, 1970
Locale: Quebec, Canada

> *Canada, a nation with a nonviolent political tradition and democratic freedoms, confronted separatist terrorism by suspending civil liberties in its French-speaking province*

Principal personages:

PIERRE ELLIOTT TRUDEAU (1919-2000), the prime minister of Canada, a French-Canadian liberal-federalist opposed to separatism

ROBERT BOURASSA (1933-1996), the premier of Quebec

JÉRÔME CHOQUETTE (1928-   ), the minister of justice in Quebec's provincial government

PIERRE LAPORTE (1921-1970), the minister of labor in Quebec's government, a terrorist kidnap victim

JAMES CROSS (1921-   ), a British trade commissioner in Montreal, kidnapped by terrorists

JEAN DRAPEAU (1916-1999), the mayor of Montreal

Summary of Event

Political violence and upheavals are very rare in Canadian history. In spite of the country's divisive tensions, generated by regionalism and by cultural and ethnic diversity, Canada has avoided the dramatic, bloody resolutions of conflict experienced by its neighbor, the United States. As a result, many Canadians have proudly referred to their country as "the peaceable kingdom." Canada's tradition of liberty, democratic stability, and tranquillity in the face of regional and cultural diversity was severely tested in October, 1970. Contributing factors to the October crisis were a rebellious trend associated with this historical period and the long-standing grievances of Canada's French-speaking community. Francophones, about 25 percent of Canada's population and largely concentrated in Quebec province, had always waged an uphill struggle against assimilation into the dominant Anglophone culture.

In spite of some gains by Quebec's French-Canadians in the 1960's, Anglophones, mainly based in Montreal and composing barely 20 percent of the province's population, still exercised disproportionate political and economic power. The phrase "white niggers of America" was employed by a Francophone radical in his famous autobiographical description of the oppression and social injustice felt by himself and many of his compatriots as second-class citizens in their own land.

Some Francophone nationalists abandoned the province's major political parties to form movements advocating much greater autonomy or independence for Quebec. In 1968, two of these groups organized the *Parti québéçois* (PQ) under René Lévesque. The PQ soon became a major vehicle for achieving separatist-nationalist goals through the legal capture of political power. Small numbers of frustrated radicals chose the more extreme course of revolutionary terrorism.

In February, 1963, the *Front de libération du Québec* (FLQ) was founded. Inspired by Third World liberation struggles, the FLQ's long-term goals were socialist revolution and an independent Quebec. Canada's FLQ operated mainly in Montreal and probably never had more than a few dozen militants or about ten active terrorists at any given time. Ad hoc cells appeared and appropriated the name FLQ when militants came up with ideas for operations. There was little or no communication between them. From 1963 to 1970, FLQ groups conducted about thirty-three armed robberies and ninety bomb attacks against military installations and various symbols of Anglo imperialism. These actions caused seven deaths and forty-nine injuries. By 1970, more than twenty FLQ members were imprisoned on criminal, not political, charges. The FLQ's smallness and extremely diffuse nature made it a difficult target for police to eradicate; its constant reappearance following capture and elimination of entire cells gave the appearance of a much larger and well-organized hydra-headed conspiracy.

The period from 1968 to 1970 was one of growing unrest and violence in Montreal. An upswing in FLQ terrorism, several traumatic labor strikes, and some unruly demonstrations by political radicals had nervous Montreal city officials and provincial leaders feeling threatened and prone to exaggerate all rumors and signs of revolutionary activity.

On the morning of October 5, 1970, the FLQ moved beyond its previous tactics when it kidnapped British Trade Commissioner James Cross from his Montreal residence. The kidnappers demanded the release of twenty-three political prisoners and their safe passage to Algeria or Cuba. The October crisis was under way.

Quebec's government, under Liberal Premier Robert Bourassa, worked closely throughout the crisis with the federal government, headed by Pierre Trudeau. Militant Quebec nationalists and separatists had not welcomed the ascendency of Trudeau, a French-Canadian native of Quebec, to the post of prime minister in 1968. This intellectual, urbane politician was a dedicated liberal-federalist who viewed Quebec separatism as a reactionary, inward-looking course. From the start, Trudeau adamantly opposed any concession to terrorist blackmail.

Feeling strong pressure from Ottawa, Quebec's justice minister, Jérôme Choquette, basically rejected all FLQ demands on October 10. In exchange for Cross's release, Choquette offered only parole for five prisoners who were eligible and safe passage abroad for the kidnappers. Fifteen minutes after this statement was broadcast, a new FLQ group, acting independently, snatched Quebec Labor Minister Pierre Laporte from his suburban Montreal home.

The kidnapping of the second most important figure in Quebec's government personalized the crisis, creating fear and panic among many of his colleagues. Bourassa momentarily wavered on the issue of a prisoner-hostage exchange but held firm. Trudeau remained uncompromising throughout. He declared that a "parallel power" would never be allowed to dictate to Canada's elected government and denounced "weak-kneed bleeding hearts" afraid to take measures to defend freedom.

As the crisis reached a climax, there were pro-FLQ mass demonstrations in Montreal and some statements of sympathy for the FLQ's political manifesto. Ottawa officials believed that the situation in Quebec was becoming chaotic and that some definitive assertion of federal power was crucial. Mayor Jean Drapeau and other Montreal city officials warned Ottawa about a threatening, organized revolutionary conspiracy. According to these sources, a state of "apprehended insurrection" existed in Quebec, requiring extraordinary police powers and assistance from the national government. On October 14, Premier Bourassa requested that the Canadian armed forces be sent into Quebec.

On October 15, the federal government dispatched troops to Montreal and a few other localities to protect public buildings and prominent individuals. Trudeau had already deployed the army in Ottawa. Bourassa offered the kidnappers the same limited terms as had Choquette and demanded a reply by 4:00 P,M.. on October 16. As soon as this deadline passed, the federal government invoked the War Measures Act, a relic of World War I which had last been used in World War II. The act gave the cabinet power to enact regulations allowing arrest, detention, censorship, and deportation in conditions of war, invasion, and insurrection. Under this authority, the cabinet introduced measures which banned the FLQ, retroactively making membership or evidence of association with that organization an offense. The Royal Canadian Mounted Police (RCMP) received extraordinary powers which overrode legal safeguards, permitting the search of premises without a warrant and arbitrary arrest on mere suspicion. The right of *habeas corpus* was suspended, allowing suspects to be held incommunicado without charges, legal counsel, or bail for up to twenty-one days. Two days after this act was proclaimed, Laporte's corpse was found in a car trunk.

Civil liberties were suspended in Quebec until April 30, 1971. Police raids hit every part of Quebec with more than forty-six hundred house searches involving confiscation of property, especially reading material. Around five hundred citizens were jailed. Armed with such broad, open-ended authority, police committed excesses. A federal cabinet minister's home was searched by mistake. No distinction was made between dissent and sedition on the RCMP's list of suspects. Many prominent persons were arrested solely on the basis of known or suspected political sympathies. More than 460 of those arrested were released, acquitted, or simply never prosecuted. Eighteen were convicted; sixteen of ordinary criminal charges (mostly for being linked somehow to Laporte's kidnapping or murder) and only two for an offense under the emergency provisions.

The act applied throughout Canada, and some arrests occurred outside Quebec. Freedom of expression was curtailed in British Columbia's schools. For individual Canadians, this was a tense period.

Impact of Event

The results and wisdom of the Trudeau government's actions are controversial subjects. Laporte's murder silenced vocal support for the FLQ in Quebec. Canadians, including Quebecers, immediately rallied behind Trudeau, who enjoyed hero status for his firmness and decisiveness in combating terrorist outrages. When the police closed in on Cross's five captors in early December, the kidnappers released him in exchange for a flight to Cuba. Within a few years, all but one had returned and received short prison terms. At the end of December, police found the hideout of Laporte's abductors, who got more severe sentences. Thereafter, FLQ activity tapered off and eventually disappeared. Canada returned to its normal status as one of the world's most tolerant and free societies.

On the negative side were the abuses of innocent persons' civil rights, the government's questionable political judgment in invoking unneeded and arguably excessive powers based on faulty intelligence, and its efforts to manipulate public opinion with misleading or exaggerated rumors. Police uncovered no evidence of an apprehended insurrection. Trudeau, whose early career was devoted to defending political dissidents, saw his reputation as a civil libertarian devastated.

The lives, employment, and families of innocent individuals were traumatically disrupted. No apology was ever made, and the public never held its leaders accountable. Angered by the Quebec situation, the majority applauded when their government took forceful action and turned a blind eye to the fact that no apprehended insurrection existed. In 1971, however, Quebec's ombudsman investigated complaints and awarded compensation in 104 cases involving police brutality, damage to property or reputation, and unjust conditions of confinement.

In Quebec, the crisis dealt a short-term setback to the separatist *Parti québéçois*, which lost members. The PQ, however, gained over the longer term. The elimination of separatist terrorism in Quebec politics made the PQ a more respectable alternative. Furthermore, the fact that English-Canadians so zealously cheered the use of the War Measures Act against a French-Canadian movement, unpopular and tiny though it was, drove many intellectuals into the separatist fold. The PQ's support rose, and from 1976 to 1985, a PQ government under René Lévesque held power. In a 1980 referendum, Quebecers rejected the choice of negotiating a new relationship with the rest of Canada by a 60 percent to 40 percent margin. Nevertheless, by 1990, the separatist option had revived because of a dispute between Quebec and other provinces concerning Quebec's status in Canada's new constitutional setup.

A positive side effect of the 1970 events may be the political lessons which thoughtful Canadians have pondered and debated. Among the most important issues is the scope of powers a democratic government needs to defend its society and the proper use of this authority. The controversial War Measures Act remained in the government's arsenal. Still, the experience of 1970 likely influenced Trudeau's decision to place restrictions on its use by future governments in the Charter of Rights associated with his 1982 constitution. Lessons learned from the October crisis are important to the preservation of Canada's free society and are instructive to other democracies.

Bibliography

Auf der Maur, Nick, and Robert Chodos, eds. *Quebec: A Chronicle, 1968-1972.* Toronto: James Lewis and Samuel, 1972. A collection of six articles which deal with the crisis and events preceding and following it. Auf der Maur, an Anglophone radio journalist, was one of the approximately five hundred persons detained by police in Quebec. Left-of-center perspective. Includes appendices containing an annotated list of major individuals and organizations mentioned in the text and a useful chronology of events.

Berger, Thomas. "Democracy and Terror: October, 1970." In *Fragile Freedoms: Human Rights and Dissent in Canada*. Toronto: Clarke, Irwin, 1981. Berger, a distinguished Canadian academic, takes the position that invocation of the War Measures Act was not warranted by the circumstances. The author argues that the government was justified in responding firmly but could have relied on ordinary police powers and criminal law combined with a strong defense of civil liberty. Bibliography, index, and chapter endnotes.

Fournier, Louis. *F.L.Q.: The Anatomy of an Underground Movement*. Translated by Edward Baxter. Toronto: NC Press, 1984. This is the most complete study of the revolutionary terrorist organization which precipitated the October crisis. The author is a Quebec radio broadcast journalist who is sympathetic to some FLQ political goals while rejecting terrorist tactics. Includes photos, select bibliography, index, and list of names of organizations.

Gellner, John. *Bayonets in the Streets: Urban Guerrilla at Home and Abroad*. Don Mills, Ontario: Collier-Macmillan Canada, 1974. This monograph includes a useful analysis of the FLQ. Chapter 3 examines the FLQ before the crisis, and Chapter 4 deals with its role and the government's exaggeration of the threat it posed. Critical of the government's handling of the affair. Bibliography and index.

Haggart, Ron, and Aubrey E. Golden. *Rumors of War*. Toronto: James Lorimer and Co., 1979. This work by two civil libertarians contains a detailed summary of events leading to the October crisis. The focus is on civil rights issues. The authors present their critique of the government in an objective, measured manner. Contains a thoughtful introduction by former Conservative Party leader Robert Stanfield. Illustrations, bibliography, and appendices with relevant documents.

Pelletier, Gerard. *The October Crisis*. Translated by Joyce Marshall. Toronto: McClelland and Stewart, 1971. One of the very rare defenses of the Trudeau government's invocation of the War Measures Act. Pelletier is a long-time political associate of Trudeau from Quebec and was secretary of state in the government during this affair. Pelletier voted to use this measure with great reluctance. Ultimate blame for the unfortunate results is placed on the FLQ. Index.

Smith, Denis. *Bleeding Hearts, Bleeding Country: Canada and the Quebec Crisis*. Edmonton, Canada: Hurtig, 1971. A forceful and sometimes passionate condemnation of Trudeau's handling of the kidnappers and invocation of the War Measures Act. The author is a Canadian academic. Contains a useful analysis of the FLQ's political aims. Includes bibliography, footnotes, and index.

Tarnopolsky, Walter Surma. "The War Measures Act and the Canadian Bill of Rights." In *The Canadian Bill of Rights*. Toronto: Macmillan of Canada, 1978. A Canadian scholar provides a good discussion of the legal and civil rights issues raised by the October crisis. Provides useful background information on the War Measures Act and its few uses by Canadian governments since it originated during World War I. Includes chapter end notes, bibliography, and index.

Trudeau, Pierre Elliott. *The Essential Trudeau*. Edited by Ron Graham. Toronto: M&S, 1998. A collection of essays, speeches and interviews by the former prime minister of Canada.

David A. Crain

Calley Is Court-Martialed for My Lai Massacre

Category of event: Accused persons' rights; atrocities and war crimes
Time: November 17, 1970-March 29, 1971
Locale: Fort Benning, Georgia

> *William Calley was convicted of murdering twenty-two Vietnamese and was the only person convicted of any crime in the aftermath of the My Lai massacre*

Principal personages:

WILLIAM L. CALLEY (1943-   ), a second lieutenant in command of a platoon of Company C at My Lai

FRANK A. BARKER (1928-1968), the commander of the unit that conducted the operation at My Lai

STEVEN K. BROOKS (1942?-1968), a second lieutenant in command of a platoon of Company C at My Lai

ERNEST MEDINA (1936-   ), a captain in command of Company C of Task Force Barker; immediate superior of lieutenants Calley and Brooks

WILLIAM R. PEERS (1914-   ), conducted the official Army inquiry of the My Lai incident

HUGH THOMPSOM (1947?-   ), a combat helicopter pilot involved in the assault on My Lai

SAMUEL W. KOSTER (1919-   ), the commander of the Americal Division

Summary of Event

The My Lai massacre occurred during the first hours of a March 16, 1968, operation carried out by a battalion-sized unit, code-named Task Force Barker, of the Americal Division of the U.S. Army. This unit, comprising three infantry companies (A, B, and C) supported by artillery, helicopters, and coastal patrol craft, was intended to sweep between two hundred and four hundred Viet Cong from a group of hamlets in the Son My subdistrict of Quang Ngai Province in South Vietnam.

Following the surprise Tet offensive launched by the Viet Cong on January 31, American commanders sought to reestablish control and to destroy known Viet Cong units. The Americal Division, including Task Force Barker, had been searching around Quang Ngai in February and March but encountered few Viet Cong.

On March 15, Lieutenant Colonel Frank A. Barker announced a three-day sweep against the Viet Cong 48th Local Forces battalion operating in and around a large, coastal fishing village. This was the third such operation against this village since February. Barker planned to move his three infantry companies into place by helicopter about 8:00 A.M., following a short artillery barrage. Helicopters were to engage fleeing or fighting Viet Cong. Offshore, small Navy patrol craft blocked any escape through the eastern seaward end of the noose.

Company C landed at 7:30 A.M., just west of another hamlet, My Lai. Lieutenant William L. Calley's platoon of twenty-five men moved first through the hamlet's south section; Lieutenant Stephen Brooks's platoon went through the north. Lieutenant Larry LaCroix's platoon remained in reserve near the landing zone.

The men of Company C expected to encounter two armed Viet Cong companies. Captain Ernest Medina, commander of Company C, had instructed his officers to burn the houses and destroy the livestock, crops, and foodstuffs in My Lai. Several men from Company C later testified that Captain Medina, who stayed at the landing zone, had specifically instructed them to kill civilians found in the hamlets. Medina denied such statements.

Calley's platoon slaughtered two large groups of villagers sometime between 7:50 A.M. and 9:15 A.M. In one instance, more than twenty people were gunned down on a pathway; in another, around 150 were systematically slaughtered with machine gun and small arms fire in a ditch about one hundred meters east of the hamlet. Soldiers later testified that Calley ordered them to kill their civilian captives. Men from all three platoons of Company C committed murder, rape, and other atrocities that morning.

About 8:30 A.M. Brooks's platoon turned northward on Medina's command to recover the bodies of two Viet Cong killed by a helicopter gunship. Brooks's platoon then entered Binh Tay, a hamlet a few hundred meters away, where they raped and murdered villagers before rejoining Company C around 10:00 A.M.

While this killing was going on, Warrant Officer Hugh Thompsom, an experienced combat helicopter pilot, was flying close overhead in an armed observation craft. At various times from 8:00 A.M. to 10:00 A.M., Thompsom attempted to aid wounded South Vietnamese civilians he saw in the fields around My Lai, saw Medina kill a wounded Vietnamese woman in a field, and landed his craft near the ditch where so many defenseless people were shot.

He urged members of Company C to stop the killing, but killings resumed after he left. Around 10:00 A.M. he landed again to protect a group of women and children who were being herded toward a bunker by men of Company C. Thompsom called in one of his gunships to evacuate some of the wounded civilians and then landed his own small helicopter to save one slightly wounded child from the heaps of bodies. In addition to his combat radio transmissions, Thompsom made reports upon his return to base to his commander about the slaughter.

The truth of these events was covered up within the American Division for a year, until a letter from a Vietnam veteran, Ronald Ridenhour, to Secretary of Defense Melvin Laird in late March, 1969, claimed "something very black indeed" had occurred at My Lai. Laird ordered an investigation. In September, 1969, William Calley was charged with murdering more than one hundred civilians at My Lai. The full dimensions of the massacre became public knowledge in mid-November, 1969, when newspapers carried Seymour Hersh's interviews with men from Company C, the *CBS Evening News* broadcast other interviews, and photographs of the massacred victims were printed in *Life* magazine.

Lieutenant General William R. Peers was assigned responsibility for conducting the official investigation of the incident. He learned that Hugh Thompsom's angry, but accurate, accusations of a civilian massacre, as well as reports by South Vietnamese officials of more than five hundred civilian deaths, were never properly investigated. Peers's report of March, 1970, contained detailed findings about what happened at My Lai and a recommendation that thirty individuals be held for possible charges.

The Army preferred charges against a total of twenty-five men: twelve for war crimes and thirteen for other military offenses. Four of the five men eventually tried on war crime charges were members of Company C. The fifth was Captain Eugene Kotouc, the staff intelligence officer of Task Force Barker. He was acquitted of torturing a prisoner. There was no evidence of any misdeeds by men from Company A, but Company B had been involved in killings of civilians at the hamlet of My Khe. Captain Earl Michles, in command of Company B, was killed in the same helicopter crash that killed Lieutenant Colonel Barker in June, 1968, so both of those men were beyond the reach of the law. Charges against Lieutenant Willingham of Company B were dismissed in 1970, in spite of evidence of between thirty-eight and ninety civilian deaths caused by his men in My Khe on the morning of March 16.

Charges were brought in 1970 against thirteen officers in the American Division for various military offenses that were less than war crimes and did not involve murder or attempted murder. Charges were dismissed against several of the officers, and several had their cases resolved in other manners. Only four men were tried for the war crimes of murdering civilians, all were members of Company C: Captain Medina, the company commander; Lieutenant Calley, in command of one of the company's platoons; Staff Sergeant David Mitchell, a squad leader in Calley's platoon; and Staff Sergeant Charles E. Hutto, a squad leader from Brooks's platoon. Lieutenant Brooks was killed in combat after the incident and so was not charged.

Initially, seven enlisted men from Company C had been charged by the Army with crimes including murder, rape, and assault. Charges against five were dropped and two men were tried. The first court-martial resulting from My Lai was that of David Mitchell, a career soldier; it began in October, 1970, at Fort Hood, Texas. Mitchell was acquitted of all charges. While Calley's trial was still in session, Charles Hutto was tried at Fort McPherson, Georgia, and found innocent. Medina's trial took place at Fort McPherson in August and September, 1971, after Calley's March, 1971, conviction. Medina was found not guilty of murder and assault.

Calley's trial was the most prominent of all the courts-martial. He had been identified from the start as ordering the shooting of women and children and was tried under article 118 of the Uniform Code of Military Justice for premeditated murder of more than one hundred Vietnamese. The trial at Fort Benning, Georgia, lasted about four months. On March 29, 1971, Calley was found guilty of three counts of murder by a panel of six officers. He was sentenced "to be confined at hard labor for the rest of [his] natural life; to be dismissed from the service; to forfeit all pay and allowances." Two days later, President Richard M. Nixon ordered Calley released from the stockade and returned to his quarters to serve his sentence. In August, 1971, the Army reduced Calley's sentence to twenty years, and in April, 1974, further reduced it to ten years. In the Army, prisoners become eligible for parole after one-third of their sentence is served. With Calley's punishment reduced to ten years, he became eligible in the fall of 1974 and parole was granted in November.

Impact of Event

The reactions both to the My Lai massacre and to Lieutenant Calley's conviction cover a tremendous range. Most Americans and many people around the world expressed horror and distress at the massacre itself; yet a great many considered Lieutenant Calley to be a scapegoat. To some, it was not Lieutenant Calley or the others who were tried in courts-martial, but the United States that was on trial for its Vietnam war.

The outcome of the courts-martial reveals that no one—not the Army, the president, Congress, or the American public—relished punishing American fighting men for their conduct in Vietnam. The Army backed away from a joint trial of the accused and did not carry through the stern spirit of justice that pervades the official Peers Report.

American official and popular statements from the time typically express outrage toward the massacre itself but suggest that it would be best to reserve judgment about Calley's or others' guilt. Some veterans and Army members believed that Calley was being punished for one of the inevitable tragedies of war. Still others believed Calley had done only what the army had trained him to do: kill communists. Many believed, in contrast, that since the United States was fighting to protect Vietnam from communism, the Army should be saving, or at least protecting, Vietnamese civilians.

Immediately following Calley's conviction for murder, the White House and Congress received a strong wave of popular sympathy for him. It was believed that Calley's conviction condemned, by implication, all Americans who had fought in Vietnam. Others believed that what occurred at My Lai were war crimes and that Calley, and others, should have been punished by death in the same way that German and Japanese war criminals were following World War II.

Beneath these opposing emotional calls for Calley's release or execution, the My Lai massacre and the subsequent courts-martial had a profound impact on the United States and the Army. Knowledge of the massacre came twenty-one months after the Tet Offensive, but it was additional confirmation that hopes for an American victory in Vietnam were unfounded. If U.S. troops were slaughtering the South Vietnamese, how could the people ever be won over to the side of the United States?

People also wondered if My Lai was only the first of many such massacres that would come to light. In fact, evidence of thousands of unnecessary and unwarranted deaths of South Vietnamese civilians caused by U.S. and other allied units have been documented, but nothing quite so horrible as that at My Lai.

Simply because of the questions raised about possible American atrocities in Vietnam, the whole discussion of the war itself took on a new color. The massacre gave proof to those antiwar protestors who called the war immoral and unjust. The atrocity marked an end, or at least a profound shock, to trust in American goodness and nobility of purpose.

In the 1970's, evidence of various hidden schemes and deadly plans by the U.S. government came to light, many of them completely unconnected with My Lai. The My Lai massacre remains a key incident that loosed the tide of self-doubt and questioning about the United States' purpose and moral stature that marked much of national life in the 1970's and 1980's. One of the most profound and lasting impacts of the My Lai massacre and the Calley court-martial was the coldness and distaste Vietnam veterans encountered after 1969 upon return to the United States. Many Americans treated all veterans as if they had joined with Company C to abuse and murder Vietnamese women and children. For those remaining in the military service, the vision of a unit running amok killing civilians in Vietnam's guerrilla war was one of several powerful forces that led to major reforms in Army military doctrine and the abandonment of the draft in favor of an all-volunteer armed services.

Bibliography

Anderson, David L., ed. *Facing My Lai: Moving Beyond the Massacre.* Lawrence: University Press of Kansas, 1997. The author provides a vivid retelling of this tragic incident in American history. Includes useful supplementary research tools.

Calley, William. *Lieutenant Calley: His Own Story, as Told to John Sack.* New York: Viking Press, 1971. After interviewing Calley at length in 1969 and 1970, the author says he took Calley's words and feelings apart and put them back together as a continuous story. Revealing.

Hammer, Richard. *The Court-Martial of Lt. Calley.* New York: Coward, McCann & Geoghegan, 1971. Although highly unfavorable to Lieutenant Calley, this is a useful summary of the trial itself, containing large amounts of verbatim testimony from Calley and men of his unit.

Hersh, Seymour. *My Lai 4: A Report on the Massacre and Its Aftermath.* New York: Random House, 1970. Hersh won a Pulitzer Prize for his reporting about the My Lai incident. Here he brings together the early evidence of a massacre in a compelling way. The book is somewhat dated by the later courts-martial and the release of the Peers Report.

Olson, James S., and Randy Roberts. *My Lai: A Brief History with Documents.* New York: St. Martin's Press, 1999. This text gathers sixty-eight primary documents to further illuminate the My Lai massacre. Illustrated and indexed, with glossary, chronology, and bibliography.

Peers, William R. *The My Lai Inquiry.* New York: W. W. Norton, 1979. Peers wrote this reflective, detailed book years after the official inquiry. A fascinating, readable summary of the massacre and its aftermath. Full of balanced, careful judgments. Indispensable.

Sim, Kevin, and Michael Bilton. *Four Hours in My Lai.* New York: Viking Press, 1992. Sim and Bilton, two British documentary filmmakers, reconstruct events leading up to the massacre, document the events, and report on the subsequent cover-ups and trials. Much of the material comes from interviews conducted in the 1980's and 1990's.

United States Department of the Army. *The My Lai Massacre and Its Cover-up: Beyond the Reach of the Law? The Peers Commission Report: Joseph Goldstein; Burke Marshall and Jack Schwartz.* New York: Free Press, 1976. In 1974, the Army released most of its official inquiry, commonly known as the Peers Report. This volume is the most convenient place to find the text of the Peers Report. Supplements deal with general war crime issues and some war crime matters relating to the Vietnam era. Be sure to distinguish between this official report and General Peer's own account.

David D. Buck

FBI and CIA Interference in Civil Rights Movement Is Revealed

Category of event: Civil rights; peace movements and organizations
Time: 1971-1974
Locale: United States

> *Overstepping their traditional boundaries of investigation, the FBI and CIA attempted to disrupt and discredit various civil rights and peace movements in the 1960's*

Principal personages:

J. EDGAR HOOVER (1895-1972), the director of the United States Federal Bureau of Investigation from 1924 to 1972

RICHARD HELMS (1913-   ), the director of the United States Central Intelligence Agency from 1965 to 1973

LYNDON B. JOHNSON (1908-1973), the thirty-sixth president of the United States (1963-1969)

RICHARD M. NIXON (1913-1994), the thirty-seventh president of the United States (1969-1974)

GERALD R. FORD (1913-   ), the thirty-eighth president of the United States (1974-1977)

RONALD REAGAN (1911-   ), the fortieth president of the United States (1981-1989)

Summary of Event

For many years, the United States Federal Bureau of Investigation (FBI) enjoyed a sterling reputation under the leadership of its longtime director, J. Edgar Hoover. In the later years of Hoover's administration, however, questions about overzealousness and abuse began to arise. Similar questions were raised about the United States Central Intelligence Agency (CIA) which always had been more controversial. Most of the CIA controversy focused on its foreign operations, for it was forbidden a domestic intelligence role. In the early 1970's, however, evidence emerged of illegal or improper domestic activity by both agencies, a significant part of that activity targeted against civil rights and anti-Vietnam War groups and individuals.

In 1971, a group calling itself the Commission to Investigate the FBI revealed a number of FBI documents which suggested that the agency had conducted intrusive, if not illegal, campaigns against a number of antiwar and leftist organizations. In October of the same year, the Committee for Public Justice and the Woodrow Wilson School at Princeton University sponsored a conference, "Investigating the FBI," which focused media attention on alleged FBI abuses in investigating civil rights and antiwar activities. Little evidence for these abuses could be produced, as the bureau closely guarded what it considered to be privileged information. After the death in 1972 of the FBI's powerful director, J. Edgar Hoover, and with the Watergate scandal in 1973 and 1974, public pressure mounted for further investigation. Finally, suits filed in December, 1973, and March, 1974, under the Freedom of Information Act resulted in publication of a number of FBI Counter Intelligence Program (COINTELPRO) files. The information in these files, coupled with documentation implicating the CIA in domestic intelligence abuses, prompted congressional investigation into the activities of both agencies. Although many FBI and CIA files had been destroyed or altered, the investigations revealed that both organizations had carried out a number of programs intended to undermine, discredit, or destroy civil rights and antiwar movements in the 1960's.

In 1964, following a number of race-related incidents, President Lyndon B. Johnson ordered the FBI to investigate the causes of racial unrest. In April, 1965, the bureau began investigating student antiwar groups for communist influence. When neither of these investigations found illegal or communist activity, Hoover intensified the programs. By 1968, the FBI had established two counterintelligence programs to gather data on black and student movements. COINTELPRO-Black Nationalist-Hate Groups extended to all forty-one FBI field offices authority for collecting information on civil rights groups. COINTELPRO-New Left attempted to undermine the activities of alleged campus radicals, with authority again given to all FBI field offices. Tactics included extensive wiretapping; planting listening devices in homes, hotel rooms, and meeting places of various organizations; infiltrating groups; and fabricating documents to create hostility within and among the organizations.

Specific evidence derived from the FBI's COINTELPRO files reveals that the bureau found certain individuals to be of particular interest. Martin Luther King, Jr., civil rights leader and recipient of the Nobel Peace Prize, was under intense FBI scrutiny from 1961 until his death in 1968. In 1964, shortly before King was to receive the Nobel Prize, the FBI sent him a tape of damaging information it had collected regarding his private life and threatened to make the data public if he did not commit suicide.

As the director of the FBI from 1924 to 1972, J. Edgar Hoover built a power base that even presidents could not challenge. (Library of Congress)

Leaders of the Black Panther Party (BPP) and the Student Nonviolent Co-ordinating Committee (SNCC) were also targets of FBI activity. When the two groups proposed a merger in 1968, the FBI engineered a rift between the groups. The rift contributed to decisions of high-ranking members of both groups, Stokely Carmichael of the SNCC and Eldridge Cleaver of the BPP, to go underground. The FBI accomplished this and other similar operations by fabricating stories and circulating them among members of targeted organizations. For example, the bureau leaked information that Carmichael was a CIA informant. It also telephoned his mother claiming that members of the BPP had threatened to kill Carmichael because of his alleged CIA affiliation. Carmichael left for Africa the next day.

FBI infiltrators at times encouraged illegal activities among groups which they had joined in order to create public disapproval of the organizations. These agents were known as provocateurs. One of the best-known provocateurs, Thomas Tongyai, traveled throughout western New York encouraging students to participate in violent activities such as bombing buildings and killing police.

The FBI's disruptive capabilities were enhanced by using local police and other federal agencies to collect data. For example, from 1968 through 1974, the FBI obtained confidential tax information from the Internal Revenue Service on 120 militant black and antiwar leaders. The CIA also became an important source of documentation and information for the FBI.

Although the CIA has no authority to gather information regarding domestic matters, that agency began collecting information on American citizens at the request of President Johnson. The agency's Special Operations Group, later known as CHAOS, was begun in August, 1967, to determine the role of foreign influence in the American peace movement. President Richard Nixon increased the demands on the CIA in 1970 by requiring that it become involved in evaluating and coordinating intelligence gathered on dissident groups. Some of the groups targeted for infiltration by the CIA included the SNCC, the Women's Strike for Peace, the Washington Peace Center, and the Congress of Racial Equality.

CIA Director Richard Helms was aware of the implications of the agency's operating outside its jurisdiction. In a cover memo to a 1968 report on student revolutionary activities around the world, including the United States, Helms noted that "This is an area not within the charter of this Agency. Should anyone learn of its existence it would prove most embarrassing for all concerned." The report concluded that student unrest was a product of domestic alienation, not of foreign manipulation, but the CIA continued to gather data on American citizens. By the early 1970's, the CIA had accumulated open files on more than 64,000 citizens and a computerized index of more than 300,000 individuals and organizations.

Impact of Event

Following the revelation of FBI and CIA abuses, there was a public outcry for curbs on both organizations. In 1975, President Gerald Ford ordered the creation of a special commission to establish the extent of CIA activities and to report findings and recommendations. The commission found that the CIA had indeed conducted improper investigations. Further, the commission recommended that the scope of CIA procedures be limited to foreign intelligence.

Also in 1975, a federal court awarded $12 million in damages to persons who had been arrested in Washington, D.C., while participating in antiwar demonstrations in May, 1971. The arrests were believed to have been a result of police coercion in which the FBI collaborated with local and national officials.

Since both the FBI and the CIA often deal with what is considered to be "sensitive" information, there has been a large amount of controversy over what the public has a right to know and what should be withheld to protect national security. In 1974, Congress amended the Freedom of Information Act (FOIA) to allow *in camera* review of documents by federal district courts in order to determine whether publication of information would pose a security risk. Although this amendment to the FOIA resulted in the declassification of many COINTELPRO documents, in many instances text was deleted. The effect of the FOIA was further modified by President Ronald Reagan's Executive Order 12356 of April, 1983. The order allowed intelligence agencies more discretionary authority over documentation and appeared to make it more difficult for the courts to review files.

Revelations of CIA abuses led to increased congressional oversight of intelligence activities, but supporters of the CIA argued that the restraints dangerously weakened the agency. The requirements were modified in 1980 to reduce to two the number of congressional committees that had to be notified of intelligence operations. Other provisions, however, increased the likelihood of information reaching Congress. For example, legislation enacted in 1978 required a judicial warrant for most intelligence agency electronic surveillance conducted in the United States.

Participants in FBI and CIA abuses during the COINTELPRO era generally went unpunished. Richard Helms, former director of the CIA, was fined only $2,000. In 1980, the only two FBI personnel tried and found guilty of COINTELPRO abuses were pardoned by President Reagan. In 1981, the FBI settled a $100 million suit for abuses committed against former members of the Weathermen, a radical student group.

Changes have been made in leadership, administrative rules, and legislation, yet recurrences of abuses are not unlikely because of the natural tensions between individual civil liberties on one hand and the demands of national security and civil order on the other.

Bibliography

Blum, Richard H., ed. *Surveillance and Espionage in a Free Society: A Report by the Planning Group on Intelligence and Security to the Policy Council of the Democratic National Committee.* New York: Praeger, 1972. This compilation of works provides information on the historical background of surveillance, the abuses that were apparent before much had been revealed publicly, and policy recommendations for eliminating and preventing further abuses. An insightful work which foreshadowed events to follow.

Caro, Robert A. *Master of the Senate: The Years of Lyndon Johnson.* New York: Knopf, 2002. Critically-acclaimed, well-researched biography of Johnson that pays special attention to his impact on civil rights legislation.

Elliff, John T. *Crime, Dissent, and the Attorney General: The Justice Department in the 1960's.* Beverly Hills, Calif.: Sage Publications, 1971. Written prior to disclosure of the extent to which the FBI violated civil liberties, the book nevertheless conveys well the tension between protecting and violating rights. Especially good coverage of black militant groups and antiwar dissent. Includes notes and index.

Garrow, David J. *The FBI and Martin Luther King, Jr.: From "Solo" to Memphis.* New York: W. W. Norton, 1981. This well-researched book provides detailed information on the FBI's relationship with King. Recommended for general readers for insight into the deviation from traditional law enforcement policies pursued by the FBI during the 1960's. Notes and index.

Kiel, R. Andrew. *J. Edgar Hoover: The Father of the Cold War.* Lanham, Md.: University Press of America, 2000. An extensive review of Hoover's career.

McKnight, Gerald D. *The Last Crusade: Martin Luther King, Jr., the FBI, and the Poor People's Campaign.* Boulder Colo.: Westview Press, 1998. Examines the FBI's surveillance of, and efforts to subvert, the Civil Rights movement.

Theoharis, Athan. *Spying on Americans: Political Surveillance from Hoover to the Huston Plan.* Philadelphia, Pa.: Temple University Press, 1978. The author, an expert on intelligence, offers a comprehensive perspective of the various ways in which the government monitors the actions of American citizens. Includes notes and index.

United States Commission on CIA Activities Within the United States. *Report to the President.* Washington, D.C.: Government Printing Office, 1975. Commissioned by President Ford, this report includes a wealth of information on illicit CIA programs and recommendations for procedural and administrative changes. Appendices.

Laurie Voice
Robert E. Biles

Amin Regime Terrorizes Uganda

Category of event: Atrocities and war crimes; civil rights; political freedom
Time: January, 1971
Locale: Uganda

> *The military coup that brought Idi Amin to power in Uganda led to the creation of one of the bloodiest regimes in African history*

Principal personages:

IDI AMIN (1925-   ), the man who ruled Uganda from 1971 to 1979
MILTON OBOTE (1924-   ), the man who was overthrown by Idi Amin in
  1971
MUTESA II (1924-1969), the king of Buganda, whose conflict with the Obote
  regime in the 1960's led to the emergence of the military as a decisive political force in the country

Summary of Event

Like many Third World states, Uganda, a former British colony in East
Africa, was an arbitrary creation of British economic, strategic, and political
interests and late nineteenth century intra-European conflicts and compro-
mises. It incorporated dozens of different linguistic and cultural groups that
had previously lived separately, although some of them maintained various
types of commercial as well as belligerent relationships. The indigenous political and social institutions included centralized monarchies in the southern
part of the country, of which Buganda was the most important, when the area
that became Uganda was declared a British protectorate (1894). Uganda also
had small-scale, clan-based social and political systems. In some parts of the
territory, a nomadic, pastoral style of life was predominant.

By the 1950's, elite groups that had emerged in various parts of the country
were demanding the right to self-determination in the form of independent statehood. The anti-imperialist movement, however, was not unified. In
Buganda and, to a lesser extent, in other kingdoms, there were strong autono-
mist and even secessionist sentiments arising from a desire to maintain special
cultural institutions and distinct identities. Throughout the colony, the emerging African elites were divided by religious rivalry, especially that between the

Roman Catholics, who were underrepresented in bureaucratic and politico-administrative positions, and the dominant Protestant Anglicans, who were overrepresented. The minority Muslims were also underrepresented but were somewhat peripheral to the rivalry within the Christian community.

On October 9, 1962, the British government granted political independence to the new state of Uganda. The government that acceded to power was a coalition dominated by the Uganda People's Congress (UPC), which was composed of elites from various parts of the country who shared a number of common aspirations and beliefs. They were mostly members of the Protestant Anglican Church, many of them secular in outlook and seeking to eliminate the socioeconomic inequalities that had emerged over the years of colonial rule among their home districts and the more prosperous southern kingdoms, especially Buganda.

The UPC's coalition partner was the all-Buganda *Kabaka Yekka* (the king above all) movement, whose primary goal was the preservation of the monarchy and the political autonomy of Buganda. The only common element between this movement and the UPC was the Anglican religious identity of the leaders and most of the followers of the two organizations. The opposition Democratic Party essentially represented the aggrieved Roman Catholics.

Uganda started independent statehood under what was in essence a parliamentary democratic system of government. There was a directly elected parliament, a cabinet headed by a prime minister responsible to parliament and, after 1963, a ceremonial president elected by parliament. The first president was Edward Mutesa II, who was also the *Kabaka* (king) of Buganda. The administrative system provided for a large degree of autonomy for the four kingdom areas and a more centralized system for most of the country. The judiciary was independent, and the military and police forces were initially nonpartisan and not directly involved in politics.

Within four years, rivalries and tensions within the ruling coalition had led the country to the brink of civil war. In early 1966, Milton Obote, the prime minister, ordered the arrest of five of his ministers on charges of plotting against him. He subsequently accused Mutesa II of participating in the alleged conspiracy and deposed him from the office of president. Obote later assumed the post. In May, he ordered the Ugandan army, then commanded by Idi Amin, to attack the palace of the *Kabaka*.

The events of 1966 had several significant consequences that were to lay the foundation for the Amin regime. First, the military was used to intervene in the political process for the first time, thus brushing aside established constitutional procedures. Second, a large number of people lost their lives in the course of indiscriminate attacks by soldiers on unarmed civilians who were identified with the ethnic group of the *Kabaka*. This established a precedent for selective military repression of civilians, which was to be one of the more sanguinary aspects of the Amin regime. Third, from this time onward, maintaining the loyalty of the army was to be the most important determinant of the exercise of political power by Ugandan leaders.

Between 1966 and 1971, Milton Obote tried to create a one-party regime. He centralized administrative and political power in his hands and forced all opposition underground or into exile through imprisonment or denial of positions of influence in the state. In the process, the military, especially army commander Idi Amin, became more prominent on the Ugandan political scene. At the same time, personal and ethnic conflict between Idi Amin and Obote developed, culminating in efforts by Obote to remove Amin from control of the army in 1970. Amin successfully resisted and in January, 1971, pushed his resistance to the point of a *coup d'état* while Obote was out of the country.

The Amin regime arose from a bloody revolt in which a number of the senior officers were either killed or forced to flee the country. During the first year, there were a number of purges of soldiers suspected of loyalty to the deposed regime. The most significant criterion used was ethnic identity. Thus, from the beginning, the Amin regime had genocidal tendencies.

In 1972, following an abortive invasion mounted by Obote loyalists from across the border in Tanzania, killings of opponents or suspected opponents of the regime spilled over into the civilian sector. People who had been senior officials of the UPC or belonged to the same ethnic group as Obote and his former military supporters became victims of brutal torture and murder. In the same year, Amin ordered the mass expulsion of citizens as well as resident aliens of Indian, Pakistani, or Bangladeshi origin. Many of them had been born in the country, and some families had lived there for several generations. Their property was taken from them without compensation and given to Amin's supporters and other Ugandans.

Impact of Event

During Amin's eight-year rule, thousands of Ugandans were killed for suspected opposition to the regime or because soldiers and members of other armed elements of the regime sought to dispossess them. Among the more prominent victims was the country's chief justice, Benedicto Kiwanuka, who was dragged from his chambers and never seen again, dead or alive. Other victims included numerous journalists, university professors, physicians, playwrights, military officers, police officers, senior civil servants, and members or former members of the regime who had fallen out of favor.

Millions of Ugandans suffered a drastic decline in their economic and social conditions. The economy rapidly deteriorated as a result of the disruption caused by the expulsion of the Asians, who had dominated commerce, and the climate of terror that discouraged investment and normal economic activities. Medical and educational services were hit hard as personnel fled the country to save their lives. Thousands of refugees fled to neighboring countries and beyond, some going as far as Europe and North America.

In late 1978, Amin sent units of his army across the border into Tanzania on the pretext that he was repelling an invasion. They killed and kidnapped civilians and looted property, thus spreading the violence and pain beyond the country's borders. The Tanzanian government decided to use this opportunity to rid Uganda and the region of the bloody tyrant. Beginning in December, 1978, the Tanzanian army, assisted by armed Ugandan exiles, steadily drove Amin's army out of Tanzania. They continued the pursuit until April, 1979, when Idi Amin and his regime were expelled from Uganda.

The impact of the eight-year rule of Idi Amin went beyond Uganda. The East African region and the African continent as a whole were affected. Apart from the thousands of lives lost or ruined, the Amin regime highlighted the enormity of the task facing countries like Uganda in creating stable, prosperous democratic states. At the regional level, Amin's often-belligerent attitude toward neighboring states led to the end of an attempt to create an East African Common Market linking Uganda, Kenya, and Tanzania.

At the continental level, the Amin regime became an embarrassment for African leaders, whose campaign against the apartheid regime in South Africa was robbed of some of its moral force by the excesses of one of their colleagues.

After the downfall of the Amin regime, Ugandans attempted to re-create civilian political institutions through multiparty elections in 1980 and a broad-based regime based on grass-roots direct participatory organizations. Obote was returned to the presidency in the 1980 elections. The lessons of the Amin regime will undoubtedly continue to influence Ugandans as they look for solutions to their intricate political, economic, and social problems.

Bibliography

Gwyn, David. *Idi Amin: Death-Light of Africa.* Boston: Little, Brown, 1977. Written under a pseudonym by a European or North American who worked in Uganda and gained intimate knowledge of the country and its people. This book combines careful analysis of the political background to the rise of the Amin regime with a passionate condemnation of its human rights outrages. One of the best works on the subject. Includes commentary in the form of an afterword. Historical chronology from the nineteenth century, maps, and appendix.

Karugire, Samwiri Rubaraza. *A Political History of Uganda.* Nairobi: Heinemann Educational Books, 1980. A good political history of Uganda that emphasizes the divisions and conflicts plaguing the country at the time of independence.

Kasfir, Nelson. *The Shrinking Political Arena.* Berkeley: University of California Press, 1976. This book focuses on the problem of interethnic and regional conflict in the period just before and following the attainment of political independence. This is an academic work. Maps, titles, selected bibliography, and index.

Kyemba, Henry. *A State of Blood: The Inside Story of Idi Amin.* New York: Grosset & Dunlap, 1977. The author served in both Milton Obote's and Idi Amin's governments. His is one of the few firsthand accounts of Amin's behavior and style. Maps, photographs, appendix, and index.

Mamdani, Mahmood. *Politics and Class Formation in Uganda.* New York: Monthly Review Press, 1976. This book analyzes the political history of Uganda up to and including the Amin regime, from a Marxist class perspective. Its analysis of the colonial period is excellent, but a rather rigid class framework renders the discussion of the postcolonial period unconvincing in many respects.

Ofcansky, Thomas P. *Uganda: Tarnished Pearl of Africa.* Boulder, Colo.: Westview Press, 1996. An examination of the government and politics of Uganda from 1962-1994, with a focus on the disintegration of Ugandan society after Idi Amin seized power in 1971. Bibliography and index.

Smith, George Ivan. *Ghosts of Kampala.* New York: St. Martin's Press, 1980. Written in the form of a personal memoir by a former United Nations official, this book provides a good description of the Amin regime. It is, however, marred by some factual errors. Map and index.

Edward Kannyo

Prisoners Riot Against Conditions in Attica

Category of event: International norms; prisoners' rights
Time: September 9-13, 1971
Locale: Attica, New York

> *A prison riot at the Attica State Correctional Facility attracted worldwide attention because of its political and racial implications and led to radical prison reforms in the United States*

Principal personages:

RUSSELL G. OSWALD (1908-1991), the commissioner of the New York State Department of Correctional Services

NELSON A. ROCKEFELLER (1908-1979), the governor of New York at the time of the Attica riot

HERMAN SCHWARTZ (1931-   ), a law professor active in prisoners' rights litigation; tried to mediate the dispute

ARTHUR O. EVE (1933-   ), A black assemblyman from Buffalo, New York; member of the observer committee

THOMAS GREY WICKER (1926-   ), a journalist for *The New York Times* who was one of the observers and who wrote in favor of prison reform

Summary of Event

On September 9, 1971, a petty scuffle between two inmates at the Attica State Correctional Facility near Buffalo, New York, triggered the bloodiest prison riot in American history. Eventually, 1,281 inmates took forty-three hostages, who were either guards or civilian prison employees. During the initial outbreak, a guard named William Quinn was knocked unconscious and eventually died of head wounds. All the rioters were potentially liable to prosecution for murder under New York state law. This motivated their demand for blanket amnesty, which was the one demand authorities were unwilling to grant.

Trouble had been brewing for a long time. With the influx of African Americans and Hispanics into New York City following World War II, the composition of New York prison populations had gradually changed from predominantly white to predominantly nonwhite. There was no corresponding change, however, in the ethnic composition of the correctional officers, who tended to be strongly prejudiced against nonwhites and particularly against blacks. The verbal and physical abuse of inmates was one of the main factors causing unrest. Other grievances included the poor quality of prison food and the facts that inmates were paid far below minimum wage for their labor in prison shops, that their communication with the outside was severely restricted, and that their attempts to appeal their sentences in the courts were punished. These and other complaints eventually were formulated in a document presented to the prison authorities and to the outside world via the news media.

The medium of television brought vivid pictures of the four-day riot into living rooms across the United States. For the first time, citizens could see for themselves what prisons and inmates as well as guards and state police really looked like; it was quite different from the picture that had been created in the popular imagination by Hollywood prison films.

Leaders of the riot took advantage of the media coverage to present a political message to the world. The essence of their thesis, which was derived largely from the Black Muslims and the Black Panthers, was that they were actually victims of society because they were poor, uneducated, and victims of discrimination.

Mainly because of the leadership by members of the Black Muslims, the riot was extremely well organized. Various committees were appointed to preserve order, distribute food, erect shelters, and dig latrines for sanitation. The center of all the rioters' activities was the section of the prison known as "D yard." There the leaders set up tables at which they issued orders and conducted negotiations with prison officials and outside observers. The authorities agreed to provide food and water in order to protect the lives of the hostages, who were generally well treated but confined to a small area entirely surrounded by inmates.

Commissioner Russell Oswald came to the negotiating table and was presented with a list of demands. One of the initial demands was for the presence of a group of outside observers, who would presumably see to it that the state lived up to any promises it made. Many of the guards and state police were disgusted with Oswald for even conferring with the inmates. Their instinct was to storm D yard with guns and tear gas and to save the hostages by the sheer weight and speed of their assault. They believed that any concessions to the prisoners would only make their jobs harder in the future.

Oswald was a progressive administrator who sincerely wanted to reform

New York State's prisons along the lines the inmates were demanding. He was handicapped, however, by the traditional attitude of the corrections officers and by a chronic unwillingness on the part of state legislators to provide the funds needed for improving facilities and hiring personnel. Many legislators, law enforcement officials, and members of the general public were strongly opposed to what they considered "coddling" of prison inmates; they believed that if prisons were unpleasant places, then people would obey the law in order to stay out of them.

Eventually, the group of observers worked out a set of "Twenty-eight Points" that Oswald was willing to accept. These points were important both because they represented the spectrum of inmate grievances at the time the riot started and because they heralded the kinds of reforms that were actually implemented after it ended. Some of the points were obvious and reasonable: The inmates wanted better food, better recreational facilities, better medical and dental treatment, and better educational and rehabilitation services. Other points were considered quite radical for the time. They called for an end to censorship of reading material, unrestricted communication with the outside world, a permanent ombudsman service to arbitrate grievances, and the application of the New York state minimum wage law to all work done by inmates, who had been paid as little as twenty-five cents an hour in prison shops. Many of the proposals were aimed at improving the quality of prison life, which was unbearably grim and tedious.

The twenty-eight proposals that were acceptable to Commissioner Oswald and to the thirty-three observers were not sufficient to satisfy the leaders of the riot. The majority of the prisoners probably would have accepted the proposals, released the hostages, and gone back to the cells under the guarantee of complete administrative amnesty; however, the leaders believed strongly that they would be the targets of legal action after the prison was restored to order.

The only person who they believed could grant them legal amnesty for all actions occurring during the riot, including the death of Quinn, was New York Governor Nelson Rockefeller. The governor believed that the riot had worldwide political implications and could lead to more prison riots and even to revolution if not handled effectively. He was a strong contender for the presidency of the United States (and later served as vice president of the United States from late 1974 through 1976, under President Gerald R. Ford). Rockefeller believed that being soft on the rioters would undermine the morale of all law-enforcement officials and alienate many conservative voters. He flatly refused to grant blanket amnesty, and the inmate leaders tore up the Twenty-eight Points. After that, a violent finale was inevitable.

State police and Attica corrections officers stormed D yard with tear gas, shotguns, deer rifles, and pistols. Twenty-nine prisoners were killed as well as ten hostages. It was later determined that all the hostages were killed by "friendly fire," although inmates had severely wounded a number of their captives with crudely fashioned knives. Three hostages, eighty-five inmates, and one state trooper were wounded. The officers took revenge for their dead in an orgy of reprisals. Forty-five percent of the inmates in D yard suffered bruises, abrasions, lacerations, and broken bones. Eventually, three leaders were charged with thirty-four counts of kidnapping, and a total of 1,289 charges of criminal activity were brought against sixty-two inmates. In 1975, however, a general amnesty was declared, mainly because of the scandal surrounding the actions of the guards and police and subsequent attempts to cover up incriminating evidence against them. Seven inmates who had plea-bargained for reduced charges were pardoned by Governor Hugh Carey. John Hill, who had been convicted of killing William Quinn, had his sentence commuted and was paroled in March of 1979.

Impact of Event

In *A Prison and a Prisoner* (1978), a study of Green Haven Correctional Facility, another upstate New York prison, author Susan Sheehan wrote that there had been more changes at New York State's maximum security prisons in the 1970's than in the preceding thirty years. Most of them were made in 1972, a few months after the Attica riot. Among the many changes instituted after the riot were improvements in living conditions. The prison's interiors were painted a neutral beige, replacing the glaring institutional green. Prisoners were allowed to select colors for their cells. Pay telephones were installed for inmates' use. Officials allowed longer visiting hours with provisions for conjugal visits. The food was improved in quality, and less pork was served in response to the protests of the Black Muslim inmates, whose religion forbade them to eat pork. More academic programs were offered that led to high school and college degrees. Vocational training in such fields as photography, plumbing, and engine repair was also made available. In the prison's "honor block," model prisoners were allowed to cook their own food and move about unescorted. A new gymnasium, weekly movies, and some live entertainment were added as well. Many more black and Puerto Rican guards were hired as a result of a statewide effort at recruitment. Prisoners were required to spend much less time in their cells, and an effective inmate grievance procedure was installed to head off future riots.

Because the Attica riot of 1971 received such heavy media coverage, it inspired similar improvements in prisons all across the United States. This did not mean, however, that prisons became pleasant places to live. One of the things that Attica proved was that the classic notion of prisons as places of so called "rehabilitation" was not only futile but hypocritical as long as society did nothing to change the conditions that produced criminals. Attica forced penologists to drop the pretense that prisons were places intended for rehabilitation and to admit that they were places of confinement and punishment, although prisoners were entitled to decent living conditions and to access to educational opportunities if they wished to make use of them. The major emphasis in criminal jurisprudence focused on finding alternatives to incarceration such as community service, halfway houses, public works projects, and restitution to victims through wage garnishments. The tendency across the United States became to sentence only the most dangerous criminals to maximum security prisons, meaning that prisons became more hostile and dangerous environments in spite of the improvements made after Attica. No doubt there will always be a need to incarcerate violent or remorseless individuals; however, the daily newspapers are full of evidence of judges' efforts to treat nonviolent offenders like rational human beings, because locking people in cages produces the opposite of rehabilitation.

Bibliography

Badillo, Herman, and Milton Haynes. *A Bill of No Rights: Attica and the American Prison System.* New York: Outerbridge & Lazard, 1972. A bitter treatment of the prison system as revealed by the events at Attica in 1971 and a detailed proposal for sweeping reforms. Badillo, a Democratic congressman from the Bronx, was one of the team of observers who tried desperately to resolve the situation without bloodshed. Many valuable chapter notes.

Bell, Malcolm. *The Turkey Shoot: Tracking the Attica Cover-up.* New York: Grove Press, 1985. The author served in the New York State special prosecutor's investigation of the Attica riot but later resigned in protest of what he considered to be a cover-up of atrocities committed by state police and prison guards in quelling the uprising. Bell charges that facts were suppressed to protect Governor Rockefeller, who had presidential ambitions.

Clark, Richard X. *The Brothers of Attica.* New York: Links Books, 1973. This is a highly emotional and biased account of the Attica riot by a black inmate who was one of its leaders. Despite its propagandistic intent, it effectively reveals the strength of the inmates' passions and their attitude that society was more guilty than the inmates themselves.

Coons, William R. *Attica Diary.* New York: Stein & Day, 1972. This is a personalized description of life at the Attica State Correctional Facility written by a college English instructor who was imprisoned there for illegal drug possession for a period of fifteen months shortly before the riot broke out. The author gives a good description of the monotony of prison life and the pent-up hostilities of the inmates.

Johnson, Robert. *Understanding and Reforming the Prison.* 3d ed. Belmont, Calif.: Wadsworth, 2001. This text provides historical information about prisons, prison life, and efforts toward prison reform.

New York State Special Commission on Attica. *Attica: The Official Report of the New York State Special Commission on Attica.* New York: Praeger, 1972. A "citizens' committee" was appointed by the chief judge of the New York Supreme Court to investigate the riot. It interviewed more than sixteen hundred inmates, four hundred guards, 270 state police, Commissioner Oswald, Governor Rockefeller, and many others to present a report that is admirable in its thoroughness's and impartiality. The report blames the 1971 uprising on the deplorable conditions in all New York prisons.

Oswald, Russell G. *Attica: My Story.* Garden City, N.Y.: Doubleday, 1972. A detailed account of the Attica riot from the point of view of the official who bore the heaviest responsibility for restoring order and saving lives. Commissioner Oswald's thesis is that the riot was orchestrated by political militants who sought a bloody confrontation for international propaganda purposes and did not sincerely desire the reforms he was willing to implement. Useful appendices.

Useem, Bert, and Peter Kimball. *States of Siege: U.S. Prison Riots, 1971-1986.* New York: Oxford University Press, 1989. Two scholars present sociological case studies of prison riots in five different states, beginning with the Attica riot of 1971, in an attempt to understand their causes and possible cure. The chapter notes at the end of the book contain extensive references to secondary source material. The authors blame feckless prison administration for the five major riots they examined.

Wicker, Tom. *A Time to Die.* New York: Quadrangle, 1975. Written in first-person fashion by a senior journalist with *The New York Times* who served on the observer committee, this excellent study of the Attica riot won an Edgar Allan Poe Award in the Fact Crime category in 1976. Extensive chapter notes at the end of the book provide a wealth of reference material.

Bill Delaney

Nations Agree to Rules on Biological Weapons

Category of event: Atrocities and war crimes; international norms
Time: April 10, 1972
Locale: Washington, D.C.; London, England; and Moscow, Union of Soviet Socialist Republics

> *The 1972 Biological Weapons Convention prohibited the production, possession, and use of biological weapons*

Principal personages:
RICHARD M. NIXON (1913-1994), the thirty-seventh president of the United States, ordered unilateral destruction of biological weapons
LEONID ILICH BREZHNEV (1906-1982), the leader of the Soviet Union from 1964 to 1982
GEORGE W. MERCK (1894-1957), the American president of Merck & Co., influential in the development of American research on biological weapons during World War II

Summary of Event

In the twentieth century, the use of chemical and bacteriological agents in warfare was unusual. The scale of destruction that resulted from these types of agents hardly compares to the loss of life inflicted in armed conflict by conventional weapons. The first large-scale use of these types of agents in warfare occurred in World War I. In 1915, German troops changed the nature of the conflict when they released chlorine gas against Allied forces in France. The Allies quickly retaliated. The human cost of this type of warfare in World War I totaled approximately one million casualties, 10 percent of which were fatal. These experiences led to the 1925 Geneva Protocol, which prohibited the use of poisonous gases and biological agents in warfare. This convention, concluded between the United States, Britain, France, Italy, and Japan, was an attempt to strengthen the 1899 Hague Gas Declaration that had prohibited the use of "projectiles the sole object of which is the diffusion of asphyxiating or deleterious gases." By the mid-1980's, this convention had 108 signatories, including all members of the United Nations Security Council.

It is important to understand the basic differences between chemical weapons and biological weapons. Chemical weapons are chemical compounds, smoke, and other materials which are designed to produce confusion, incapacitation, or death. Most chemical weapons fall into the categories of choking agents, blood agents, blistering agents, or incapacitating agents. Many experts would also include the use of nonlethal agents on populations and the use of herbicides to destroy forests or agriculture as examples of chemical warfare.

Biological warfare, often referred to as bacteriological or germ warfare, is the dissemination of pathogenic microorganisms in an attempt to incapacitate or kill military or civilian populations, animals, or plants. The primary difference from chemical weapons is that biological compounds kill humans by fostering diseases among entire populations. Biological weapons utilize pathogenic microorganisms that enter the body and produce illness through the ability of the microorganisms to replicate inside the body of the person exposed to these agents. Microorganisms that can be utilized in these weapons are bacteria, viruses, and parthenogenetic microscopic fungi.

Epidemics are possible with these types of weapons because the individuals that come into direct contact with contagious microorganisms are capable of transmitting these diseases to unaffected populations. Disease can also be spread through food contamination and insect bites. Examples of bacteriological agents that can produce incapacitation are viruses that can induce influenza and diphtheria. Potentially lethal agents that can be used in biological warfare are microorganisms that cause cholera, typhoid, and smallpox. Occupying a middle ground between chemical and biological agents are toxins, microorganisms produced originally by living organisms or manufactured synthetically that are not capable of multiplying inside infected individuals.

Efforts to control the production and possession of these types of weapons were not specifically addressed in the 1925 Geneva Protocol. Although the first use of asphyxiating or poisonous compounds was banned, poison gas was used by Italian forces in 1936 against Ethiopian forces who did not possess chemical capabilities. There is also evidence that gas was used by Japan in the late 1930's against the Chinese.

The fact that poison gas was not used extensively in World War II appears to have been the result of fear on both sides that chemical warfare would escalate, as it had in World War I. Both sides seemed to be reluctant to be the first to violate the Geneva Protocol in attacking states with chemical warfare capabilities. By the 1940's, advances in chemical weapons and tactics had also made the potential costs of this type of warfare enormous. Fearing German advances in biological warfare, in 1942 the United States began research into the production of weapons that utilized anthrax, botulism, and other biological agents. Although few biological weapons were produced by the United States, and later evidence established that Germany had done little to establish a biological arsenal, Allied forces inoculated approximately one hundred thousand soldiers against botulism toxins to convince the Axis Powers that biological retaliation was possible.

Research on and production of chemical and biological weapons by the Soviet Union and the United States escalated soon after the end of the war. Citing the failure of the United States to ratify the 1925 Protocol, the Soviet Union falsely charged the United States with the use of biological weapons in Korea. In response to Soviet research and development, the United States increased its expenditures on chemical and biological weapons nearly twenty fold between the early 1950's and 1969. There are also indications that by the mid-1950's, official U.S. policy on the use of chemical and biological agents had been modified to decouple the United States from any treaties that prohibited first use.

In the 1960's, there was increased international support for stronger controls on the development and possession of chemical and biological weapons. A 1966 resolution of the United Nations General Assembly called for continued observance of the 1925 Protocol and urged the acceptance of its principles by all states. The use of defoliants in Vietnam by the United States began to focus worldwide attention on the environmental risks involved with development and testing of chemical and biological weapons. In response to congressional criticism, President Richard Nixon directed National Security Adviser Henry Kissinger to review chemical and biological policy. A 1969 National Security Council report recommended dividing the issues of chemical and biological weapons as well as maintaining the renunciation of the first use of chemical and biological agents as a separate issue. Nixon announced in November, 1969, that the United States would unilaterally destroy its biological weapons, would confine biological research to strictly defensive purposes, and would submit the 1925 Geneva Protocol to the Senate for ratification.

The U.S. support for controls on biological weapons closely resembled an existing resolution in the United Nations that dealt with the prohibition of the possession of biological weapons. In 1970, the head of the U.S. Arms Control and Disarmament Agency, Gerald Smith, stated that the best hope for an international convention on biological weapons was contained in the British resolution to the U.N. Conference of the Committee on Disarmament that dealt with the prohibition of the production and possession of biological weapons, with chemical agents treated separately. By 1971, the Soviet Union and its allies reversed their previous position and agreed to treat the issue of biological arms separately from that of chemical weapons. The separation of the two issues drew criticism from a number of states in the General Assembly which favored a comprehensive convention that would address both chemical and biological weapons.

The actions of the Soviet Union greatly facilitated flexibility in the negotiations on the possession and use of biological weapons. Although the 1972 treaty was intended to be a first step in an overall agreement that would limit the possession of chemical weapons, some toxic agents previously defined as chemical weapons were included in the 1972 agreement. The Convention on the Prohibition, Development, Production and Stockpiling of Bacteriological and Toxic Weapons of 1972 declared that the forty-six signatory states would refrain from developing or stockpiling "microbial or other biological agents, or toxins whatever their origin or method of production." The convention was historic because it was the first modern treaty to prohibit the possession and use of an entire class of weapons.

Impact of Event

Because biological weapons have not been used extensively in warfare, it is difficult to estimate precisely how the 1972 convention has influenced human rights. Critics have frequently referred to the lack of verification procedures as a major weakness in the 1972 convention. By the mid-1970's, Western observers identified sites inside the Soviet Union as facilities capable of producing biological weapons. In 1979, Western intelligence sources pointed to an anthrax epidemic in the Soviet city of Sverdlovsk as evidence of military research and possible production of offensive biological weapons. The Soviets did not deny that the anthrax outbreak occurred but attributed it to the consumption of contaminated meat. Although many in the West used the epidemic at Sverdlovsk as proof of Soviet noncompliance with the 1972 convention, the evidence was far from conclusive.

Additional Western criticism of the Soviet Union was related to the controversy over "yellow rain." In 1981, U.S. defense officials announced that Western intelligence sources had identified traces of biological material related to the trichothecene toxin in Southeast Asia. American officials charged the Soviet Union and its allies with the use of bacteriological weapons in Laos, Cambodia (Kampuchea), and Afghanistan. Although there was considerable debate about these charges, many leading scientists in the West concluded that these reports of yellow rain were not examples of biological warfare but rather naturally occurring environmental changes related to bee droppings.

In 1984, the United States proposed building a $1.4 million laboratory to conduct secret research on "substantial volumes of toxic biological aerosol agents." Citing continuing Soviet research into biological agents in the 1980's, the United States expanded its research on biological warfare. Congressional critics of the Reagan administration's funding of biological research introduced legislation that suggested continued U.S. compliance with the 1972 convention.

It should be understood that the 1972 protocol did not prohibit research on or the possession of biological agents for protective or peaceful purposes. The problem with research of this kind is that similar processes are employed to develop offensive biological weapons and defensive vaccines. Research into these agents also makes it possible for governments to develop bacteriological weapons quickly in periods of international crisis.

Bibliography

Adams, Valerie. *Chemical Warfare, Chemical Disarmament.* Bloomington: Indiana University Press, 1990. An excellent introduction to the subject of chemical and bacteriological weapons by a specialist in defense and arms control issues who has worked in the United Kingdom's ministry of defense. Includes notations, tables, bibliography, and index.

Geissler, Erhard, ed. *Biological and Toxin Weapons Today.* New York: Oxford University Press, 1986. Briefly examines the 1972 convention and the renewed military interest in chemical weapons in the 1980's. Because a great deal of the book examines modern scientific research on chemical and bacteriological agents, this book is useful primarily to students interested in the scientific aspects of the topic. Includes notations, suggestions for further reading, a copy of a U.N. history of the negotiation of the 1972 convention, appendices, and index.

Lawler, William. "Progress Towards International Control of Chemical and Biological Weapons." *The University of Toledo Law Review* 13 (Summer, 1982): 1220-1253. Written by a senior political affairs officer in the United Nations Centre for Disarmament. An excellent history of U.N. efforts to promote the establishment of controls on biological and chemical weapons. Includes notations.

Lederberg, Joshua S. *Biological Weapons: Limiting the Threat.* Cambridge, Mass.: MIT Press, 1999. Explores the history of attempts to control the use of biological weapons.

Mangold, Tom, and Jeff Goldberg. *Plague Wars: The Terrifying Reality of Biological Warfare.* New York: St. Martin's Press, 2000. An authoritative and exhaustive report on biological weapons and the biological warfare situation as it currently exists.

Seagrave, Sterling. *Yellow Rain: A Journal Through the Terror of Chemical Warfare.* New York: M. Evans and Company, 1981. An account of research and stockpiling of chemical and biological agents by the United States, the Soviet Union, and other countries. Examines in detail allegations of noncompliance with the 1972 convention. Includes notations, bibliography, and index.

Sims, Nicholas A. *The Diplomacy of Biological Disarmament: Vicissitudes of a Treaty in Force, 1975-85.* New York: St. Martin's Press, 1988. An excellent account of the 1972 convention and its impact on the international community. Includes notations, appendices, charts, bibliography, and index.

Stockholm International Peace Research Institute. "Chemical and Biological Disarmament." In *World Armaments and Disarmament: SIPRI Yearbook 1972.* New York: Humanities Press, 1972. A brief examination of the essential provisions of the draft convention on the development, production, and stockpiling of biological weapons approved by the U.N. General Assembly in December of 1971. Includes appendices and index.

_____. *The Problem of Chemical and Biological Warfare: A Study of the Historical, Technical, Military, Legal, and Political Aspects of CBW, and Possible Disarmament Measures.* Vols. 3-4. New York: Humanities Press, 1973. A detailed account of the Geneva Protocol and other international efforts to outlaw chemical and biological warfare. Includes notations, a number of appendices, and an index.

Zilinskas, Raymond, ed. *Biological Warfare: Modern Offense and Defense.* Boulder, Colo.: Lynne Rienner, 2000. Includes an assessment of how to stop the augmentation of biological weapons on an international level.

Lawrence Clark III

Burundi Commits Genocide of Hutu Majority

Category of event: Atrocities and war crimes; racial and ethnic rights
Time: May-August, 1972
Locale: Burundi

> *The atrocities begun by the government of Burundi against its own citizens, the Hutu majority, were implicitly condoned by African statesmen and ignored by the outside world*

Principal personages:

THOMAS PATRICK MELADY (1927-   ), the United States ambassador to Burundi from November, 1969, to June, 1972
MICHEL MICOMBERO (1940-   ), the president of Burundi
JULIUS NYERERE (1922-1999), the president of Tanzania

Summary of Event

The historical background to the Hutu people (also known as Bahutu) is important. Burundi achieved independence from Belgium in 1962. It had a population estimated at about 3.5 million in the 1970's and a land area of slightly more than ten thousand square miles.

The original inhabitants of the area of modern-day Burundi were probably the Twa (Batwa), a subgroup of the Twide pygmies. The Hutus compose nearly 85 percent of the population in Burundi. Another group, the Tutsis (also called Watutsi) arrived in the area later but dominated both the Twa and the Hutus. They composed about 14 percent of the population of Burundi.

The Tutsis dominated the Hutus for more than four hundred years. They came as invaders and quickly established themselves as the ruling class. The Tutsis were pastoralists (nomads with cattle as their chief commodity and status symbol) and warriors; in time they shaped and controlled a feudal society with the Hutus at the bottom. The two groups share a common language, Kirundi. Educated members of the two groups, including literate peasants, speak French. The Tutsis regarded themselves as an elite minority, constantly on guard against real and imaginary plots by the Hutu majority. The Tutsis established a rigidly stratified society to retain their prestige and privileges.

Germany was the first European colonial power in the Burundi area. The

Germans established indirect rule over the central African territory by permitting the Tutsi aristocracy to retain its dominance over the feudal structure. Hutus, consequently, remained at the bottom. Tutsis relished Germany colonialism and saw themselves as equals to the Germans; they revered the Germans for abetting their rule over the Hutus while being unconscious of the subjugated people's plight.

The Allied victory in World War I led to Belgian military rule in Burundi in 1916, known then as Ruanda-Urundi. The area was of little economic value to the Belgians. They had hoped to trade Ruanda-Urundi for a piece of northern Angola to add to their southern colony of the Congo. This did not happen. The territory became a Belgian Mandate under the League of Nations. The switch in European "ownership" of the territory had no salutary effect for the situation of the Hutus. Belgium copied the German practice of working through the Tutsi minority in governing the region. There was little or no economic incentive for the Belgians to settle in the area or to make any substantial investments in a subsistence economy that lacked even a rudimentary infrastructure. The economy was household based, and villages were isolated from each other. Burundi did not offer Belgium a market for manufactures, and the region had almost nothing worth extracting for local use or for transport to Europe or America.

After World War II, Ruanda-Urundi was changed from a League of Nations Mandate to a trust territory under the United Nations. This change had real importance, as the U.N. trust criteria required Belgium to prepare the population for self-rule. This meant majority rule. The new requirement threatened the Tutsi minority and gave the Hutus hope of doing through representative government what they had been unable to accomplish through armed conflict over the centuries.

Tutsi-Hutu relations were uncertain when limited self-government was granted by Belgium in 1961. The Belgian Foreign Office was hopeful that the monarchy would be a stabilizing institution in Burundi. In July, 1962, Belgium recognized Burundi as an independent monarchy. It was assumed by Belgium and by U.N. officials that the monarchy had considerable support among both the Tutsis and Hutus. Hutus generally had been neglected by their European colonizers in the educational system and in government service. A feudal society had, apparently, bred a docile and politically muted people.

A major setback for ethnic harmony and representative government in Burundi was generated by events outside the country, in neighboring Rwanda. Hutus and Tutsis accounted for similar proportions of the population of Rwanda as they did in Burundi. Selective genocide was launched in Rwanda by the Hutu elite against the Tutsi minority. Between 1962 and 1963, Hutus murdered twenty thousand Tutsis. It took a few weeks before news of the Rwanda genocide reached Burundi and the rest of the outside world. The Rwanda government never admitted the genocide of the Tutsi minority, claiming that only 870 people were killed.

An atmosphere of trepidation was created among the Tutsis in Burundi by the slaughter of their brothers in Rwanda. Whatever sanguine expectations were held by leaders of both tribes for a pluralistic and harmonious society were shattered by the Hutu killings in Rwanda. Hutus, nevertheless, were making some political gains in Burundi. Hutus held twenty-three of the thirty-three seats in the National Assembly. Hutu presence in government and in other institutions, such as the army, was symbolic rather than a genuine effort to reflect demographic reality. This fact was not wasted on educated Hutus, who were increasingly aware of their political potency.

Growing political awareness among Hutus and enthusiasm to command Burundi society led to an attempted *coup d'état* in October, 1965. Tutsi revenge was quick. Attacks on Hutu leaders and people continued for more than a year. Eighty-six high-ranking Hutu officials were executed in late 1965; in all, between twenty-five hundred and five thousand Hutus were killed during this dress rehearsal for a more horrendous genocide of the Hutu people by Tutsis.

On April 29, 1972, Hutu rebels, allied with Zairian exiles, attacked southern Burundi in an attempt to establish a Hutu-dominated republic. They struck at Tutsi soldiers and civilians in an attempt to overthrow the minority government. There had been ongoing antagonism between the two groups since Hutu plotters were foiled in a 1969 attempted coup. The 1972 attempted coup was better organized and was carried out at many points throughout the country, including the capital, Bujumbura. In the first week of fighting, between two and three thousand were killed on each side. Government sources erroneously claimed that Hutus killed more than fifty thousand Tutsis. This government account maintained that the aim of the Hutu rebels was to exterminate the Tutsi race.

By mid-May, Tutsi soldiers had completed their military operations against the rebels. The threat to civil peace was over, but the killings of Hutus by the Tutsi authorities continued. Soldiers and paramilitary, as well as ordinary citizens, killed about three thousand Hutus in the first week of the fighting. At least two thousand Hutu government workers were arrested and later executed by Tutsi soldiers. Two dozen Hutu army officers were executed by orders of the Burundi government. Tutsi violence was generated by fear of losing political power and the possibility of a massacre of their people or expulsion from Burundi. President Michel Micombero encouraged this sentiment.

By mid-May, President Micombero had sanctioned a policy of selective genocide of educated Hutus. On May 10, U.S. ambassador Thomas Patrick Melady informed his country's Department of State that the period of civil strife appeared to be over and that what the government was now doing approached an official government policy of selective genocide of elite Hutus. The Belgian government agreed with Ambassador Melady's assessment. It declared on May 19 that the army was engaging in a "veritable genocide" and demanded that the killings stop.

Ambassador Melady was the first to appeal personally to President Micombero to stop the killings. President Micombero told Ambassador Melady that he had evidence detailing Hutus' intentions to kill "every mother and child of the Tutsi race." He declined to produce the evidence. Ambassador Melady's main consideration, expressed to President Micombero, was simply to stop the killing. Africa, Ambassador Melady observed, would lose its moral standing in the Third World; the genocide would also undermine black Africa's condemnation of apartheid in South Africa.

The failure of the international community, including the Organization of African Unity (OAU) and the United Nations, to denounce the atrocities in Burundi gave a green light to other African governments wishing to use a "final solution" to historical intertribal rivalries. Ambassador Melady proposed to the U.S. State Department a three-pronged approach to stopping the genocide in Burundi. The United States should work first through direct contacts with African leaders, then through appeals to the OAU, and last through the United Nations. Melady believed that if the United States rushed into the Burundi situation it would face resentment for decades to come. The State Department acceded to Ambassador Melady's policy recommendation.

Impact of Event

Genocide was almost a constant in the evolution of nation-states in Africa following the collapse of European colonialism. African states, more ethnically heterogeneous than Western European nation-states, exhibited a paranoia about their independence and national security, and African leaders saw malevolent plots by the West against their independence. This misapprehension of world affairs handicapped African governments in confronting dangerous and complicated social, economic, and political problems within Africa. As a matter of fact, the United States and Europe by the 1970's had generally agreed to refrain from intervening in the internal affairs of African states.

The OAU, founded in May, 1963, was considered by policymakers within and outside Africa as the legitimate forum for African states to settle African problems, although its charter outlawed military intervention into the internal affairs of other African states. The United States and European nations had on many occasions reaffirmed their determination to support the OAU members in controlling their own affairs. In the Burundi crisis, the OAU was inept. A fact-finding team dispatched by the OAU practically endorsed genocide of the Hutus by the Burundi government.

International efforts, especially those of the United States government, to get the OAU to mediate an end to the slaughter of Hutus in Burundi was a failure. During the critical months of June and July, when most of the killings took place, OAU leaders assured the outside world that Africans would stop the genocide in Burundi, if indeed it were occurring. The position of the OAU merely lengthened the genocide and did nothing to deter future bloodbaths. President Micombero was pleased with the OAU endorsement of his government's policies: The OAU pledged full support for the Burundi government.

The United Nations sent a fact-finding mission to Burundi on June 22. On July 4, U.N. secretary-general Kurt Waldheim announced the findings of the team. Waldheim called for humanitarian aid to Burundi refugees and noted estimates of the dead that ranged from eighty thousand to two hundred thousand. The United Nations failed to devise any swift measures to stop the killing.

U.N. secretary-general Kurt Waldheim. (Library of Congress)

Numerous factors contributed to the eventual end of the genocide. Publicity by the United Nations of the atrocities probably played a role. The Tutsis in power also became convinced that the Hutus had been taught their lesson, and that they no longer posed a threat to the power structure. Julius Nyerere, the president of Tanzania, invited President Micombero to Tanzania on August 6 and urged him to end the genocide. By then, the killing had slowed but not stopped.

Nyerere also took a more direct approach to an outbreak of atrocities in Burundi in May and June of the following year, 1973. He demanded that the OAU "concern itself actively" in the civil strife in Burundi. The OAU, Nyerere insisted, must mediate in Burundi to prevent another bloodbath. President Nyerere's strong stance might have prevented another episode of genocide by the Tutsis against the Hutus in 1973.

Bibliography

Bowen, Michael. *Passing By: The United States and Genocide in Burundi, 1972.* Washington, D.C.: Carnegie Endowment for International Peace, 1973. A behind-the-scenes account of the State Department's attempts to influence Burundi to stop the Hutu genocide.

Hatch, Charles J. *Julius K. Nyerere.* London: Becker & Warburg, 1976. Praises President Julius Nyerere's efforts to start socialism in one country and his willingness to challenge the OAU's doctrine of official apathy and opposition to intervention or public condemnation of atrocities within African countries.

Lemarchand, Rene. *Burundi: Ethnic Conflict and Genocide.* New York: Cambridge University Press, 1996. Explores the origins of ethnic conflict in Burundi.

_____. *Burundi: Ethnocide as Discourse and Practice.* New York: Cambridge University Press, 1994. Informative account of historical events in Burundi. Focuses on the 1972 and 1988 massacres. Bibliography and index.

Melady, Thomas Patrick. *Burundi: The Tragic Years.* Maryknoll, N.Y.: Orbis Books, 1974. This American ambassador was the first to urge the diplomatic corps to pressure President Micombero to stop the killing. He was also involved in shaping United States government policy to bring a halt to the Tutsi genocide of the Hutus.

Newbury, Catharine. *The Cohesion of Oppression: Clientship and Ethnicity in Rwanda, 1860-1960.* New York: Columbia University Press, 1988. Examines the historical background to ethnic conflict between the Tutsis and Hutus and the impact European colonialism had on each group.

Claude Hargrove

United States Supreme Court Abolishes Death Penalty

Category of event: International norms; prisoners' rights
Time: June 29, 1972
Locale: United States Supreme Court, Washington, D.C.

> *In* Furman v. Georgia, *the Supreme Court decided that the death penalty as applied in 1972 constituted cruel and unusual punishment in violation of the United States Constitution*

Principal personages:

WILLIAM HENRY FURMAN, the condemned man whose name was used to identify the case *Furman v. Georgia*

ANTHONY AMSTERDAM (1935-   ), the attorney who argued on behalf of Furman before the Supreme Court

ARTHUR J. GOLDBERG (1908-1990), the Supreme Court justice whose 1963 dissenting opinion gave impetus to the movement to abolish the death penalty

HUGO ADAM BEDAU (1926-   ), a philosopher, historian, and opponent of the death penalty who provided scholarly information to the attorneys who represented Furman before the Supreme Court

Summary of Event

Since biblical times and the injunction of "an eye for an eye," capital punishment has been an accepted practice. In the United States, there have been periods during which there have been efforts to abolish capital punishment balanced by periods during which the trend was to sanction its use. From the end of the eighteenth century until the U.S. Civil War, abolitionists worked to reduce the number of crimes punishable by death. With the Civil War came a period of acceptance of capital punishment. There was another movement in the early twentieth century to abolish the death penalty. This movement ended with the beginning of World War I. After 1920, however, there was a gradual decline in any interest in or use of the death penalty. In 1930, 155 persons were executed. In 1960, the death penalty was used only 56 times.

Around this time, in 1959, the American Law Institute (ALI), an organization of legal scholars that was little known to the public but widely respected among lawyers, recommended that if the death penalty were to be retained, there should be changes in the statutes allowing its use. The ALI recommended that when there was the possibility of the death penalty, the defendant should have a bifurcated trial: one trial to establish innocence or guilt and another trial to determine the penalty if guilty. The reason for this was to allow the defendant a chance to testify at the penalty phase while still retaining a constitutional right not to speak during the first trial. In addition, the ALI suggested that the death penalty could not be imposed unless the jury found that aggravating circumstances were present and mitigating circumstances were absent. The reason for this recommendation was to provide some guidelines for jurors when they imposed the death penalty.

In 1963, in a case involving a rapist sentenced to death, Supreme Court justice Arthur Goldberg disagreed with the majority of justices, who confirmed the rapist's sentence. Goldberg stated that it was the Supreme Court's task to determine whether or not the death penalty was constitutional. Lawyers in the Legal Defense Fund (LDF), a branch of the National Association for the Advancement of Colored People (NAACP), were encouraged by this statement. Fresh from battles to enforce desegregation, LDF lawyers saw that the death penalty, particularly as it was applied to black men convicted of raping white women, was an area in which they next wanted to become involved. By 1967, the LDF had decided to undertake the representation of all inmates on death row. It brought several class action suits on behalf of these inmates. From that date until after the *Furman* decision in 1972, there was a moratorium on any executions. In the cases which they brought, attorneys for the LDF were determined that eventually the Supreme Court would have to answer the question that Goldberg had asked: Was the death penalty constitutional?

One commentator has said, regarding these cases, that the LDF lost every battle except the first and the last. The first battle came in *Witherspoon v. Illinois* in 1968. At issue in this case was whether or not a potential juror who expressed misgivings about the death penalty could be dismissed automatically from jury duty in a capital case. This was the common practice at the time. The Supreme Court ruled that such a practice was improper. A number of death row inmates were thus entitled to new trials.

This case was the only success for several years. Anthony Amsterdam, a professor at Pennsylvania Law School at the beginning of this period and later a professor at Stanford Law School, was the key strategist for the LDF in bringing and arguing the cases. Several times before *Furman*, Amsterdam argued in the

Supreme Court that juries should have standards, such as aggravating or mitigating circumstances, before them when imposing the death penalty, just as
the ALI had recommended. Amsterdam also argued for a bifurcated jury,
again as the ALI had suggested. The Supreme Court rejected both arguments
in 1971 in *McGautha v. California.* The LDF's only remaining theory with which
to challenge the death penalty after this was to declare that it was cruel and unusual punishment, prohibited by the Eighth Amendment to the Constitution.
On June 28, 1971, the Supreme Court announced that it would answer this
challenge to the death penalty in the case of *Furman v. Georgia.*

Furman v. Georgia consisted of four cases involving four African-American
defendants, all of whom had been sentenced to death. Two of the defendants
were murderers, and two were rapists. All of the victims were white. The man
who gave his name to the case, William Henry Furman, had entered his victim's home to commit burglary. When his victim discovered him, Furman
tried to run away. In the process, Furman's gun accidentally discharged. A bul-
let hit and killed the victim. Although Furman was found competent to stand
trial, it was discovered after the shooting that he was mentally subnormal and
subject to psychotic episodes. Nevertheless, he was convicted and sentenced to
death. The fate of more than six hundred prisoners on death row depended
upon the way the Supreme Court would decide his case.

Several times in the twentieth century, the Court had decided that a punishment meted out to a convicted criminal was cruel and unusual. In the most
important case, *Trop v. Dulles*, in 1958, the Court decided that loss of citizenship for a defendant who had deserted the armed forces during war was cruel
and unusual punishment. The Court stated that the Eighth Amendment pro-
hibiting cruel and unusual punishment takes its meaning "from evolving standards of decency that mark the progress of a maturing society." Implicit in this
statement was the sense that the meaning of cruel and unusual punishment
could change over time. The justices in *Furman* were to decide if the "standards of decency" in 1972 had evolved to the point that capital punishment
must be abolished.

Anthony Amsterdam argued on behalf of Furman before the Supreme
Court in January, 1971. Before the Supreme Court delivered its opinion in
June, 1972, the California Supreme Court decided in another case which Am-
sterdam had argued that the death penalty in California was unconstitutional.
Tension mounted concerning what the United States Supreme Court would
decide in *Furman.*

On June 29, 1972, the Supreme Court announced its decision. A five-to-
four majority of the justices found that as it was currently applied, the death

penalty constituted cruel and unusual punishment in violation of the Constitution. Each of the nine justices wrote a separate opinion. Two of the justices in the majority, Justice William Brennan and Justice Thurgood Marshall, declared that the death penalty was unconstitutional under any circumstance. Justices William Douglas, Potter Stewart, and Byron White stated that the death penalty was cruel and unusual punishment because it was arbitrary and capricious in the way it was currently imposed. Some of the dissenters, although personally opposed to the death penalty, stated that it was not up to the Court but to state legislatures to decide the question. Thus, by the narrowest of margins, the Supreme Court in 1972 answered the question that Justice Goldberg had urged it to answer in 1963, whether the death penalty was constitutional. In deciding that it was not, the Supreme Court allowed more than six hundred prisoners to leave death row.

Impact of Event

Although America briefly joined the rest of the Western world when it abolished capital punishment in *Furman v. Georgia* in 1972, there were indications in the decision itself that under certain circumstances the death penalty might be constitutional. One immediate reaction to the decision was that states started rewriting their death penalty statutes. Two years after *Furman*, twenty-eight states had new statutes. By 1976, thirty-five states had rewritten their death penalty laws. By that time, there were 450 inmates on death row.

In 1976, the Supreme Court agreed to hear the case of *Gregg v. Georgia* in order to decide whether one of these new statutes was constitutional. The defendant had been convicted of murder and sentenced to death under a new statute. This statute required a bifurcated jury, with separate trials to determine guilt and punishment. It also required that the jury find aggravating circumstances to condemn and consider mitigating circumstances to reprieve, and that there be an automatic appeal of any death sentence imposed, to the highest court in the state. The Supreme Court found that this statute was constitutional. Capital punishment was thus reinstated. In 1977, Gary Gilmore became the first man to be executed since the moratorium on executions which the LDF had created in 1967.

Since that time, there have been continuing challenges to various aspects of the death penalty. In 1977, the Supreme Court decided that the death penalty was a disproportionate punishment for the crime of rape. In 1987, the Court decided that studies showing that blacks received the death penalty more frequently than whites did not necessarily mean that any racial bias was involved, so the death penalty was not unconstitutional on grounds of discrimination. In 1989, the Court upheld the imposition of the death penalty for a convicted murderer who was mildly to moderately retarded as well as deciding that the death penalty could be imposed on those who were minors at the time of their crime. In June, 1991, the Court decided that victim impact statements are permissible at the sentencing of the defendant. The euphoria that accompanied the *Furman* decision had long since abated. There were about thirty-seven hundred inmates on death row in 2002, with no indications that the Supreme Court was moving toward ruling against the death penalty.

Bibliography

Banner, Stuart. *The Death Penalty: An American History.* Cambridge, Mass.: Harvard University Press, 2002. A well-researched, comprehensive examination of the history of the death penalty in America.

Bedau, Hugo Adam. *The Courts, the Constitution, and Capital Punishment.* Lexington, Mass.: Lexington Books, 1977. A clear analysis of the cases appearing before the Supreme Court in the period surrounding the *Furman* decision. Gives all possible constitutional theories against the death penalty and how they have been used, successfully or not. The author is an ardent abolitionist but presents balanced, well-reasoned arguments both for and against the death penalty. Some of the essays in the volume were written before *Furman*. Thus, it is hard at times to keep track of the time framework.

Bedau, Hugo Adam, and Chester M. Pierce. *Capital Punishment in the United States.* New York: AMS Press, 1975. A comprehensive survey of capital punishment after the *Furman* decision. These essays were collected because the *Furman* decision left open the constitutionality of the death penalty. The aim was to get as many social scientists as possible to comment on it, particularly concerning its deterrent effects. Contains a complete list of references and an index.

Berger, Raoul. *Death Penalties: The Supreme Court's Obstacle Course.* Cambridge, Mass.: Harvard University Press, 1982. A scholarly account arguing that the Court exceeded its proper boundaries in deciding *Furman*. Berger posits that the cruel and unusual punishment clause should be interpreted as it was when the Framers wrote the Constitution. The Supreme Court should not be making this decision; it should be up to Congress and the state legislatures. Extensive footnotes.

Friendly, Fred W., and Martha J. H. Elliott. "Willie Francis' Two Trips to the Chair, Punishment and the Death Penalty." In *The Constitution: That Delicate Balance.* New York: Random House, 1984. A moving account of one of the times before deciding *Furman* when the Supreme Court considered the death penalty as cruel and unusual punishment. Francis did not die the first time he was electrocuted. The Court ruled that it was not cruel and unusual punishment to electrocute him a second time. Francis was so worn down by the appeals process that he acquiesced to the second try and died. Brief mention of *Furman* and *Gregg.*

Furman v. Georgia. 408 U.S. 238 (1972). The lengthy opinion by the Supreme Court. Includes nine different opinions. Justices William Brennan and Thurgood Marshall find the death penalty unconstitutional in and of itself. Justices William Douglas, Potter Stewart, and Byron White argue that, as applied, the death penalty is wanton, capricious, and freakish. The dissenters, Justices Warren Burger, Harry Blackmun, Lewis Powell, and William Rehnquist, all think that the Court overstepped its boundaries in deciding this case and that the decision should be in the state legislatures' hands.

Gregg v. Georgia. 428 U.S. 153 (1976). The first time the Supreme Court considered the constitutionality of the death penalty after *Furman.* Gregg, convicted of murder, was condemned under a statute newly enacted in Georgia. The Supreme Court found that the statute was constitutional.

Meltser, Michael. *Cruel and Unusual: The Supreme Court and Capital Punishment.* New York: Random House, 1973. Complete coverage of the cases, individuals, legal issues, and social trends which led to *Furman.* Good analysis of cases preceding *Furman* and the strategy of the LDF in bringing them. Although this is the best account of cases leading to *Furman,* changes in the law require an update.

Jennifer Eastman

Marcos Declares Martial Law in the Philippines

Category of event: Atrocities and war crimes; political freedom
Time: September, 1972
Locale: Philippines

> *Ferdinand Marcos's declaration of martial law imposed an authoritarian rule on the Philippines that primarily benefited the Marcos family, the military, and the financial elite*

Principal personages:

FERDINAND MARCOS (1917-1989), the president of the Philippines from 1965 until 1986, when he sought asylum in Hawaii

IMELDA MARCOS (1929-   ), the wife of Ferdinand Marcos, notorious for her ostentatious wealth

JAIME SIN (1928-   ), a church leader who moved from moderation to outspoken criticism of Marcos and martial law

FABIAN VER (1920-1998), an alleged half-brother of Ferdinand Marcos, head of the secret police, and army chief of staff

JUAN PONCE ENRILE (1924-   ), a lawyer who held many high-ranking positions under Marcos, considered to be the architect of martial law

JOSE DIOKNO (1922-1987), a senator and prominent human rights lawyer who founded the Free Legal Assistance Group, providing services to human rights victims

Summary of Event

On September 21, 1972, President Ferdinand Marcos signed Proclamation No. 1081, placing the Philippines under martial law. The president justified his decision with his concern that the country was in peril from communist and Islamic insurgencies. Through a series of general orders, he gave himself the power to govern the nation and direct all operations. These powers included limitations on the judiciary, restrictions on the press, and special personal constitutional authority to create new governmental institutions. He declared that he would develop a "New Society" under a new style of government, "constitutional authoritarianism."

Ferdinand Marcos had been elected to a four-year term as president in 1965 and won an unprecedented second-term election in 1969. According to the constitution of the Philippines, the president can serve only two terms. The imposition of martial law nullified this limitation. Circumventing the constitution and the National Congress, Marcos utilized Citizens' Assemblies (*Barangays*) to ratify martial law. Marcos gave himself the right to legislate by personal decree. He issued more than nine hundred major decrees during his presidency.

The first consequence of martial law was political repression. Within days after Marcos's proclamation, thousands of his critics were arbitrarily arrested for being subversives and were held without trial. They included several senators, three members of congress, two governors, four delegates to the Philippine Constitutional Convention, three newspaper publishers, and several journalists. Marcos arbitrarily dismissed four hundred government employees and demanded resignations from thousands more. To repress all public criticism, Marcos closed all but one of Manila's fifteen daily newspapers, six of the city's seven television stations, and nine of the major radio stations.

Under Marcos, the autonomy of the judicial branch was destroyed. He had ultimate power over the justice system because he could remove any judge or judicial official by fiat. He packed the Supreme Court by expanding it and adding his own judges. Civil courts were superseded by military courts. Decisions of these tribunals became final only upon Marcos's approval. A report of an Amnesty International mission in 1975 concluded that the judiciary of the Philippines had become totally ineffective in preventing violations of human rights. Amnesty International saw the rule of law under martial law as authoritarian, unchecked by constitutional guarantees or limitations.

Prisoners of the military were subject to torture and harassment. They often were not charged with any crime and were held without trial. Under the command of General Fabian Ver, the military and police employed torture methods against critics and so-called subversives. These methods included "salvaging," or kidnapping and murder; electric shock treatment; "telephone," a euphemism for breaking the eardrums; "hamletting," the forced evacuation of villagers to special camps; and sexual attacks.

The abuses of individuals included women, students, and even social workers. In 1977, Vilma Riopay, a twenty-one-year-old female catechist, was taken into custody and severely tortured. As a result of her beatings she became an invalid. Thousands of brutalized and mutilated bodies have been found. A student leader who had criticized Marcos, Edgar Jopson, was captured in 1974. He escaped from prison in 1979. Four years later, he was again captured. Later, his battered corpse was turned over to his father. The government suppressed a popular demonstration of sympathy and support for the young man. A leader of a slum-based Manila organization, Trinidad Herrera, was arrested for challenging government relocation efforts. She was tortured, but because of pressures from the World Bank, she was released from jail.

Strict press controls robbed the press of its function as an independent agent for information and analysis. Official censorship and punitive licensing procedures created a press that lacked credibility. Relatives and friends of the Marcos family established their own television and radio stations and their own newspapers. They used these institutions to attack their opponents and to promote loyalty to the government. No criticism was allowed of the president and Mrs. Marcos, the regime, or the military. The secrecy allowed for deception, especially concerning the Marcos family's corruption, official embezzlement, and the crimes of the police and armed forces.

The two pillars justifying martial law were the needs to suppress insurgencies and to promote economic reform. To counter the communist and Muslim uprisings, military forces expanded in number from less than 50,000 to 225,000. The military budget increased from $129 million in 1973 to $676 mil-

Philippine president Ferdinand Marcos during a state visit to the United States. (Library of Congress)

lion in 1977. This amount accounted for 20 percent of the national budget. In addition, U.S. military aid more than doubled, from $80 million in 1972 to $166 million in 1976.

Marcos's economic policies were designed to increase foreign investment and tourism. To create stability, Marcos outlawed strikes in "vital industries" and curtailed the activities of labor unions. To promote tourism, Mrs. Marcos rebuilt large parts of Manila. This effort required the removal of urban slum dwellers. The police and military were used to dump the so-called squatters in empty fields miles from water, job opportunities, and adequate housing. In May, 1976, two thousand demonstrators in front of the Manila Cathedral were arrested for opposing the first lady's urban renewal projects.

The only major institution that effectively criticized martial law was the church. Just a month after the announcement of martial law, Father Edward Gerlock, a Maryknoll priest active in social action programs, was arrested on charges of subversion. His order mobilized to defend him and criticized martial law as being incompatible with the social justice program outlined by Pope Paul VI and the Asian Bishops Conference of 1970. The torture of Father Primitivo Hagtad and the arrest, torture, and interrogation of the Reverend Toribio of the United Methodist Church in early 1974 resulted in a united Protestant and Roman Catholic attack on martial law. The government, however, continued to arrest and torture church leaders and laity. By 1975, there was vigorous church opposition to Marcos's rule. Cardinal Jaime Sin mobilized the Catholic Church in criticizing Marcos's policies.

The maintenance of martial law required a large international propaganda machine and a well-supplied secret police abroad. The Office of Media Affairs hired American public relations companies and conservative academicians to defend Marcos against his international critics. In addition to the open acts of propaganda, many Filipino critics charge that Fabian Ver's secret police engaged in acts of intimidation and even murder. The mysterious disappearances in 1977 of Primitivo Mijares, a former Marcos aide who testified before the U.S. Congress regarding the corrupt practices of the Marcos regime, and the murders of two outspoken Filipino-American labor activists in Seattle are examples of Marcos's network of terror outside the Philippines.

In 1981, Marcos lifted martial law and, despite charges of election fraud and corrupt practices, was reelected president. He did not reform any of the repressive institutions that had developed since 1972. The assassination of Marcos's chief rival, Benigno Aquino, in 1983 led to political destabilization and ultimately resulted in the popular uprising that forced Marcos, his family, and his major supporters to find asylum in Honolulu in 1986.

Impact of Event

The irony of the martial law proclamation was that initially many Filipinos seemed to welcome the new order. At first, Marcos's authoritarian rule brought some order to Manila. Strict military and police rule greatly curtailed the activities of criminal elements in Manila. Murder and robbery rates dropped. The city was beautified and garbage was collected. Many Filipinos considered the national legislature weak and disorderly, the media filled with sensationalism, and the insurgencies a threat to social order. Thus, closing of the legislature and restricting press freedom were not causes for great concern.

Within a few years, however, the public came to believe that Marcos's New Society was really a new plutocracy that was destroying the Philippines financially and creating a large, impoverished lower class. Foreign debt rose from $2.5 billion in 1970 to $10 billion in 1980. By 1985, the debt was $30 billion. The proportion of the urban population living below the poverty line rose from 24 percent in 1974 to 40 percent in 1980.

The establishment of martial law led to widespread abuses of human rights. Every sector of the society was affected by the militarization of the Philippines. The suspension of *habeas corpus* gave security forces power to arrest and hold anybody without any legal challenge. For example, health workers in rural areas had been accused by the military of aiding and abetting the insurgents. Without any recourse to legal due process, doctors and nurses were arrested, tortured, and killed. According to a 1985 report by the International Commission of Jurists, for example, one doctor was shot while working in his clinic by a military man in civilian clothes. The intimidation of medical personnel aggravated the already significant "brain drain" of health workers from the Philippines to foreign countries. This emigration greatly reduced domestic availability of health care, especially for the poor.

Despite the government's widespread abuse of human rights, it still won support from the Nixon and Reagan administrations. When Vice President George Bush attended Marcos's inauguration in June, 1981, he offered a toast to President Marcos that became a symbol for what some saw as America's disrespect of human rights issues: "We love your adherence to democratic principles and to democratic processes." The U.S. government's close relationship to Marcos produced a strong antiforeign and nationalistic backlash in the Philippines. Filipino leaders and mass organizations called for the termination of American military bases, and terrorist attacks were made against American forces.

The major consequence of martial law was its self-destruction. Except for a small but militarily and economically powerful group of followers, Marcos lost all popularity with the Filipino people. Lawyers throughout the Philippines, under the leadership of Senator Jose Diokno, actively represented victims of Marcos's rule. Marcos overwhelmingly lost the 1986 presidential election to Corazon Aquino, wife of the assassinated Benigno Aquino, and was forced to flee the Philippines in ignominy.

Bibliography

Celoza, Albert F. *Ferdinand Marcos and the Philippines: The Political Economy of Authoritarianism.* Westport, Conn.: Praeger, 1997. Examination of the period between 1972 and 1986, the year in which Marcos was ousted from the Philippines.

Hamilton-Paterson, James. *America's Boy: A Century of Colonialism in the Philippines.* London: Granta Books, 1998. Comprehensive analysis of the rise and fall of Ferdinand and Imelda Marcos.

Karnow, Stanley. *In Our Image: America's Empire in the Philippines.* New York: Random House, 1989. A well-documented study of U.S.-Philippine relations. Focuses on American support of Marcos despite his corruption and human rights violations. Karnow, an outstanding journalist on East Asian affairs, has personally interviewed the Marcoses, General Ver, Benigno Aquino, Juan Enrile, and other political leaders both in the Philippines and in the United States.

Leary, Virginia A. *The Philippines: Human Rights After Martial Law.* Geneva: International Commission of Jurists, 1984. Investigates the abuses of the armed forces and the police, critiques the criminal law and the judicial system, and provides excellent documentation of the abuse of economic and social rights. The report provides a unique survey of the abuse of tribal people.

Rosenberg, David A., ed. *Marcos and Martial Law in the Philippines.* Ithaca, N.Y.: Cornell University Press, 1979. A collection of scholarly works on New Society ideology and policies concerning the legal system, land reform, freedom of the press, and the economy. Most useful is the appendix, which contains key documents on the proclamation of martial law and the responses of human rights and religious groups.

Seagrave, Sterling. *The Marcos Dynasty.* New York: Harper & Row, 1988. A muckraking investigation of the Marcos family and their cronies. Seagrave provides lurid details on the venality, corruption, and repression of the regime. Although some of his data have been questioned, his study remains the most thorough and substantial critique of the alleged atrocities of Marcos, General Fabian Ver, and other members of the regime.

Richard C. Kagan

Arab Terrorists Murder Israelis at Munich Olympics

Category of event: Atrocities and war crimes; religious freedom; refugee rights
Time: September 5-6, 1972
Locale: Olympic Village, Munich, West Germany

> *In a massacre of eleven Israeli athletes at the 1972 Olympic Games, Palestinian terrorists committed murder in the name of nationalism*

Principal personages:
YASIR ARAFAT (1929-   ), the leader of al-Fatah guerrillas who later became the chair of the PLO
GOLDA MEIR (1898-1978), a founder of the state of Israel and its prime minister
HANS-DIETRICH GENSCHER (1927-   ), the chief negotiator for the West German government during the crisis
AVERY BRUNDAGE (1887-1975), the president of the International Olympic Committee during the 1972 games

Summary of Event

As soon as the state of Israel was created by the United Nations in 1948, Palestinian guerrilla organizations sought to destroy it. In 1949, the Egyptians were the first to use Palestinian guerrillas against Israel. By 1956, attacks inside Israel were also directed from Palestinian enclaves in Jordan, Syria, and Lebanon. After Israel's overwhelming victory in the Six-Day War of 1967, the Arab states were reluctant to allow the Palestinians the use of their territory to stage attacks on Israel. As a result, the Palestinians lost the ability to wage war and therefore shifted their activities to daring international acts of terrorism. Financed by Arab oil money and with the help of the Communist bloc, the Palestinians shocked the world with dramatic political assassinations and extortions. Terrorists hijacked passenger aircraft and offered hostages in exchange for freedom for their fellow fighters imprisoned in Israel and Europe. The hijackings were also used to attract world attention to the cause of obtaining a Palestinian homeland. The sequence of events that took place on September 5 and 6, 1972, was another such attempt.

432

In the darkness of predawn hours on September 5, eight Palestinian *feda-yeen* (fighters for the faith) entered the Israeli residence at the Olympic Village, taking nine Israeli athletes hostage and killing two others. By the time the drama ended some twenty hours later, a German police official, five Palestinian terrorists, and eleven Israeli athletes were dead.

The body of Israeli wrestling coach Moshe Weinberg was dragged outside onto the steps leading to the Israeli compound. Wrestler Joseph Romano lay dead inside. The nine Israeli hostages were bound hand and foot in groups of three. In exchange for the Israelis, the Palestinians demanded the release of two hundred Arab prisoners in Israel, of the two leaders of a notorious German leftist terrorist gang, and of Kozo Okamoto, a Japanese terrorist who had taken part in the massacre of twenty-six people at Israel's Lod airport only four months earlier.

Billed as the "Games of Joy," the Twentieth Olympiad was a festival in which twelve thousand athletes participated. More world records were set in Munich than in any previous Olympic Games. This was the Olympics of Mark Spitz, the Jewish-American swimmer who won seven gold medals for the United States. The most spectacular Olympics yet, with unprecedented worldwide media coverage, the Munich Olympiad was the ideal stage for the eight *fedayeen,* who simply climbed over a six-foot fence and entered the village.

The perpetrators belonged to the most extreme Palestinian terrorist group, Black September. Although al-Fatah, the dominant Palestinian guerrilla organization, and its leader, Yasir Arafat, denied any collusion with Black September, there is evidence to the contrary. Al-Fatah wanted its connection to Black September to remain secret, so that its image in Europe and America would not be tarnished. Arafat, fully aware that al-Fatah had been infiltrated by Israeli intelligence, concealed the connection, allowing only the nine Central Committee members to deal with Black September matters.

Black September was created at the end of 1970 by a handful of survivors of the "ten terrible September days" of fighting against the forces of King Hussein of Jordan in a futile attempt to turn that country into a Palestinian homeland. Exiled in Lebanon, they committed themselves to total war against the Jews of the world and to the elimination of King Hussein. Black September was not a splinter terrorist group but rather a state of mind. The name "Black September" also implied inter-Arab hatred. Arafat himself was said to have chosen it.

Palestinian animosity toward the Arab states stemmed from the first Arab-Israeli war in 1948-1949. The Arab states, overconfident and with their own territorial designs on Palestine, were defeated by Israel, leaving some 650,000

Palestinian refugees in Arab territory. Instead of absorbing the Palestinians, the Arab states abandoned them in refugee camps and shanty towns.

One thing all the Arabs, including the Palestinians, agreed upon was that the existence of the state of Israel was the main problem. They perceived the creation of Israel as an invasion and another humiliation imposed upon them by Western powers and sanctioned by the American-controlled United Nations. Moreover, Arabs believed that they were being forced to pay the price for Europe's collective guilt over the Holocaust, in which nearly six million Jews were killed.

The Jewish minority in Palestine had lived alongside the Arabs for centuries, enduring various degrees of persecution. The emergence of Zionism, the Jewish quest to return to their biblical homeland in Palestine and to re-create Israel, changed that equation. The British, who administered Palestine after World War I, tried to limit Jewish immigration to appease the Arabs. The Jews, however, could not be stopped from escaping persecution in Europe during the 1930's and 1940's. After World War II, in their desperation to resettle some half million survivors of the Nazi death machine, the Zionist leaders chose to see Palestine as a land without people for a people without a land.

The Arab world, wanting to keep Palestine for itself, responded violently to the creation of Israel. Terrorist groups such as Black September were only part of that reaction, and the Munich massacre was only one of a series of terrorist acts committed in the battle for Palestine.

Negotiations with the Black September terrorists in the Olympic Village continued into mid-afternoon on September 6, and were covered on worldwide television. Athletes were seen tirelessly training, and the village hot spots remained full. Most Arab countries applauded their courageous brothers. Communist bloc countries remained silent. East Germany's residences, adjacent to the Israeli compound, refused to evacuate and blamed the whole affair on Israel.

Israeli prime minister Golda Meir refused to capitulate to the Palestinians, leaving the matter to be resolved by the West German authorities. Israel once again affirmed its conviction that giving in to terrorism leads to more terrorism. The *fedayeen*, suspicious of German claims that the Israeli parliament was still debating, pressed negotiators for an aircraft to fly them and their hostages to Cairo. Afraid of losing their nerve and stamina, the terrorists decided to retreat to friendlier grounds.

Hans-Dietrich Genscher, who later became the foreign minister of unified Germany, took over the negotiations. He offered the terrorists unlimited sums of money in exchange for the Israelis. When that failed, he offered himself

Golda Meir, prime minister of Israel at the time of the Munich massacre. (Library of Congress)

and other West German officials as hostages instead of the athletes but was again rebuffed. Realizing that time was running out, Chancellor Willy Brandt telephoned the Egyptians, but neither Anwar Sadat nor his foreign minister were available in Cairo.

The International Olympic Committee (IOC), the governing body of the Olympiad, was faced with the prospect of stopping the games. Avery Brundage, the controversial president of the IOC, was bent on continuing the games and made decisions on his own, without the consent of the Executive Board. In 1936, as president of the U.S. Olympic Committee, Brundage had drawn criticism for speaking favorably about Nazi Germany. Brundage was dismissed as a man who did not understand democracy.

The virulent anti-Semitism of the Nazis was very much a part of Black September's mentality. Yasir Arafat and some of the leaders of Black September were related to Haj Amin al-Husayni, the preeminent Palestinian leader during the 1930's who had thrown in his lot with Hitler. A bitter anti-Zionist, Husayni spent World War II in Germany working as a Nazi propagandist for the Middle East and as a guerrilla organizer in the Balkans. Husayni became a philosophical tutor to Black September and al-Fatah. Later al-Fatah was to merge with the Palestine Liberation Organization (PLO), with Arafat in charge. The young men sent to Munich for the mission in the Olympic Village were not wild-eyed, gun-toting madmen, but were educated, highly trained, and disciplined. They spoke various languages and could easily get along inconspicuously in Europe. In fact, Issa and Tony, the two leaders, were employees of the Olympic Village.

The terrorists set their final deadline for 9 P.M. on September 5. While a crowd watched and television cameras zoomed, the eight *fedayeen* and nine Israelis walked out close together, with the athletes at gunpoint. The group was driven by bus to two helicopters, which flew them to an airbase outside Munich where a fueled 707 waited. Five sharpshooters were also waiting at the airport. After the terrorists inspected the jetliner, it became evident to the Germans that the *fedayeen* sensed a trap. With the lives of the two German helicopter pilots also in jeopardy, the snipers opened fire. During the firefight, one of the terrorists tossed a grenade into a helicopter, incinerating five athletes. The other four Israelis were machine-gunned while sitting, tied up, in the second helicopter.

Impact of Event

A silent and troubled audience of eighty thousand filled the Olympic Stadium for a hastily arranged memorial service the following morning. For the first time in Olympic history, the podium was draped in black and the flags of 122 nations flew at half-staff. The representatives of the Arab countries were absent. The delegations from the Soviet Union, East Germany, Poland, and Yugoslavia also did not attend. The surviving Israeli athletes were on the stand next to eleven empty chairs honoring their dead teammates.

Only days later, on the eve of the Hebrew New Year, Israel retaliated with air strikes inside Syria and Lebanon, inflicting sixty-six deaths and wounding dozens, according to Arab sources. In what was the heaviest fighting since the 1967 war, Israeli ground troops broke through the Lebanese border to battle the guerrillas. The harsh Israeli response threatened the fragile peace in the Middle East as Syria quickly mobilized and deployed its forces at the frontier.

Although the Munich massacre was not the first Black September attack on Israel, it marked a turning point in the way Israel would react to the challenge of combating terrorism. To prevent attacks, all Israeli embassies became fortresses. Walls were reinforced with concrete capable of withstanding an all-out terrorist attack. The latest security systems were installed, and state of the art screening devices were implemented. The embassies were stocked with large amounts of weapons and ammunition. Israeli diplomats carried pistols, and most foreign governments assisted with additional protection and intelligence.

Three top Israeli security officials were fired. Prime Minister Golda Meir called in Major General Aharon Yariv to launch an antiterrorist war to wipe out Black September, al-Fatah, and their accomplices, whom the Israelis considered to be one and the same. Assassination squads were sent to hunt down and kill Black September operatives in Europe and elsewhere.

The terrorists succeeded in forcing the world to take note of their plight. In the Arab view, the operation was a supreme success despite the deaths of the five *fedayeen.* Moreover, Arafat could revolve in diplomatic circles pretending to have no knowledge of, or connections to, Black September.

Libya requested the bodies of the five dead commandos, and the funeral there attracted tens of thousands of mourners. All Arab ambassadors assigned to Tripoli were present. The three surviving *fedayeen* were set free the following month, when the hijackers of Lufthansa 727 demanded their release. Black September threatened to blow up Lufthansa jetliners until the commandos were let go, and the West Germans gave in.

Immediately after the Munich slayings, the problem of terrorism was placed on the agenda of the General Assembly of the United Nations. The United States called for an international pact against terrorism. Another resolution proposed the condemnation of terrorism followed by an international conference. Believing that the resolutions were directed against them, the Arab states supported a third resolution to defeat the other two, blaming the West for causing terrorism.

The Olympic Games were canceled once during World War I and twice during World War II. In 1980, the United States boycotted the Moscow Games, protesting the invasion of Afghanistan. In 1984, the Soviet Union boycotted the Los Angeles Games in kind. In 1972, in Munich, the polarization caused by the Arab-Israeli conflict and East-West rivalry resulted in the paralysis that allowed the tragedy to occur. Willi Daume, president of the organizing committee for the Games, summed up the general feeling at the memorial service for the Israelis: "Even in the world of crime, there are still some taboos, a final limit of dehumanization beyond which one dares not go. This limit was crossed by those guilty of the attack on the Olympic Village."

Bibliography

Dobson, Christopher. *Black September: Its Short, Violent History.* New York: Macmillan, 1974. A complete account of the beginning and the end of Black September. Dobson offers a historical account and a philosophical explanation of the activities of this group. Attempts to show how cruel and counterproductive Arab terrorism is. Includes an index.

Groussard, Serge. *The Blood of Israel: The Massacre of the Israeli Athletes, the Olympics, 1972.* Translated by Harold J. Salemson. New York: William Morrow, 1975. Provides an enormously detailed chronological account of this tragic event. Includes brief biographies of the athletes who were killed and of the various personalities involved. Supplemented by appendices and maps of the Olympic Village and Olympic Park.

Kamenka, Eugene, and Alice Erh-Soon, eds. *Human Rights: Ideas and Ideologies.* New York: St. Martin's Press, 1978. Composed of nine essays by nine separate authors. Discusses the origin of human rights; their strengthening and eventual transformation; human rights and international law; Marxism, socialism, and human rights; and individual rights against group rights. Includes a list of suggested reading and an index.

Parry, Albert. *Terrorism: From Robespierre to Arafat.* New York: Vanguard Press, 1978. Discusses the nature of terrorism, examines terrorism in history and in modern times, and explores the potential for destruction that new technology offers terrorists. Supplemented by an appendix, a bibliography, notes, and an index.

Reeve, Simon. *One Day in September: The Full Story of the 1972 Munich Olympics Massacre and the Israeli Revenge Operation "Wrath of God."* New York: Arcade, 2000. Arab-Israeli relations are examined in this gripping account of the hostage crisis.

Geoffrey Bar-Lev

Vietnam Releases U.S. Prisoners of War

Category of event: Atrocities and war crimes; peace movements and organizations; prisoners' rights
Time: 1973
Locale: Vietnam and the United States

> *The release of United States prisoners of war by Vietnam and the simultaneous withdrawal of U.S. military forces from Indochina signaled the end of U.S. military involvement in a war that had become increasingly unpopular*

Principal personages:

RICHARD M. NIXON (1913-1994), the president of the United States from 1969 until 1974

HENRY A. KISSINGER (1923-   ), the national security adviser to President Nixon who acted as chief U.S. negotiator during the Paris peace talks

LE DUC THO (1911-1990), a North Vietnamese politburo member who acted as chief negotiator for Vietnam during the Paris talks

MELVIN LAIRD (1922-   ), the secretary of defense under President Nixon who urged that the United States "go public" on prisoners of war

NGUYEN VAN THIEU (1923-2001), the president of South Vietnam from 1967 until 1975, when South Vietnam was taken over by North Vietnam

MARTIN LUTHER KING, Jr. (1929-1968), a prominent U.S. civil rights leader who linked the Civil Rights movement with the antiwar movement

JANE FONDA (1937-   ), a U.S. actor who was prominent in the peace movement and traveled to Hanoi in 1972

Summary of Event

The opinions of the United States government and the peace movement about the prisoner of war (POW) issue mirrored different approaches to understanding the Vietnam War. The government viewed publicizing the incarceration of POWs as one way to arouse indignation of U.S. citizens toward Hanoi. The peace movement attempted to deflect attention from the problems of POWs in North Vietnam by stressing the U.S. responsibility for torture of prisoners held in South Vietnam. While the U.S. government sought a military solution in Vietnam and mechanisms to contain dissent at home, the peace

439

movement criticized U.S. domestic and foreign policies in social, political, and cultural terms.

The peace movement in the United States was influenced heavily by the Civil Rights movement of the early 1960's. Especially influential was the Student Nonviolent Coordinating Committee (SNCC), which worked to oppose racial segregation in the southern states. Students of all races who had been active in the Civil Rights movement through freedom rides, boycotts, and voter-registration projects learned to demonstrate their discontent and to integrate nonexclusive organization and nonviolent protest.

Students for a Democratic Society (SDS) became one of the largest organizations associated with the peace movement during the late 1960's. In 1962, leaders of SDS drafted the Port Huron statement, which called for nonexclusion of socialist and communist groups and for participatory, grass-roots democracy. The rejection of "red-baiting" and promotion of democratic decision making and nonexclusion by SDS became hallmarks of the peace movement and were used to define a "New Left," which rejected dogma and the fragmentation of the "Old Left." The prominence of SDS dramatically increased as a result of its decision to protest the U.S. intervention in Vietnam by sponsoring the first national demonstration against the war in Washington, D.C., and by organizing teach-ins, at which people would learn about Vietnam and U.S. policy. By June, 1969, however, SDS had become factionalized to the point that it dissolved.

Despite popular perceptions, the peace movement had a broader base than student organizations. Groups of African Americans protested U.S. involvement in Vietnam as well. Since the combat soldiers who were sent to Vietnam were disproportionately black, and since many blacks were upset at the federal government for not protecting their rights while it was using rhetoric that the United States was defending the rights of Vietnamese, many blacks (especially the youths involved with the SNCC) were strongly involved in the antiwar movement. Martin Luther King, Jr., became an active leader in the peace movement in 1967, stressing that the importance of his emphasis on promoting nonviolence in the Civil Rights movement paled when compared to the level of violence the United States was using in Vietnam.

Prominent Hollywood personalities also became involved with activities in support of the peace movement. In 1970 and 1971, Jane Fonda and other entertainers toured under the name "Free the Army Antiwar Troupe" in areas around U.S. military bases in order to encourage military personnel to protest U.S. policies. When Fonda visited Hanoi in 1972, she made numerous antiwar radio broadcasts to U.S. troops. Although Fonda had seen POWs, upon returning to the U.S. she did not defend them. In reaction to her trip and reports, leaders in Colorado and Maryland tried to ban Fonda from entering their states.

An intellectual wing, embodied in the Community of Concerned Asian Scholars (CCAS), became a large factor in the peace movement. Consisting of academics and graduate students who had been trained in various aspects of Asian studies, the CCAS broke from the larger academic community (particularly the Association for Asian Studies), which refused to take an official stand on the war. Seeing complicity in silence, CCAS members were determined to take responsibility for the results of their research. Once organized, the CCAS became a source for vital information on Vietnam for a movement (and a society) that had little understanding of the country or its people. Through books, lectures, periodicals, and conferences, the CCAS served as a counter to the governmental disinformation about Vietnam and U.S. policy.

Utilizing many different tactics, the peace movement was able to exert considerable influence on public opinion. Large marches became a major way in which the movement was able to show its strength and gain media attention. On April 24, 1971, one million protesters crowded Washington, D.C., in the largest demonstration in U.S. history. Parts of the movement also used direct action, especially targeting the draft. Youths burned their draft cards at the risk of imprisonment, and priests destroyed draft boards' records in symbolic protest. The use of teach-ins to spread information about Vietnam spread to college campuses across the United States. On October 15, 1969, millions of people participated in a day of moratorium by not working.

The governmental response to the peace movement was multifaceted. Most visibly, the U.S. government, especially under President Richard Nixon, countered demonstrators with strong rhetoric, painting the demonstrators as unpatriotic radicals. This rhetoric sprang from the attitude that protesters were students who were self-indulgent and morally rudderless, allowing officials to discredit their actions. In addition to this criticism, the government instituted harsh policies against the peace movement. More than three thousand draft resisters were imprisoned for burning draft cards or tampering with draft records. Further, the Nixon administration established domestic espionage and infiltration programs, using both the Federal Bureau of Investigation (FBI) and the Central Intelligence Agency (CIA). The FBI and CIA systematically spied on and attempted to subvert activist organizations by planting agents. The information gathered or created was then used to blacklist antiwar activists and, in some instances, was used to bring charges against organizations, diverting their resources from opposing the war. A major target was the Committee of Concerned Asian Scholars. Evidence suggests that the agencies used provocateurs to participate in illegal activities, thereby entrapping activists.

Part of the Nixon administration's response to defuse public opinion was to open public negotiations and to implement "Vietnamization," which called for an increased reliance on Vietnamese troops and a reduction in the number of U.S. troops deployed in Vietnam. The chief proponent of Vietnamization, Melvin Laird, also recommended that the administration make the prisoners of war a public issue, breaking the silence on the issue that had prevailed during the Lyndon Johnson administration. The United States intended to use the POW issue "to bring world opinion to bear on the North Vietnamese" by charging that the Vietnamese had maltreated and tortured prisoners. In accordance with this goal, in 1969 and 1970 the United States brought up the issue with the International Red Cross and the United Nations. Finally, some prisoners who were released early were used to broadcast charges of maltreatment by their captors. Making the POWs a public issue in tandem with negotiations also allowed the administration to dismiss immediate withdrawal plans as unrealistic, since they did not resolve the issue of the POWs.

Critics of the administration's policy charged that the rhetoric used against the Vietnamese merely increased the value of the prisoners as hostages. Another charge of the peace movement was that the Nixon administration manipulated the issue of the prisoners to expand the war and to continue to keep U.S. forces in Vietnam.

Both sides in the war violated international standards for treatment of prisoners. The recounting of torture by U.S. prisoners, the early parading of prisoners as "war criminals" in Hanoi, and the lack of information given about the prisoners by the government of North Vietnam all were clear violations of international conventions. In South Vietnam, however, treatment was as harsh if not harsher. It was revealed that prisoners were kept in "tiger cages" on Con Son island. Guerrillas who were captured were classified as political dissidents, not prisoners of war (and thus were not protected by international conventions). Aside from the evidence of torture of prisoners, there was strong evidence showing that U.S. forces often killed prisoners in the battlefield in order to raise body-count figures.

On January 27, 1973, the Paris Agreement on Ending the War and Restoring Peace in Vietnam and a protocol on prisoners of war were signed by the United States, the Democratic Republic of Vietnam (North Vietnam), the Provisional Revolutionary Government of South Vietnam (National Liberation Front), and the Republic of Vietnam (South Vietnam). When the POWs were returned to the United States, the treatment they received was less than honorable. They were not allowed to speak freely for a period after their return, and when they were allowed to speak it was in controlled press conferences. Some prisoners who had made statements against the war while captives were charged with aiding the enemy. These charges were dismissed after one of the accused shot himself to death. Since there no longer existed any clear issue around which the peace movement could organize, the diverse groups had no reason to continue to work together and returned to separate domestic concerns.

Impact of Event

The peace movement in the Vietnam era changed the way people in the United States thought about government and politics. Foremost among these changes was that a large segment of the population grew to distrust the federal government, especially the presidency. A direct result of this sentiment was the War Powers Act of 1973, which was intended to curb the power of the president to commit U.S. troops abroad.

For the first time since the founding of a bipartisan consensus on foreign policy after World War II, the public grew to challenge the assumptions that underlay U.S. policy. The congressional consensus broke down, resulting in the U.S. decision not to send troops to Angola. The change in perspective about the public's right to debate foreign policy also led to a larger segment active in challenging presidential and State Department decisions.

The methods of the peace movement in the Vietnam era permeated society to such an extent that the ideals of nonviolent resistance and grass-roots organizing became mainstays of social movements. Not only did progressive organizations continue to use these protest tactics, but conservative organizations, notably antiabortion groups, also adopted similar strategies in pursuit of their goals.

Scholars who were blacklisted for their antiwar activities in the Vietnam era continued to feel the war's impact, as some still were unable to get jobs within the field of Asian studies. In large part, these scholars' input on governmental decisions was limited, as was their access to research and grant money. Their prolific output of information during the war changed the context of academic debate, however, and helped to encourage a strain of activist scholar.

The division in society did not end with the war but continued to manifest itself in various ways in the United States. Conflict continued over the issue of whether there were any living prisoners of war or soldiers missing in action (MIA) remaining in Indochina. In large part, however, the numbers of MIA included a significant number of people known to have been killed in action. Still, some organizations such as the National League of Families of American Prisoners and Missing In Southeast Asia continued to demand a full accounting of every MIA. Strongly related to the issue of MIAs was the dispute over whether and when the United States should normalize relations with Vietnam. Those who believed that U.S. prisoners were still being held in Vietnam and who accused Vietnam of not cooperating on the POW and MIA issues often used this to dismiss the possibility of normalization, expressing continued hostility toward the country of Vietnam.

Bibliography

Karnow, Stanley. *Vietnam: A History.* 2d rev. ed. New York: Penguin Books, 1997. An exhaustive history of the strife in Vietnam. Features an annotated bibliography, index, and photos.

Rochester, Stuart I., and Frederick T. Kiley. *Honor Bound: American Prisoners of War in Southeast Asia, 1961-1973.* Annapolis, Md.: Naval Institute Press, 1999. An inclusive, scholarly account of the experiences of almost eight hundred prisoners of war.

Rosas, Allan. *The Legal Status of Prisoners of War: A Study in International Humanitarian Law Applicable in Armed Conflicts.* Helsinki: Suomalainen Tiedeakatemia, 1976. Despite a legalistic approach, pages 167-185 provide an excellent, balanced summary of issues relating to prisoners of war during the Vietnam War, showing how the U.S. experience in Korea shaped POW negotiations and how the issue of POWs in the Vietnam War differed from standard practice. The book utilizes a balance of official and primary source material from many perspectives.

Sales, Kirkpatrick. *SDS.* New York: Random House, 1973. Traces the history of the organization from its beginning as an offshoot of the League of Industrial Democracy to its factionalized stage. A definitive history of the group made possible by the use of the SDS archives.

Young, Marilyn B. *The Vietnam Wars: 1945-90.* New York: Harper & Row, 1991. Highly accessible and readable overview of the U.S. involvement in and with Vietnam. This well-documented account provides a balance of social and political angles of U.S. involvement.

Richard C. Kagan

Military Rule Comes to Democratic Uruguay

Category of event: Political freedom; revolutions and rebellions
Time: June 27, 1973
Locale: Uruguay

> *The long-standing democratic political system in Uruguay evolved into one of Latin America's more brutal military dictatorships*

Principal personages:

JOSÉ BATLLE Y ORDÓÑEZ (1856-1929), the father of modern Uruguay, whose innovative reforms ultimately led to chaos and dictatorship

JUAN MARÍA BORDABERRY (1928-   ), the president of Uruguay who presided over the demise of Uruguayan democracy

RAUL SENDIC (1927-   ), a law student who organized the Tupamaro urban guerrilla movement

JORGE PACHECO ARECO (1920-   ), the president of Uruguay who set in motion the precipitous decline of Uruguayan democracy

JULIO MARÍA SANGUINETTI (1936-   ), the first president of Uruguay after control of the government was returned formally to civilian rule

Summary of Event

In 1945, 1950, 1955, and 1960, a panel of Latin American experts was asked to rate the twenty Latin American republics in order of their democratic attainment. On all four occasions, Uruguay ranked as the most democratic. The criteria included a number of factors, such as freedom of the press and an independent judiciary, that are germane to human rights. Had a similar poll been conducted during the 1970's, the outcome would have been very different. A 180-degree turn had changed Uruguay from one of Latin America's most democratic countries to a cruel military dictatorship.

Three decades of democracy in Uruguay eroded over the course of one decade. The seeds in which one of Latin America's more brutal military regimes germinated had been sown decades earlier. The catalyst was an urban guerrilla group known as the Tupamaros. (Formally named the National Liberation Movement, the group acquired a label derived from the name of the last Inca

chieftain, Tupac Amarú.) Disenchanted socialists who had given up on the peaceful path to reform, they declared that progress had been subverted to the interests of the few, and they embraced the life of the urban guerrilla. The demise of democracy in Uruguay was acquiesced to, even encouraged, through the processes of the Uruguayan democratic system.

José Batlle y Ordóñez, the "father of modern Uruguay," was a leader of the Colorado political party who served as president of Uruguay from 1903 to 1907 and again from 1911 to 1915. A forceful, innovative leader, he transformed the nature of the Uruguayan political, economic, and social systems. His reforms led to increased democracy and social betterment—improved education, more public social welfare programs—and they enhanced governmental participation in the economy. Ultimately, however, these changes, which earlier had created the "Switzerland of South America," contributed to a collection of destabilizing conditions—a factionalized political system, a welfare state that exceeded the financial capabilities of the government, inefficient industry, and runaway inflation. The resulting dissatisfaction was reflected in an increase in left-wing radicalism.

In September, 1970, after more than one hundred Tupamaros had escaped from a penitentiary, President Jorge Pacheco Areco took the next step in dealing with armed violence in Montevideo. He lifted control of the antiguerrilla campaign out of the hands of the police to make it the responsibility of the armed forces. This move was followed by a period of relative tranquility, but the explanation did not lie in the escalation by the government. Rather, it was attributable to the fact that the Tupamaros had made a political decision to suspend violent activities during the upcoming political campaign in the hope that this would improve the chances of the left-wing coalition that was contesting the election. A questionable election count led to the selection of Colorado candidate Juan María Bordaberry as the president who would have the dubious honor of presiding over the snuffing out of democracy in Uruguay.

President Bordaberry, with the willing cooperation of the military, continued the tough policies of his predecessor. By early 1973, the military had moved out of an ostensible support position to become a part of a new National Security Council structure that, jointly with the elected president, exercised executive power in Uruguay. In June of 1973, the combined president-military closed the parliament and formally instituted dictatorial rule. By that time, the Tupamaros had been defeated; they no longer were a threat. The military, however, had become politicized to the point that it continued and augmented its role in running the country. It had decided to extirpate not only the Tupamaros—the symbol of a failing economic, political, and social system—but also the system itself.

There was no single or simple explanation for the transformation of one of Latin America's most apolitical and least visible military institutions into an activist ruling party. A deteriorating economy; a middle class at risk to inflation, strikes, and chaos; and an ineffectual political system that long had demonstrated a lack of will to resolve Uruguay's problems all were evident. On the other hand, there were also motivations within the military leadership to embrace the political forum. Among the motivations suggested were that the military traditionally had been recruited from among the most conservative elements within Uruguay, that the experience of being brought into contact with the complaints that gave rise to Tupamaro rebellion was a traumatic one (even though ideologically the Tupamaros and the military were at opposite poles), and that Uruguay's military leadership had absorbed the so-called national security doctrine associated with the governing military in bordering Brazil. That doctrine, simply stated, saw the world as polarized between Christian free enterprise and Marxist socialism, with the military serving as the ultimate arbiter of the right choice.

Not atypically, Uruguay's military regime never was purely military. Several military-civilian structures were established through which the functions of government were carried out. Major decision-making power was, however, held jointly by the heads of the separate services. Less typical was the fact that no single military figure ever rose to a position of dominance; there was no Gamal Abdel Nasser, as in Egypt, nor an Augusto Pinochet, as in Chile. Internal security, the police function, was carried out by the military and the civilian police, with the military in control.

The human rights and political freedoms records of military rulers in Uruguay were abysmal. Torture, disappearances, and murders were used, as well as imprisonment for political reasons. People in general were categorized in terms of their political reliability. Those at the low end of the scale were denied jobs and passports. Military courts were used for trials of civilians. Publications offensive to the military regime were banned from school libraries. Public meetings and festivities, even family reunions, had to be conducted with the knowledge and approval of the security authorities. Labor unions were banned. Censorship was instituted for all types of news and cultural publications and events. The military government took on the trappings of a tyrannical system.

The end result of all of this was a regime of fear. Probably fewer than three hundred persons actually were killed, and the modes of torture used—electric shock, beatings, simulated executions—could be called conventional. The internal security apparatus grew, however, and it became more pervasive and more draconian. People came to feel that a seemingly arbitrary hand of authority hung over their heads. Many cowered, and many fled.

Lip service had been given from the beginning to the redemocratization of Uruguay. The regime's performance, however, did not lend credence to a real dedication to re-creating democracy in Uruguay. As the military encountered growing problems in ruling the country—difficulty in gaining political compliance from the politicians, who resisted military proposals for a new order, an initially apparently successful but soon failing economic policy, and an outright rejection by the electorate of a proposed new constitution that would have ensured a continued political position for the military—the time ripened for the military to bow out, even if not gracefully. In the eleventh year of the military regime, elections were held that resulted in the selection of a longtime Colorado politician, Julio María Sanguinetti, as president, to take office on March 1, 1985. The leading opposition candidate had been jailed and excluded from the plebiscite.

Impact of Event

In a region in which Uruguay, Chile, and Costa Rica were the traditional democratic states, the failure of democracy in Uruguay was a blow to the image of democratic government in Latin America. The blow was compounded by the fact that, on September 11 of the same year (1973), President Salvador Allende of Chile was murdered during the course of a successful military coup that instituted a brutal military regime. To add to the tragedy, the military governments of Argentina, Chile, and Uruguay developed records of brutal human rights violations that became major political concerns in all three countries and were not forgotten in the international community. These remained as dark stains on the escutcheons of the three most ethnically and racially European of all Latin American countries. This was Latin America's holocaust.

Most of Latin America long had strived for democratic sobriety but often had fallen by the wayside. It was, nevertheless, progressing. The long-term military dictatorship of Alfredo Stroessner in Paraguay was only a pale image of cruel nineteenth and twentieth century dictatorships in Argentina, Venezuela, and Mexico. Countries such as Colombia and Venezuela appeared on the road to a permanency of democratic government. Over the first seventy years of the twentieth century, there had been a cyclical alternation of periods of predominant civilian and military rule in Latin America. Even military governments paid lip service to democracy and often were moderate in their violations of human rights. Then elements of "Nasserism" infiltrated the zone; long-term military governments with major political and economic agendas blossomed in countries such as Brazil and Peru. The proclamation of the military as defenders of the constitution was being replaced by a psychology that gave precedence to the military institution as the best setting for government—

the corrector of the weaknesses and evils of civilian government. Scholars observing Brazil and Peru have attributed this effect to teachings in the higher-level military schools. The Uruguayan military seemed to have taken the journeyman's route; they learned on the job that their destiny was to rule. The fragile fabric of Latin American democracy was rent by events in Chile and Uruguay, the bastions of democracy in South America.

Alternatively, another lesson may have been learned. The military that governed soon discovered that military professionalism was no match for problems that seemed endemic to Latin American society. Even something as astounding as the Brazilian boom of the 1960's and 1970's soon yielded to economic difficulties that did not respond to further public ministrations. Military governments learned what empirical studies have proved to scholars, that the records of military regimes essentially were no better than those of civilian regimes.

The question remained, however, whether Latin America finally was committed to democratic systems. Even longstanding democratic polities, like that in Uruguay, could fail. In the 1980's, the Ronald Reagan administration in the United States declared that democracy was here to stay in Latin America, that the course of history had been broken. On the other hand, scholars of the area were more pessimistic. More than thirty years of democracy in Uruguay and Chile were not sufficient to sustain democracy there. Why place faith in the future?

Bibliography

Brito, Alexandra Barahona de. *Human Rights and Democratization in Latin America: Uruguay and Chile.* New York: Oxford University Press, 1997. The author provides a scholarly examination of the challenges of governmental transition, comparing the Uruguayan situation to that of Chile. Bibliography and index.

Kaufman, Edy. *Uruguay in Transition: From Civilian to Military Rule.* New Brunswick, N.J.: Transaction Books, 1979. This is a methodologically explicit, decision-making case study of variables that help to account for the transition of democratic Uruguay to a military dictatorship. Despite the academic trappings, the text is readily understandable to the general reader.

Servicio Paz y Justicia, Uruguay. *Uruguay nunca más: Human Rights Violations, 1972-1985.* Translated by Elizabeth Hampsten. Philadelphia: Temple University Press, 1992. A Uruguayan peace organization documents the human rights atrocities that occurred under military dictatorship. Includes useful appendices, bibliography and index.

Sosnowski, Saúl, and Louise B. Popkin, eds. *Repression, Exile, and Democracy: Uruguayan Culture.* Translated by Louise B. Popkin. Durham, N.C.: Duke University Press, 1993. Cultural examination of the Uruguayan dictatorship and its aftermath. Bibliography.

Weinstein, Martin. *Uruguay: Democracy at the Crossroads.* Boulder, Colo.: Westview Press, 1988. From the vantage point of twenty years of close study of Uruguay, political scientist Weinstein presents an insightful summation of political events in Uruguay as they have played themselves out in recent times. This is the best single source in English on the subject of this article.

Thomas I. Dickson

Chilean Military Overthrows Allende

Category of event: Atrocities and war crimes; revolutions and rebellions
Time: September 11, 1973
Locale: Santiago, Chile

> *The Chilean armed forces overthrew the leftist Popular Unity government, headed by a democratically elected Marxist president, Salvador Allende, who died during the violent coup*

Principal personages:

SALVADOR ALLENDE (1908-1973), the legally elected Marxist president of Chile (1970-1973) and head of the Popular Unity coalition of leftist parties

AUGUSTO PINOCHET (1915-   ), the commander of the Chilean army and a leader of the coup; became head of the armed forces and dictator of Chile (1973-1989)

CARLOS PRATS (1915-1974), the army commander in chief and interior minister under Allende (1972-1973)

EDUARDO FREI (1911-1982), the Christian Democratic president of Chile (1964-1970)

ORLANDO LETELIER (1932-1976), the Allende foreign minister assassinated by the Pinochet regime in Washington, D.C.

JORGE ALESSANDRI (1896-1986), the Conservative president of Chile (1958-1964) and candidate in the 1970 election

Summary of Event

The Chilean presidential election of 1970 plunged the country into a political crisis which culminated three years later in a brutal military coup and imposition of a ruthless dictatorship which lasted until 1989. In the election of 1970, Salvador Allende Gossens, the Marxist leader of the Socialist-Communist Popular United (UP) coalition, won a plurality, but not a majority, of the popular vote. He had lost closely contested presidential elections in 1958 and 1964. According to the constitution, in cases when no candidate received a majority of votes, the Chilean Congress decided the victor. It adhered to the country's political tradition by confirming Allende as president.

Allende entered office to rule over a polarized nation. Jorge Alessandri, the

Conservative candidate, had received almost 35 percent of the vote, compared with Allende's 36 percent, and the opposition dominated the national congress. Although ineligible for reelection, outgoing Christian Democratic (CD) president Eduardo Frei retained wide support, and the CD candidate, Radomiro Tomic, had won 28 percent of the vote. Thus, the electorate was roughly split into thirds, with both the UP and CD calling for radical change in Chile. The situation called for conciliation, a traditional Chilean political virtue. This time, the politicians rejected compromise. More revolutionary in rhetoric than in action, Allende tried to use the political process rather than brute force to establish socialism. He planned to redistribute land to peasants who owned no property, nationalize foreign companies and Chile's financial system, replace the congress with a popular assembly, and convert the educational system to socialist schools. In foreign affairs, he steered a procommunist course, visiting Moscow, sending his foreign minister to China, and hosting a month-long visit by Fidel Castro.

At the level of the individual Chilean citizen, Allende's presidency provoked feelings of high hope and intense animosity. Both industrial and agricultural laborers believed that Allende would rapidly break the power of the traditional Chilean economic elite, and they were impatient with the president's insistence upon legal niceties. Throughout Chile, and especially in the poverty-stricken south, peasants began to occupy farmlands, refusing to wait for legal title. Such seizures increased when it became obvious that the government would not use its security forces against the peasants. Workers also took over textile factories, largely owned by Middle Eastern immigrants. In the arid north, miners reveled over the nationalization of the copper mines. To both the workers and the new socialist managers, nationalization seemed to be an end in itself. State ownership meant social justice in the mines or on the farms. Workers initially benefited from higher wages imposed by the government. Output, however, began to slip because workers lacked incentives to increase production. At the El Teniente copper mine, for example, absenteeism on Mondays soon climbed to more than 30 percent of the work force.

Allende's support remained strong among such laborers, but his appeal within the middle class soon dissipated. Landholders who managed to retain their property faced higher government-mandated labor costs on one hand and price controls on the foodstuffs they produced on the other. With profits declining, many cut food production, some with the intent of undermining Allende. When the government financed its expenditures by printing huge quantities of currency, inflation soared, and prices outstripped the initial increases in salaries and wages. Middle-class homemakers took to the streets of

Santiago, banging pots and pans to protest shortages of basic commodities, but were ridiculed by working-class Allende supporters who had known scarcity for years.

As opposition to Allende's programs and government multiplied from within and outside the country, violence and chaos engulfed the populace. The extreme left accused Allende of moderation and reformism. By 1973, it was resorting to terrorism, illegal seizures of land and businesses, and illicit strikes. It also began to organize militias as a counterweight to the armed forces. The Chilean right, opponents of Allende's Marxist vision for the nation, criticized the government through the media and organized thugs into Fatherland and Liberty gangs to attack and kill targets on the left. Much of the political center waited to see if the president could deliver his promised changes. By 1973, however, the economy was in shambles, with government spending up by one-third from the previous year, inflation running in triple digits, real wages down to one-quarter of what they had been in 1970, and shortages of food and consumer items provoking popular demonstrations against the government.

In the United States, the Nixon administration watched apprehensively what it perceived as the latest Soviet challenge in the Cold War, worrying over the ramifications should Allende succeed in turning Chile into a communist state. The American Central Intelligence Agency had financially supported Allende's opponents in the 1970 election, tried to bribe Chilean Congress members to prevent Allende from becoming president, and encouraged the Chilean military to overthrow the regime, all without success and with considerable damage to the image of the United States. When Allende nationalized American copper interests and other economic holdings, the United States retaliated by delaying or stopping loans, although international agencies and European governments still made financing available. Some American companies with interests in Chile, such as International Telephone and Telegraph, actively tried to subvert the Allende government.

Chile devolved into turmoil, with the citizenry's civil and human rights under siege from left and right extremists. Allende could not implement his program because his opponents controlled the congress. Strikes from the left and the right crippled the economy. Most serious was a nationwide truckers' strike in October, 1972, which gained wide support. Congressional opponents impeached four of Allende's ministers. Frei announced open Christian Democratic opposition to Allende's policies. To quell the mounting insurrection, Allende appointed as minister of the interior General Carlos Prats, who helped guarantee honest congressional elections in March, 1973. Allende hoped to win a majority, which would enable him to push ahead, and his opponents aimed to garner a two-thirds majority, which would enable them to impeach the president. Allende's Popular Unity coalition slightly increased its congressional representation in the election but failed to achieve the desired majority.

Meanwhile, empty store shelves and the fear that the government might confiscate their properties and businesses turned the middle class against Allende. The threat of expropriation implicit in Allende's Marxism left Chileans insecure in their property rights and devastated the economy. Convinced that there was no peaceful road to socialism—that it could only be established by force—the Movement of the Revolutionary Left (MIR) stepped up its campaign of violence. In June, 1973, elements of a tank regiment attacked the presidential palace but failed to overthrow the government.

Trying to ensure order on August 9, 1973, Allende named to his cabinet the commanders of all three branches of the armed forces plus the head of the national police. Amid widespread strikes, again including the truckers, and new waves of violence and terrorism by the right and the left, the opposition in Congress called on the traditionally nonpolitical military to intervene to guarantee civil order. Military wives demonstrated against General Prats, whom they perceived as too sympathetic to Popular Unity aims. Prats and the other military members of the cabinet resigned.

This opened the way for conservative elements in the military to move against Allende. A four-man *junta*, dominated by army commander General Augusto Pinochet Ugarte, gave Allende an ultimatum to resign. The president refused, and the coup began on September 11. Rather than taking refuge with the leftist militia, Allende went to La Moneda, the presidential palace. Allende died during a bomber and tank attack, allegedly from a self-inflicted gunshot wound. He had previously threatened to commit suicide rather than submit to a coup d'état.

Impact of Event

Overthrow of the Allende government did not solve the Chilean crisis. Pinochet and the armed forces imposed a political calm on the nation through a brutal dictatorship worse than anything the nation had experienced. Vowing to eliminate the Marxist threat to Chile, the military arrested thousands of Allende supporters and suspected subversives, many of whom were murdered. One of the *junta*'s first acts was to broadcast a list of sixty-eight prominent Socialist and communist leaders who were ordered to turn themselves in at the Defense Ministry. Hundreds of party members were arrested.

More than one thousand people died when armed industrial workers tried to resist the coup. Security forces turned the Santiago soccer stadium into a temporary prison and execution chamber, and makeshift detention centers sprang up around the country. Of those not immediately executed, many leading pro-Allende politicians were incarcerated in a frigid concentration camp on Dawson Island, near the Antarctic.

Some prisoners received summary trials, but many were simply murdered. Security forces took famed guitarist and folksinger Victor Jara to the Santiago stadium, broke both of his hands, and later killed him, dumping his corpse at a morgue for his wife to identify. A few prisoners were taken aloft in helicopters and dropped to their deaths. Many were killed while allegedly attempting to escape their captors.

As many as five thousand people were murdered, tortured, or "disappeared" at the hands of the *junta*. These included communists, politicians opposed to the dictatorship, and especially union leaders. Countless others suffered lesser violations of their rights, with the dictatorship jailing suspects without trial, outlawing Marxist political parties, censoring the news media, forcing into exile thousands who feared for their lives, and looting suspects' homes. Even critics of the regime living outside the country were at risk. Among those killed in 1974 were General Prats and his wife, who were in exile in Argentina. In Washington, D.C., on September 21, 1976, a Pinochet hit-squad blew up the car of Orlando Letelier, foreign minister under Allende. Letelier and an American associate died.

In 1980, the Pinochet regime imposed a new constitution on the nation. It included a weak Congress, with many of the legislators to be chosen undemocratically by the regime. The constitution also gave the military a veto over most congressional decisions and permitted the government to suspend individual civil rights to deal with threats to national security. A clandestine offshoot of the Chilean Communist Party, the Manuel Rodríguez Patriotic Front, began a campaign of urban terrorism which the Pinochet government used to justify its claims of a totalitarian threat. To protect itself, the dictatorship declared an amnesty on all atrocities and abuses of civil rights committed prior to 1978.

Pressure against the regime mounted, with sporadic outbursts of terrorism coming from the extreme left. On September 7, 1986, guerrillas attacked Pinochet's motorcade, killing four bodyguards, although the general escaped unscathed. Under terms of the 1980 constitution, the regime agreed to hold a plebiscite in 1989, with the people approving or rejecting a presidential candidate proposed by the government. In the referendum, 54 percent voted against Pinochet. He was then constitutionally obliged to hold an open election for a successor in 1989. That election was won by Christian Democrat Patricio Aylwin, but Pinochet continued as commander of the army, with the power to prevent any thorough retribution against the military.

Pinochet remained the head of army until 1998, when he was appointed senator for life. However, during that same year, he was detained in England, where he went for medical treatment, when the Spanish government sought to have him extradited to Spain for trial on charges of human rights abuses. This incident triggered an international tug of war to bring Pinochet to trial in Spain, Chile, and Argentina, but efforts to hold him accountable for his past actions effectively ended after Chile's highest court rule him mentally incompetent to stand trial.

Bibliography

Arriagada, Genaro. *Pinochet: The Politics of Power.* Translated by Nancy Morris. Boston: Allen and Unwin, 1988. A concise and essential study of Chile under Pinochet, analyzing the overthrow of Allende and how it destroyed the traditional professionalism of the Chilean military and denied respect for human and civil rights. Arriagada's discussion of Pinochet's political savvy is perceptive.

Chavkin, Samuel. *The Murder of Chile: Eyewitness Accounts of the Coup, the Terror, and the Resistance Today.* New York: Everest House, 1982. A passionate account which blends excerpts from interviews with pro-Allende figures to convey the drama and pathos of 1973 from a leftist perspective. It is sometimes uninformed or inaccurate about later events and says little about the two-thirds of Chileans who did not adhere to the Popular Unity coalition.

Cleary, Edward L. *The Struggle for Human Rights in Latin America.* Westport, Conn.: Praeger, 1997. Good coverage of Chile.

Cockroft, James D., ed. *Salvador Allende Reader: Chile's Voice of Democracy.* New York: Ocean Press, 2000. An anthology of Allende's interviews and speeches, predominately given during his three-year presidency.

Davis, Nathaniel. *The Last Two Years of Salvador Allende.* Ithaca, N.Y.: Cornell University Press, 1985. Written by the U.S. ambassador to Chile when the coup occurred, this study accords Allende sympathy although faulting him for failing to check the extreme left. Attempts to exculpate Davis and the United States for the bloody overthrow of 1973.

Falcoff, Mark. *Modern Chile, 1970-1989: A Critical History.* New Brunswick, N.J.: Transaction Publishers, 1989. Blames the overthrow of the government on the Popular Unity coalition's internal contradictions and redistributionist populism while downplaying U.S. involvement. Argues that there was no peaceful path to socialism and that Allende's stature as a leading socialist derives solely from the brutality of the Pinochet regime.

Inter-American Commission on Human Rights. *Report on the Situation of Human Rights in Chile*. Washington, D.C.: Organization of American States, 1985. Compares the provisions for human rights and civil liberties in the Chilean constitutions of 1925 and 1980 and analyzes how the Pinochet dictatorship abrogated them. Cites a number of individual cases to illustrate the violations.

Kaufman, Edy. *Crisis in Allende's Chile*. New York: Praeger, 1988. By a political scientist, this is the most thorough and detailed account thus far on the Allende presidency. Without hard evidence, Kaufman speculates that the United States played a more sinister role than is generally thought and that Allende was especially naïve regarding motives of the military and the United States.

Sigmund, Paul E. *The Overthrow of Allende and the Politics of Chile, 1964-1976.* Pittsburgh: University of Pittsburgh Press, 1977. A serious, fair-minded history of the Allende years, accessible to the general reader. It faults Allende for choosing revolutionary ideals over political compromise and holds the U.S. government responsible for exacerbating the crisis but not for causing the coup.

Valenzuela, J. Samuel, and Arturo Valenzuela, eds. *Military Rule in Chile: Dictatorship and Oppositions*. Baltimore: Johns Hopkins University Press, 1986. A collection of articles on Chilean society, politics, and economics under Pinochet. While dealing with human rights only in a peripheral way, these studies are essential to understanding the dynamics of the dictatorship and the difficulties in organizing a strong opposition.

Kendall W. Brown

United Nations Votes to Punish South Africa for Apartheid

Category of event: Civil rights; international norms; racial and ethnic rights
Time: November 30, 1973
Locale: United Nations, New York City

> *The International Convention on the Suppression and Punishment of the Crime of Apartheid was adopted by the United Nations in 1973*

Principal personages:

FREDERIK WILLEM DE KLERK (1936-   ), the president of South Africa
JULIUS NYERERE (1922-1999), the former president of Tanzania
KENNETH D. KAUNDA (1924-   ), the former president of Zambia
SALIM AHMED SALIM (1942-   ), the former chair of the United Nations General Assembly Decolonization Committee

Summary of Event

The apartheid system in South Africa evolved over time as the African and European populations fought for control over this area. From 1910 to 1939, a racial order evolved that kept the African majority outside the central decision-making institutions in society. The year 1948 marked the ascension of the National Party to power in South Africa and the introduction of the formal apartheid policy.

The apartheid system rested on two laws passed in 1950. One is the Population Registration Act, which categorized every individual living in South Africa as belonging to one of four racial groups: whites (14 percent, about three-fifths of whom were Afrikaners); blacks (73 percent); Coloureds (10 percent); and Indians (3 percent). The other was the Group Areas Act, which required each racial group to live in a segregated area. Whites were separated from nonwhite townships by distances of more than five miles.

Black resistance to apartheid took different forms after the end of World War II. Black Africans in South Africa adopted the Gandhian method of nonviolence as a strategy of change throughout the 1950's. The African National Congress (ANC) spearheaded the defiance campaign protesting against the repressive apartheid laws. During a demonstration on March 21, 1961, in front

459

of a police station in Sharpeville, police killed sixty-nine unarmed protesters. This event sparked widespread protest throughout South Africa against the killings. The government banned the African National Congress and the Pan Africanist Congress (PAC) from any political activity inside South Africa. At this juncture, the ANC, under Nelson Mandela's leadership, launched a guerrilla campaign and gave up on the nonviolent approach to changing South Africa. Nelson Mandela was arrested in 1962, along with leaders of several other organizations, on the charge of treason. He was sentenced to life in prison.

From 1946 to 1960, the Western nations controlled the United Nations General Assembly and the Security Council. They supported South Africa's claim that the racial situation and the apartheid policies were a domestic affair. The West, in general, was defensive with reference to racial and colonial issues. The Sharpeville massacre was a critical event that changed the world's perception of Pretoria's apartheid policies from being considered a domestic issue to violating various United Nations human rights conventions and threatening international peace.

Even prior to that, attitudes were shifting. On April 1, 1960, the Security Council passed Resolution 134, condemning apartheid. The change in the tone and thrust of the United Nations at this juncture was the result of the admission of eighteen newly independent African states in 1960. The new membership altered the balance of voting power within the United Nations General Assembly and gave a new saliency to the Afro-Asian movement's demands to end colonialism, racism, and apartheid. Starting in 1963, the Organization of African Unity began to press the United Nations to take a bolder stand against apartheid and move toward isolating South Africa from the international community. Such efforts resulted in the United Nations vote for the suppression and punishment of the crime of apartheid on November 30, 1973.

In the late 1960's, black people began to respond to their oppression through the Black Consciousness movement. This movement was influenced by Stephen Biko, Barney Pityana, and Harry Nengwekulu. The obvious philosophical contributions of black consciousness derived from contemporary African Americans (Malcolm X, Stokely Carmichael, and Bobby Seale) and the writing of Frantz Fanon were pivotal to the development of this new political generation. This movement sought to address and change the Afrikaner definition of nonwhites in South Africa. This ideology challenged the Afrikaner attempt to divide the nonwhite population along racial, linguistic, and ethnic lines. Following the tradition of the Haitian revolution, the Black Consciousness movement redefined all nonwhites as black.

In June, 1976, student uprisings began in Soweto against requiring the Afrikaans language in secondary schools. Student protest spread to other townships around the country. Stephen Biko was arrested in May, 1977, and died in police custody, provoking widespread protest throughout the country and from the international community. The government responded by banning all Black Consciousness organizations from political activity.

The government crackdown on the Black Consciousness movement created a political vacuum which was filled by a labor movement, the United Democratic Front, and the ANC in the late 1970's. As a result of a number of wildcat strikes and pressure from the business community, the government moved to recognize trade unions. The government's attempts to co-opt the black trade unions and get them to focus on shop-related issues met with little success. Activists began to demand the release of Nelson Mandela.

The United Democratic Front evolved in the mid-1980's into a potent political force which included a multiethnic and multiracial coalition. The Reverend Desmond Tutu and the Reverend Allan Boasek became major players in this organization and in exporting the antiapartheid struggle beyond the borders of South Africa. The government responded to challenges by imposing a state of emergency in thirty-six areas, most of them black townships. In August, 1985, international banks refused to extend credit to Pretoria, causing serious economic dislocation. The government repealed the pass laws, which had restricted the freedom of black South Africans to travel within the country, and lifted the state of emergency as a response to domestic and international critics. In June, 1986, a new state of emergency was declared nationwide. Antiapartheid forces were successful in getting the United States and the European Economic Community to impose economic sanctions on the apartheid regime.

Desmond Tutu's outspoken leadership in South Africa's antiapartheid movement received international acknowledgment in 1984, when he was awarded a Nobel Peace Prize. (© The Nobel Foundation)

Between 1986 and 1989, the economic sanctions began to take their toll on the South African economy. In August, 1989, South African president Frederik de Klerk replaced President Pieter Botha, who had suffered a stroke. The business community and many other sectors of the white population began to articulate the need for the government to enter negotiations with the ANC to resolve the political and economic crises. The new president outlined several conditions under which negotiations with the ANC could begin.

The demise of communism in Eastern Europe and the retreat of Soviet support for Third World radicalism provided the de Klerk government with an advantageous bargaining position vis-à-vis the ANC. The Soviets and Cubans had agreed to depart from the region and cease supporting the ANC through Angola as part of the political settlement leading to black majority rule in Namibia. The ANC agreed to close its bases in Angola as part of the settlement.

Nelson Mandela was released on February 11, 1990, after serving twenty-seven years in prison. The ANC and representatives of the de Klerk government entered into negotiations to bring an end to apartheid and to work out an arrangement for black empowerment. In 1991, South Africa repealed a number of apartheid laws but avoided releasing political prisoners and enacting policies allowing black participation in the political process. Some elements of the de Klerk government were engaged in covert support of Chief Buthelezi's Inkatha movement, which countered the ANC, in an attempt to keep Nelson Mandela from consolidating his position and getting a political foothold among black South Africans. Buthelezi, in return, expected to participate in the negotiations.

In July, 1991, U.S. president George Bush removed U.S. sanctions against South Africa, stating that Pretoria was making satisfactory progress toward eliminating apartheid. After more than three centuries of growing political, economic, and social domination by a minority of white European settlers, South Africa finally adopted a system of nonracial democracy in 1994, and Nelson Mandela was elected president of the country.

Impact of Event

The 1973 United Nations International Convention on the Suppression and Punishment of the Crime of Apartheid globalized the struggle against apartheid policies in South Africa. In 1976, the U.N. General Assembly welcomed the coming into force of this international convention and proclaimed June 16 as the International Day of Solidarity with the Struggling People of South Africa. The action by the General Assembly in 1973 placed this international institution at the forefront in the global battle against apartheid. After the 1973 convention, the United Nations emerged as the most dynamic international institution mobilizing world opinion against South Africa's continued violation of the 1948 United Nations Universal Declaration of Human Rights through apartheid laws and regulations. The 1973 convention played a decisive role in making the attainment of human rights in South Africa a United Nations issue as well as one concerning the global community.

The African National Congress, the Pan-Africanist Congress, and other South African antiapartheid movements were able to mobilize support on a global scale in their efforts to end apartheid as a direct result of the General Assembly action. Opponents of apartheid initially encountered a number of bottlenecks in their efforts to deploy sanctions and arms embargoes through the United Nations General Assembly and Security Council during the late 1960's and early 1970's. The mid-1970's, however, witnessed the growth and escalation of a broad, multiracial coalition in the United States and to some extent in Western Europe. This coalition was successful in mobilizing opposition to continued U.S. corporate investment in South Africa. It was also successful in getting local and state municipalities and in some cases university pension funds, to divest themselves of relationships with companies doing business in South Africa.

In the mid-1980's, this coalition was able to build bipartisan and multiracial support for a veto-proof sanction bill in the U.S. Congress. This same group employed direct action strategies against the South African diplomatic corps in the United States. Its success in generating economic sanctions contributed to a decline in South Africa's fortunes as banks and multinational corporations began to divest. Western economic support for the apartheid regime was dealt a mortal blow by the ability of the ANC and other South African antiapartheid liberation movements to build a broad-based coalition within the United States, the Commonwealth, and to some extent the European Economic Community.

The African Group pressed its case against apartheid in a variety of international institutions, ranging from the Nonaligned Movement to the Group of 77. The African Group joined forces with other Third World nations and launched a concerted campaign to isolate Pretoria from the international community and press it to abandon its racist policies. This effort bore fruit in the International Labor Organization and the United Nations Educational, Scientific and Cultural Organization. These actors could also count on support from the Soviet Bloc. The African Group was also successful in mobilizing support in the Arab League, the Organization of Petroleum Exporting Countries, and the Afro-Asian Peoples Solidarity Organization. The Special

Committee Against Apartheid and the U.N. Centre Against Apartheid also emerged as important diplomatic instruments in the battle against apartheid. Through such efforts, the apartheid issue was kept before the international community, thereby creating an environment conducive to the eradication of this gross violation of human rights.

Bibliography

Beinart, William, and Saul DuBow, eds. *Segregation and Apartheid in Twentieth-century South Africa.* New York: Routledge, 1995. This volumes compiles ten important essays on the development and growth of segregation and apartheid in South Africa. Includes a helpful glossary.

Callaghy, Thomas M., ed. *South Africa in Southern African: The Intensifying Vortex of Violence.* New York: Praeger, 1983. Examines the South African conflict with reference to Pretoria's aggressive posture in the Southern African region.

Denoon, Donald, and Balam Nyeko. *Southern Africa Since 1800.* 2d ed. London: Longman, 1984. Provides a critical and insightful history of the region.

Hanlon, Joseph. *Apartheid's Second Front: South Africa's War Against Its Neighbors.* New York: Penguin Books, 1986. Examines South Africa's policy of low-intensity war against its neighbors.

Özdemir, Özguer. *Apartheid: The United Nations and Peaceful Change in South Africa.* Dobbs Ferry, N.Y.: Transnational Publishers, 1982. Examines the role of United Nations agencies in pressing South Africa toward peaceful resolution of the conflict concerning apartheid.

Thompson, Leonard M. *A History of South Africa.* 3d ed. New Haven, Conn.: Yale University Press, 2000. A thorough review of the apartheid era. An indispensable tool for understanding the history of the conflicts in South Africa.

United Nations. *The United Nations and Apartheid 1948-1994.* Author, 1994. An account of the campaign against apartheid in South Africa.

Worden, Nigel. *The Making of Modern South Africa: Conquest, Segregation and Apartheid.* 3d ed. Malden, Mass.: Blackwell, 2000. A detailed examination of the primary issues that have shaped South Africa. Includes a bibliography and an index.

Darryl C. Thomas

Medical Group Exposes Torture in Greece and Chile

Category of event: Atrocities and war crimes; health and medical rights
Time: 1974
Locale: Denmark, Greece, Chile

A team of Danish medical experts helped to substantiate allegations of the widespread use of torture by military dictatorships in Greece and Chile

Principal personages:

SALVADOR ALLENDE (1908-1973), the first elected Marxist leader in the Western Hemisphere, who died during a U.S.-sponsored coup in September, 1973

CONSTANTINE II (1940-   ), the king of Greece, deposed in 1973

RICHARD M. NIXON (1913-1994), the thirty-seventh president of the United States (1969-1974)

GEORGE PAPADOPOULOS (1919-1999), the leader of the 1967 coup in Greece who became the *junta*'s prime minister from 1967 to 1973

AUGUSTO PINOCHET (1915-   ), the general in the Chilean army who led the overthrow of the democratically elected government of Allende in 1973

Summary of Event

Although separated by thousands of miles and located in different hemispheres, the nations of Chile and Greece shared many common features in 1974. Both nations were ruled by brutal military regimes that had come to power by forcibly overthrowing constitutionally elected governments. Both nations' military governments were supported by U.S. president Richard M. Nixon as bulwarks against communism. In addition, citizens in both countries were systematically subject to torture if they dared to voice any criticism of the military government or express any thought deemed "subversive."

On the morning of April 21, 1967, the people of Greece awoke to discover that their elected government had been overthrown by a swift military coup led by Colonel George Papadopoulos. Using the excuse that a communist conspiracy to seize power was about to unfold, the new military dictatorship quickly attacked not only the communists but all individuals who opposed

465

their rule. Even King Constantine II, a confirmed anticommunist, was forced to flee Greece after falling out with the military *junta* under Papadopoulos. Resting on only a narrow base of support, the military quickly turned to fierce repression as the means to prolong its rule. In the more than seven years that the regime ruled Greece, torture was honed to a fine art.

In much the same manner, on September 11, 1973, the constitutionally elected Chilean government of Salvador Allende was ousted in a swift and violent military coup led by General Augusto Pinochet. Claiming that Socialist president Allende's Marxist program was a prelude to a communist revolution, the coup ended a longstanding tradition of democratic government and nonintervention by the Chilean armed forces in political affairs. In the aftermath of the coup, thousands were killed and as many as forty thousand Chileans were arrested. Political parties, the Congress, trade unions, and any other organizations that opposed Pinochet were soon outlawed. To maintain his regime in the face of massive resistance, Pinochet's government turned to torture as an accepted procedure during the interrogation of political prisoners.

Since neither the Greek nor the Chilean military government was subject to any type of democratic checks while both enjoyed the backing of President Nixon and the United States, it was extremely difficult to bring pressure on them to respect human rights. Utilizing twentieth century technology, the dictatorship in Greece developed torture into a sadistic art form euphemistically termed "scientific techniques of interrogation." Rather than feeling embarrassment over such methods, the Greek regime let its methods become public knowledge, understanding that this alerted all potential members of the resistance to the fate that awaited them should they be arrested.

In many cases, individuals who merely mildly criticized the government were arrested, tortured, and released as a warning to others. Even assisting the families of political prisoners and deportees had to be done secretly, since so much as a financial donation to the wrong hungry family was a crime. The suppression of open opponents of the military was not surprising, but the fact that such minor infractions of the new order as owning a book written by Karl Marx or saying that Plato was a homosexual could land one in jail was a testament to the rigidity of the regime. Once in custody, political prisoners were subject to unspeakable cruelties designed to break their spirit and force them to implicate others.

In these circumstances, the job of attempting to make the Greek *junta* recognize human rights was extremely difficult. International pressure was dismissed as communist-orchestrated, and human rights violations were portrayed as exaggerations. When political prisoners with obvious injuries were produced by impartial investigations, the official response was inevitably the same, that the injuries had been suffered during the course of arrest when the accused resisted lawful authorities. Every documented case of torture that could not be factually disproved or blamed on the victim's own resistance was dismissed as a rare exception.

In Chile, the Pinochet government had been established in an atmosphere of bitter social and political conflict that had resulted in an almost complete disregard for the rights of political prisoners. Not only was torture widespread, but confessions obtained by these methods were considered admissible evidence in trials held by military tribunals. Torture was more than merely an individual option for members of the armed forces dealing with supporters of the ousted Allende government. Among the most noted torturers were the intelligence services, which were responsible to Pinochet and the ruling *junta* alone.

Within days of the coup that brought the military to power, torture seemed to have become an official policy, a fact indicated by the uniformity of torture incidents reported by released political prisoners. Further, the International Red Cross noted a large number of military detention camps to which they were denied access in the first months after Allende's overthrow.

At first, Chilean military officials denied that torture was taking place. Later, they claimed it occurred only in isolated incidents involving individual soldiers mainly at the time of arrest. Although local excesses on individual or local initiative did take place, it seems clear that there was a consistent policy of torture that was approved at the highest levels of the military command structure. As evidence of torture reached the outside world, the Chilean government sought to minimize these reports by arguing that the accusations were politically motivated.

Thus, in both Greece and Chile, a systematic program of torture was carried out by the military governments in power with little regard for outside condemnation. This made the task of helping the thousands of political prisoners in these nations extremely difficult. Amnesty International intervened in both situations with impartial commissions composed of internationally respected jurists and others. Given the cynicism of both military regimes when it came to human rights, this approach had less impact than desired.

To outside condemnations of human rights violations and denunciations of widespread torture, the response of both military dictatorships was strikingly similar. Both the Papadopoulos-controlled press in Greece and its counterpart in Pinochet's Chile vigorously disputed the facts in every case in which political prisoners were said to be tortured. The two standard objections to charges of torture were that the accusers were politically motivated or that they had no medical expertise to determine whether injuries observed were the results of accidents or deliberate mistreatment.

It was at this point, in the spring of 1974, that a Danish medical group was organized that helped to increase the pressure on both regimes. The composition of the team answered both the major objections that had been raised to past investigations. The Danish medical group was composed of a number of highly respected medical personnel, which made it impossible for either the Greek *junta* or Pinochet's dictatorship to argue credibly that the inspectors did not know the difference between a fall and a beating. In addition, the impartiality and moral integrity of the individuals made charges of political bias difficult to sell.

Impact of Event

As part of long international campaigns to expose the torture policies of both the Greek and Chilean governments, the Danish medical group played a vital role. After public hearings in the parliament building in Copenhagen, world public opinion shifted to a more widespread awareness that what was happening in Greece and Chile was not a few minor infractions of human rights. Rather, it was revealed that systematic torture was being utilized as a matter of governmental policy in both dictatorships.

The impact of these findings was most clearly felt in Greece. The military government in Athens, although unconcerned about human rights, was sensitive to its increasing isolation from the rest of Europe. This was particularly a problem for the Greek dictatorship, as ongoing tensions with neighboring Turkey made European acceptance a practical matter of concern.

In addition, the Danish medical findings struck a chord with the increasingly discontented Greek population. The large number of Danish tourists who traditionally vacationed in Greece increased the findings' importance. Tourists stayed away in significant numbers or voiced their objections to the Greek government privately during their visits. The fact that King Constantine's wife was a Danish princess made it difficult for the Greek *junta* to paint outspoken Danes as "tools of Moscow." Thus, the Danish medical group contributed to the process that ended the military dictatorship in Greece in the summer of 1974 and eliminated torture as an accepted method of behavior there.

In Chile, the results were not so immediately dramatic. All the same, the Danish investigations played a vital part in isolating the Pinochet regime from

Europe. Because the late president Salvador Allende had been a leader of the Socialist Party who governed with the support of the Chilean communists, many conservative Europeans had at first greeted reports of torture with skepticism.

Many international campaigns were organized by European communist parties to gain freedom for political prisoners in Chile. Although these efforts played a vital part in raising awareness among the general public, the participation of the left strengthened conservative suspicions. These doubts were eroded greatly when the evidence compiled by the Danish medical group began to bolster the findings of politically neutral Amnesty International.

Although torture was not ended in Chile, a certain restraint appeared to have developed as a result of the exposé. The military dictatorship in Chile realized the damage these revelations were doing to the government's image and attempted to limit the use of torture to specific cases.

Bibliography

Amnesty International. *Chile: An Amnesty International Report.* London: Amnesty International Publications, 1974. A clear, concise documentation of the human rights violations taking place in Chile in the first months after the overthrow of Allende. Without reference features.

Clogg, Richard, and George Yannopoulos, eds. *Greece Under Military Rule.* New York: Basic Books, 1972. A collection of essays on topics ranging from politics to culture, this work is highly recommended even though it was compiled two years before the Greek *junta* fell. Offers reference notes, bibliography, and index.

Kaloudis, George Stergiou. *Modern Greek Democracy: The End of a Long Journey?* Lanham, Md.: University Press of America, 2000. Comprehensive analysis of the military regimes in power from 1967-1974.

O'Shaughnessy, Hugh. *Pinochet: The Politics of Torture.* New York: New York University Press, 2000. Fascinating account of the disturbing Pinochet regime. Index.

Uribe, Armando. *The Black Book of American Intervention in Chile.* Boston: Beacon Press, 1975. Written by a former member of the Allende government, this work details the involvement of the United States in the destruction of democracy in Chile. Includes reference notes and an index.

Valenzuela, J. Samuel, and Arturo Valenzuela. *Military Rule in Chile.* Baltimore: The Johns Hopkins University Press, 1986. This collection of essays covers a wide range of important areas and is useful for anyone interested in the Pinochet dictatorship. Offers reference notes and an index.

Verdugo, Patricia. *Chile, Pinochet, and the Caravan of Death.* Translated by
   Marcelo Montecino. Coral Gables, Fla.: North-South Center Press, 2001.
   Written by a journalist whose father was murdered by the Pinochet regime,
   this is a highly readable, well-researched book about the atrocities that occurred under Pinochet.

                                                          William A. Pelz

Soviet Union Expels Solzhenitsyn

Category of event: Civil rights; political freedom
Time: February 13, 1974
Locale: Moscow, Soviet Union

In 1974, the Soviet government charged Russian writer and critic Aleksandr Solzhenitsyn with treason and sent him into exile

Principal personages:

ALEKSANDR SOLZHENITSYN (1918-   ), a Nobel Prize-winning author

NIKITA S. KHRUSHCHEV (1894-1971), a Soviet leader who approved publication of Solzhenitsyn's *One Day in the Life of Ivan Denisovich*

ALEKSANDR TVARDOVSKII (1910-1971), a liberal editor who published Solzhenitsyn's writings and supported him in the face of official criticism

LEONID ILICH BREZHNEV (1906-1982), the general secretary of the Communist Party whose repressive cultural policies forced Solzhenitsyn into exile in 1974

Summary of Event

Aleksandr Solzhenitsyn, one of Russia's and the world's greatest writers, is the author of plays, poetry, and essays. He is best known for his novels, particularly *V kruge pervom* (1968; *The First Circle*, 1968) and *Rakovy korpus* (1968; *Cancer Ward*, 1968), the novella *Odin den Ivana Denisovicha*, (1962; *One Day in the Life of Ivan Denisovich*, 1963), the historical novel *Avgust chetyrnadtsatogo* (1971; *August 1914*, 1972), and the monumental three-volume literary investigation *Arkhipelag gulag* (1973-1975; *The Gulag Archipelago*, 1974-1978). The underlying theme of Solzhenitsyn's writings is humanity's struggle for truth and decency against the forces of oppression and corruption.

Although he is a critic of the materialism and license of contemporary Western society, the dominant struggle of his life was against the hollowness and brutality of the Soviet regime. By virtue of his writings and the life he lived, Solzhenitsyn became one of the great moral prophets of the twentieth century. In October, 1970, he was awarded the Nobel Prize in Literature with the citation "For the ethical force with which he has pursued the indispensable traditions of Russian literature."

471

Solzhenitsyn's struggle with the Soviet state began during World War II, when, as a battery commander fighting the Germans, he wrote some oblique remarks critical of Stalin in a private letter to a friend. For this, Solzhenitsyn was arrested, charged with engaging in "anti-Soviet propaganda," and sentenced to eight years of imprisonment in corrective labor camps. After his release, he was again sentenced (in absentia) to perpetual exile. The harsh experience of prison life provided Solzhenitsyn with material for some of his most important later writings.

Another source for material was his life in exile in a remote, primitive village in Southern Kazakhstan. While there, he was struck with cancer (for a second time), miraculously surviving with the aid of hormone and X-ray treatments. The novel *Cancer Ward* recorded some of his experiences in the Tashkent hospital.

Stalin's death in 1953 marked the beginning of a change in the Soviet Union's political life. As Nikita Khrushchev, Stalin's successor, consolidated his power, he initiated a process of de-Stalinization which involved ending some of the worst features of Stalin's terror. In 1956, Solzhenitsyn was released from exile, and in the following year he successfully petitioned the Soviet Supreme Court to overturn his original conviction. One feature of Khrushchev's de-Stalinization was a cultural "thaw," which permitted Soviet writers to tread upon subjects that previously had been forbidden. During this period, Solzhenitsyn wrote *One Day in the Life of Ivan Denisovich*, a gripping account of life in Stalin's labor camps. He submitted the manuscript to *Novy Mir*, one of the country's most respected literary magazines whose editor, Aleksandr Tvardovskii, was an active proponent of using literature to examine honestly the problems of Soviet society. Tvardovskii persuaded Khrushchev to permit publication of Solzhenitsyn's novella. The book was a sensation in the Soviet Union and abroad and made Solzhenitsyn an instant celebrity. He was even invited to join the Writer's Union, the official organ for accepted Soviet writers.

Solzhenitsyn's literary success brought mixed results. On one hand, he became the hero and spokesman for those critics of Soviet life who sought to use the literary weapon to enlarge the realm of free thought and speech. On the other hand, he was opposed by many of the conservative elements who did not support Khrushchev's policy of de-Stalinization. Even during the Khrushchev years, Solzhenitsyn became the object of public attacks in the press.

The coup in 1964 that replaced Nikita Khrushchev with Leonid Brezhnev led to an abandonment of the de-Stalinization campaign and a renewal of political and cultural repression. The repression intensified in September, 1965, when the writers Yuli Daniel and Andrei Sinyavsky, whose satirical attacks on the Soviet establishment and Socialist Realism had been published abroad, were arrested for anti-Soviet slander. In that atmosphere, Solzhenitsyn himself became more outspoken and uncompromising in his criticism. In 1965, KGB surveillance and harassment of the writer began. On September 11, the KGB devastated Solzhenitsyn by raiding his apartment and confiscating his personal archive, an action that provoked momentary thoughts of suicide in the writer. Solzhenitsyn's antagonisms toward the regime deepened as he sought without success to publish several of his major works, including *The First Circle* and *Cancer Ward*. In May, 1967, he made an unprecedented public condemnation of censorship in the Soviet Union with an open letter to the Fourth Congress of Soviet Writers. In 250 copies sent to key delegates, Solzhenitsyn decried the fact that "Our writers are not supposed to have the right . . . to express their cautionary judgments about the moral life of man and society . . ." Notwithstanding the public support of eighty writers, the Congress bowed to Communist Party authorities and ignored the challenge to censorship.

Meanwhile, though his novels could not be published legally, many were read in the Soviet Union as *samizdat,* a form of publication by means of typed reproductions circulated to an underground readership. Both *The First Circle* and *Cancer Ward* were eventually published in the West (without Solzhenitsyn's authorization) from such *samizdat* editions. Worldwide distribution of these writings added to the author's already distinguished reputation as a writer and social critic. Indeed, his global reputation became so great that the Brezhnev regime was constrained from taking harsh measures—such as imprisonment—to stop him. The government could and did see that he was vilified in the government-controlled press, and it forced Solzhenitsyn's expulsion from the Writer's Union in November, 1969.

Further support from the West came in 1970, with the Nobel Prize in Literature. Moscow treated the award

Aleksandr Solzhenitsyn. (© The Nobel Foundation)

as a deliberate provocation by the West. Those in the Soviet Union who dared to send congratulatory telegrams to the Russian writer were summoned by KGB and Communist Party officials for warnings. Solzhenitsyn seriously considered going to Oslo to accept the award but ultimately decided not to for fear that he would not be permitted to return. That year, the historical novel *August 1914* was completed. It was offered to seven Soviet publishers, all of whom rejected it. With all avenues for publication blocked at home, Solzhenitsyn decided to authorize, for the first time, publication of his writings abroad. *August 1914* was published in Paris in June, 1971. It immediately became a best-seller in several countries.

Pressure against Solzhenitsyn intensified during 1973. He was barred from living in Moscow, and threats were made against his life. A rumor that the KGB planned for him to be "accidentally" killed in an automobile accident induced Solzhenitsyn to give up driving altogether. Unquestionably the most devastating blow was the KGB seizure of a copy of his *The Gulag Archipelago*. The authorities obtained the manuscript by tortuously interrogating Solzhenitsyn's close associate, Elizabeth Voronyanska, for five days, forcing her to reveal the manuscript's location. Upon her return home, Voronyanska hanged herself. Solzhenitsyn defiantly authorized the publication of the first two parts of *The Gulag Archipelago*, which went on sale in Paris in December, 1973.

From that point, war between the writer and the Soviet state was virtually total. Twice he was summoned to the state prosecutor's office, and twice he refused the summonses. Finally, on February 12, 1974, seven KGB officers arrested Solzhenitsyn in his apartment. He was taken to the infamous Lefortovo prison, stripped of his clothing, searched, and informed that he was charged with treason, a crime punishable by death. The next day, Solzhenitsyn was told that he had been deprived of his citizenship and ordered deported. Without being informed of his destination, he was put on an Aeroflot plane. Several hours later, he arrived in Frankfurt, Germany. Thus began the great author's exile.

Impact of Event

Solzhenitsyn was exiled because he was too respected abroad to be imprisoned, but one way or another the Soviet regime was determined that Solzhenitsyn's subversive voice at home would be silenced. Although he was only one of many domestic critics, his campaign had been particularly insistent, uncompromising, and eloquent. The more Solzhenitsyn was threatened, the greater was his defiance. As a convict, he had refused an assignment at a privileged research institute and willingly accepted the life of an ordinary prisoner; when denied publication, he read chapters of his prohibited works in public; he ignored official summonses from the police. It became evident that he meant it when he told his persecutors in the Writers Union, "No one can bar the road to truth, and to advance its cause I am prepared to accept even death."

The truth he propagated undermined the regime. He debunked the myriad falsehoods that had become the foundation of Soviet communism. Most devastating was his critique of Lenin, who symbolized Soviet legitimacy. It was not only Stalin and the "personality cult" that created "distortions" in socialism. Solzhenitsyn traced the long evolution of terror, the labor camps, the frame-up trials, the mass shootings, and the secret disappearances back to the period of Vladimir Ilich Lenin. By comparison, Solzhenitsyn showed that czarist autocracy was benign, even humane. Decades before anyone even suggested that the roots of Stalinism were in Lenin, Solzhenitsyn had debunked the myth of a humane Lenin.

Exile did not silence Solzhenitsyn's voice, though it broadened the range of his critique. Solzhenitsyn chose Zurich as his initial place of residence, possibly to gather materials for his historical volume *Lenin v Tsyurikhe* (1975; *Lenin in Zurich*, 1976). Life in Switzerland, however, dissatisfied him, in part because of the difficulty of living a fully private life. In the summer of 1976, he moved to the United States, settling on a fifty-acre tract in Cavendish, Vermont. Although Solzhenitsyn fought tenaciously for his privacy, he became involved in some of the political currents of his adopted country. He traveled, spoke in public on occasion, was lionized by his admirers, and was scathingly criticized by some members of the press who disagreed with his ideas. Solzhenitsyn was a critic of détente, which was in vogue in the mid-1970's. No détente was possible, he said, with a country that continually perpetuated "acts of cruelty and brutality" against its own citizens and neighboring peoples. A notable event was the commencement address which he gave at Harvard University on June 8, 1978. In it, he attacked the Western world, which he charged had lost its "civic courage." He condemned the press for misguiding public opinion, popular culture for its television stupor and intolerable music, and the West as a whole for its loss of religious faith. As a result of these and other observations, Solzhenitsyn was a controversial figure during his stay in the United States.

Throughout his exile, the one enduring theme behind all of his jeremiads was the oppression and aggression of the Soviet regime and the fundamental dishonesty of Marxism-Leninism. In the end, history justified his crusade. Solzhenitsyn lived to see the collapse of communism he had predicted. He had the satisfaction of having the charges of treason against him dropped, of seeing his works published in his native country, and of being invited to return home. In May, 1994, he returned to Russia to live.

Bibliography

Carter, Stephen. *The Politics of Solzhenitsyn.* New York: Holmes & Meier, 1977. Hewing closely to Solzhenitsyn's writings, the author dissects Solzhenitsyn's critique of the impact of Marxism-Leninism on Soviet society. He also examines the writer's critique of Western democracy.

Feuer, Kathryn, ed. *Solzhenitsyn: A Collection of Critical Essays.* Englewood Cliffs, N.J.: Prentice-Hall, 1976. These are thirteen essays on either specific works of Solzhenitsyn or important themes in his writings. Most are purely literary, but a few examine his politics. An interesting collection.

Labedz, Leopold, comp. *Solzhenitsyn: A Documentary Record.* New York: Harper & Row, 1971. A useful and interesting collection of documents covering the period 1956-1970. Among the subjects highlighted are Solzhenitsyn's literary debut, struggles with the authorities, expulsion from the Writer's Union, and the Nobel Prize.

Pearce, Joseph. *Solzhenitsyn: A Soul in Exile.* London: HarperCollins, 1999. A comprehensive, readable account of Solzhenitsyn's life.

Scammell, Michael. *Solzhenitsyn: A Biography.* New York: W. W. Norton, 1984. This is the best English-language biography to date. The author had limited cooperation from Solzhenitsyn and his first wife. This volume examines the writer in the context of the society in which he lived.

Joseph L. Nogee

Khmer Rouge Take Over Cambodia

Category of event: Atrocities and war crimes; political freedom; revolutions
and rebellions
Time: April 17, 1975
Locale: Phnom Penh, Cambodia

> *The 1975 takeover of Cambodia by the Khmer Rouge led to one of the bloodiest peri-
> ods of genocide in modern history*

Principal personages:
POL POT (1928-1998), leader of the Khmer Rouge
NORODOM SIHANOUK (1922-   ), the elected leader of Cambodia, deposed
    in a coup by Lon Nol
LON NOL (1913-1985), a Cambodian general who, with the support of the
    United States, deposed Norodom Sihanouk in a 1970 coup
RICHARD M. NIXON (1913-1994), the thirty-seventh president of the United
    States (1969-1974)
HENRY A. KISSINGER (1923-   ), the U.S. secretary of state during the Nixon
    administration

Summary of Event

In the late 1960's and early 1970's, the United States was still embroiled in a
long war, supporting the South Vietnamese government against communist
Vietnamese forces (the Viet Cong and the North Vietnamese army). For much
of this time, the North Vietnamese and Viet Cong forces used border areas of
Cambodia as sanctuaries from American ground and air forces.

North Vietnamese use of Cambodian border areas began to create substantial political difficulties for Cambodia's government, headed by Prince
Norodom Sihanouk. The president of the United States, Richard Nixon,
and U.S. secretary of state Henry Kissinger applied increasing pressure on
Sihanouk to deny use of the border areas to the Vietnamese. This pressure was
brought to a higher level when President Nixon and Secretary of State
Kissinger instituted a secret bombing campaign in 1969 and 1970.

A turning point for Cambodia came in 1970, when American ground
forces crossed the border in an attempt to destroy North Vietnamese army

units in their Cambodian strongholds. Cambodians, long at odds with the Vietnamese, were at first in favor of the invasion. The United States did not succeed in destroying the Vietnamese, however, and as a result Cambodia found itself in an even more precarious position.

There were several consequences of the American invasion. North Vietnamese forces, which had previously ignored Cambodian government troops, began attacking on sight. When combined with the long-standing ethnic tensions between the Cambodians and the Vietnamese, the situation became intolerable.

On March 11, 1970, with Norodom Sihanouk out of the country, a series of civil disturbances began in Phnom Penh. They started as ethnically oriented riots against the Vietnamese but soon escalated into a full military coup, led by General Lon Nol, to remove Sihanouk from power. The coup succeeded.

The United States supported the new Lon Nol regime with weapons, ammunition, and air power. Air strikes, often disastrously inaccurate, were directed by the American embassy. So extensive was the American support for the new regime that many Cambodians believed that the United States had taken over rule of their country.

The new regime became increasingly unpopular. Prince Norodom Sihanouk had been regarded as a god-king by the peasantry of his country. Consequently, his removal from power guaranteed a certain level of unpopularity for the new government. Sihanouk, whose government had been fought by small bands of Khmer Rouge, a communist guerrilla force, since the late 1960's, announced soon after the coup that he was supporting the Khmer Rouge. The power and size of the group began to grow. The Khmer Rouge previously had been limited to a few thousand fighters isolated in remote parts

Made king of Cambodia by the French government in 1941, when he was only nineteen, Norodom Sihanouk was overthrown by the Khmer Rouge in 1970. However, he reestablished himself as king during the 1990's. (National Archives)

of the country. They soon became an army of tens of thousands who were able to win victories against the American-supported government of Lon Nol.

Throughout the early 1970's, the Khmer Rouge, despite devastating American air attacks on behalf of the Lon Nol regime, consistently pushed the Cambodian government's forces back. It was during this period that many of the infamous policies of the Khmer Rouge were formulated. Khmer Rouge harshness developed from having withstood the withering American bombing during this period. The policy of civilian evacuation, later to shock the world, was developed during the early 1970's as a device for controlling villages that they had captured.

The end of the war and the victory of the Khmer Rouge came early in 1975. By early April, Khmer Rouge forces were on the outskirts of Phnom Penh. On April 12, 1975, the last Americans evacuated their embassy. The Khmer Rouge entered Phnom Penh on April 17, 1975.

Almost immediately on completing the conquest of Cambodia, the Khmer Rouge, led by Pol Pot, began to implement, on a far more sweeping scale, their practice of uprooting the populace of cities and towns. This time, however, the intent of the movement of the population was not just to pacify and to control the countryside. What the Khmer Rouge intended was to remove the entire population from the cities, move it to the countryside, and create a new social order based on agriculture and free of outside, imperialist influences.

In implementing this policy of evacuating the populace from the cities, huge numbers of people were moved from the capital. Phnom Penh, which before the war had a population of 600,000, had grown to 2.5 million people by the end of the war. Almost all were taken to the countryside. This exodus included the infirm, the sick, and the elderly. Many thousands died as a result of this forced movement.

In addition to forcing people to leave the cities, the Khmer Rouge began a systematic campaign of eliminating Western influences. This campaign included killing those Cambodians who were educated, individuals associated with the government and army of the Lon Nol regime, and anyone who had Western associations. Uncounted thousands died in this vengeance of the Khmer Rouge.

In moving the population to the countryside, the Khmer Rouge rapidly began to implement their version of a new social order. This concept of society was military in format and was based on continual struggle. All citizens were to give complete allegiance to an abstract concept called *Angka*, which has been interpreted as "organization" or, alternatively, as "the people's will."

People were executed for the smallest infractions of the rules set down by the Khmer Rouge. Children were separated from their parents and were encouraged to inform upon them for the sake of *Angka*. Marriages were arranged by the Khmer Rouge, also in the name of *Angka*.

In the countryside, the people who had been uprooted were given small plots of land, typically seven acres in size. On these plots of land, the transportees were encouraged to grow crops such as maize, cassava, and yams. Rice paddies, the source of the heart of the Cambodian diet, and the tractors necessary to work them on a large-scale basis were kept under the strict control of the Khmer Rouge.

The workday for those who had been transported was long. Typically, the Khmer Rouge forced people into the fields at 5:00 A.M. Once in the fields, people worked until 11:00 A.M. The Khmer Rouge then permitted a break for lunch until 2:00 P.M. Workers finally finished the day's labors at 5:00 P.M.

The lengthy workday was quite strenuous—even for those physically able to do the labor. Many were not, and consequently, many died. Even those who were able to stand the rigorous labor found conditions difficult. Food, because of Khmer Rouge policies of isolation and self-sufficiency, was in short supply. This lack of food and a corresponding lack of medicine contributed to the death of many more people.

Cambodians of all ages, both genders, and varied backgrounds came to fear and hate the soldiers of the Khmer Rouge. Many observers stated that they feared the younger soldiers more than the older ones, because the younger Khmer Rouge were more thoroughly indoctrinated than their older counterparts. Therefore, there was a much higher probability of execution when younger soldiers enforced the rules.

The time of terror finally came to an end in early 1979 when, after a period of border skirmishes, Vietnam invaded and rapidly conquered Cambodia. After quickly driving the forces of Pol Pot from power, the Vietnamese installed a puppet government. It was only then that the world began to get an inkling of the true extent of the horrors of the Khmer Rouge regime.

Impact of Event

The greatest impact of the Cambodian takeover was the huge number of people who died as a result of Khmer Rouge neglect and vengeance. Most estimates state that approximately one million people died in Cambodia as a result of the Khmer Rouge terror. Some believe that 1.6 to 1.8 million people were victims of the followers of Pol Pot.

The consequences of this event remain difficult to gauge. The world has again discovered that it has a profound ability to ignore dreadful events as they occur. The circumstances of the Cambodian genocide do not convey a message of hope about the world's ability to forestall such disasters in the future.

Many ironies have resulted from the Khmer Rouge dominance in Cambodia. First, the Khmer Rouge are still among several groups contending for power in Cambodia. A number of these groups organized to fight the puppet government installed by Vietnam. This alliance has put democratic forces, backed by the United States, on the same side as the Khmer Rouge. Furthermore, Norodom Sihanouk, former leader of Cambodia, found himself aligned with the Khmer Rouge. Sihanouk, after his January, 1979, liberation by the Vietnamese, denounced the Khmer Rouge in a memorable press conference.

The personal basis is perhaps a better indicator of the extent of the tragedy in Cambodia. Entire families were exterminated by the Khmer Rouge because one member was employed by Westerners. Physicians had to conceal their profession for the fear that, once discovered, they would be killed for being educated. Another indicator of the personal tragedy's extent came from the fact that for some Cambodians there was more than one relocation. The Khmer Rouge, during the first evacuation, moved people to the countryside in random patterns. Consequently, some were transported to areas that could not support them. Khmer Rouge officials discovered the problem and rectified their mistakes by ordering second transports of some refugees. Many Cambodians were in weakened condition because of short rations and the first forced movement. To avoid the horrors of a second transportation, some committed suicide.

The horrible personal and societal consequences of Khmer Rouge victory were manifested by waves of Cambodian refugees who struggled across Thailand's border. Tens of thousands languished in Thai refugee camps. The Cambodian refugee problem proved difficult to solve. Thailand found it a strain to take care of large numbers of refugees, and refugee Cambodians were reluctant to return to homes that were in a war zone. Therefore, finding a solution to the refugee problem was predicated on ending the war. Unfortunately, ending the war proved difficult because of the groups contending for power. Peacemakers found it impossible to reconcile the Khmer Rouge, the advocates of democracy, and the supporters of the Vietnamese-backed government. Therefore, it appears that years after the American invasion of Cambodia, peace and security in Cambodia remain the captive of the regional politics of Southeast Asia.

Bibliography

Chandler, David. *A History of Cambodia.* 3d ed. Boulder, Colo.: Westview Press, 2000. This is a broad history of Cambodia that is well researched and comprehensively presented. The author does a good job of placing the conflict in a larger context of Cambodian history and development. For example, he discusses the Indian roots of Cambodia, which are in part responsible for the long history of tension between Vietnam (Chinese in origin) and Cambodia.

Kamm, Henry. *Cambodia: Report from a Stricken Land.* New York: Arcade, 1998. A detailed account of Cambodia's history beginning with the establishment of the Khmer Rouge.

Kiernan, Ben. *The Pol Pot Regime: Race, Power, and Genocide in Cambodia Under the Khmer Rouge, 1975-79.* New Haven, Conn.: Yale University Press, 1996. A comprehensive account of the reign of Pol Pot and the Khmer Rouge regime.

Ngor, Haing, and Roger Warner. *A Cambodian Odyssey.* New York: Macmillan, 1987. This is the autobiography of a Cambodian holocaust survivor who became famous by becoming an actor and by portraying another survivor in *The Killing Fields* (1984). While primarily a personal story, this book contains some interesting observations about the roles of certain important characters, notably Norodom Sihanouk, in the victory of the Khmer Rouge.

Ponchaud, François. *Year Zero.* Translated by Nancy Amphoux. New York: Holt, Rinehart and Winston, 1978. One of the books that helped reveal the full extent of the horrors of the Khmer Rouge regime in Cambodia. Based on dozens of interviews with Cambodian witnesses. This book was very controversial when it was first published and is now regarded as a pioneering work in the field.

Shawcross, William. *The Quality of Mercy: Cambodia, Holocaust, and Modern Conscience.* New York: Simon & Schuster, 1984. One of the more detailed approaches to the Cambodian tragedy. It examines the political causes and consequences of the Khmer Rouge victory. In particular, the book focuses on the role, past and present, of Vietnam, the United States, the Soviet Union, and China in the Cambodian tragedy.

Lyndon C. Marshall

Tokyo Declaration Forbids Medical Abuses and Torture

Category of event: Health and medical rights; international norms
Time: October 10, 1975
Locale: Tokyo, Japan

> *A global organization of physicians developed and passed a declaration stating that doctors should not "countenance, condone or participate" in torture or cruel, inhuman, or degrading punishment*

Principal personages:

P. A. FARRELLY (1928-   ), an Irish physician who called the WMA's attention to physicians' participation in torture

DEREK PAUL STEVENSON (1911-   ), the secretary of the British Medical Association and member of the WMA's council

ANDRÉ WYNEN, a Belgian physician, WMA council member, and later WMA secretary-general

Summary of Event

Physicians possess special abilities to heal the sick and wounded; they may also compound their patients' suffering. Some physicians have been perpetrators of torture; others have played roles that enabled the military or police to carry out torture. A physician, for example, could advise the torturer on methods which will leave few conclusive marks of torture. A physician may also heal the victim, for that person's benefit or instead so that he or she can endure more torture. Other practices include the prescription of drugs to facilitate use of sensory-deprivation techniques and filing of fraudulent medical reports. None of this is new: In the Holy Roman empire of 1532, the *Constitutio Criminalis Carolina* referred to "medical complicity" in torture.

The Declaration of Tokyo was passed by the World Medical Association (WMA) on October 10, 1975, the last day of its five-day conference. The declaration contains a preamble and six guidelines. The preamble states that practice of medicine is a privilege, and that "utmost respect for human life is to be maintained even under threat." It also defines torture: "the deliberate, systematic or wanton infliction of physical or mental suffering,"

The guidelines first declare that "the doctor shall not countenance, condone or participate in the practice of torture or other forms of cruel, inhuman or degrading procedures" regardless of the victim's alleged offense, beliefs, or motives. This applies equally during international or civil wars. The next two guidelines help define when a doctor might be accountable for another's actions. A doctor is not to "provide any premises, instruments, substances or knowledge" to facilitate torture or maltreatment, nor shall he or she be present during any procedure in which torture or maltreatment is used or threatened. A fourth guideline proclaims that the doctor must have complete clinical independence—the doctor is to alleviate distress, a higher purpose than service of personal, collective, or political motives. The fifth provision specifically mentions forcible feeding. It stemmed from British treatment of Irish Republican hunger strikers. When patients refuse nourishment, medical personnel should not provide it. Before deciding that a prisoner lacks the capacity to make an informed refusal, a doctor should seek confirmation from another physician. In the sixth and final provision, the WMA promises to support and encourage doctors who refuse to condone torture and inhuman punishment.

The Declaration of Tokyo addressed recurrent abuses by physicians, occurring in recent decades in Chile, Uruguay, Syria, Colombia, Spain, South Africa, the Soviet Union, Great Britain, Iraq, and elsewhere. Many torture victims were examined at the Rehabilitation and Research Centre for Torture Victims in Copenhagen. In one report, 4 percent of torture victims examined described nontherapeutic administration of drugs by doctors, and 5 percent said that a doctor was present during their torture. Some doctors gave advice as to whether the torture should continue.

The World Medical Association was planned at an informal meeting of physicians held in London in July of 1945. Its first general assembly met in Geneva, Switzerland, two years later. It included delegations from all continents, but the membership varied over time. At the 1975 assembly, the United States was not represented, but Canada and Great Britain were. Each continent sent at least one delegation.

The Declaration of Tokyo built on earlier WMA resolutions. The Declaration of Geneva, adopted by the 2d General Assembly (1948), declared: "I will not use my medical knowledge contrary to the laws of humanity." The International Code of Medical Ethics, adopted in 1949 at the 3d General Assembly in London, added such directives as: "A physician shall act only in the patient's interest when providing medical care which might have the effect of weakening the physical and mental condition of the patient." Similar language is included in the WMA's Regulations in Time of Armed Conflict, adopted in 1956 (later edited and amended) by the 10th Assembly, held in Havana; these regulations also strictly forbid human experimentation on prisoners and populations under occupation.

Allegations of British abuses in Northern Ireland placed the torture issue on the WMA agenda. Such abuses accounted for the specific mention of forcible feeding. These issues had been raised by P. A. Farrelly and Derek Stevenson at the 1974 Congress. They and other members of the Irish and British associations collaborated in the Tokyo Declaration's composition. Those associations drafted a working paper, as did the French Medical Confederation and WMA council chair André Wynen.

When the council met in Paris in March of 1975, it revised the declaration and placed it on the agenda of October's World Medical Assembly. The British Medical Association had wanted specific mention of regimes that equated opposition with mental disorder, thereby justifying "treatment" in a hospital or prison. The French working paper urged that physicians maintain an attitude of "active neutrality." The declaration hints at both concerns, but neither was expressly included.

The WMA's concern coincided with actions against torture in other forums. One spur was the United Nations General Assembly session in the fall of 1974. A resolution as phrased initially would have directed the World Health Organization (WHO) to draft ethical guidelines for physicians concerning torture and interrogation. The WMA lobbied successfully for language that would allow it to assume a major role in drafting such guidelines.

The U.N. General Assembly addressed the practices of torture by unanimously adopting the Declaration on Torture on December 9, 1975. Amnesty International called it "the most important human rights document since the. . . Universal Declaration of Human Rights," adopted in 1948. Amnesty International's Campaign Against Torture publicized the issue through publications and conferences. The International Council on Nurses issued a policy statement in August, 1975, clarifying nurses' obligation to take action should they be made aware of ill-treatment of detainees.

The Tokyo Declaration was approved by the 350 delegates in attendance. One who did not attend was the secretary-general, Sir William Refshauge. The Japanese government would not issue entry visas to delegates from South Africa, and Sir William was committed to a conference which included all national sections of the WMA, regardless of politics. South Africa's apartheid policies, and the proper role of professional associations such as the WMA, would continue to be debated as physicians sought to give meaning to the Declaration of Tokyo.

Impact of Event

The WMA proclaims that "its voice is authoritative, being the considered opinion of many medical experts from every region of the world." The Declaration of Tokyo is accorded great authority by professional associations; the reputation of the WMA, however, has been called into question.

Physicians' associations and publications praised the declaration. *The Medical Journal of Australia* called it a "courageous and responsible statement"; and indicated that "by it WMA has enhanced its own stature as the one existing world voice for a profession which has much to give to the world, but which is to some extent under siege." The American Medical Association (AMA) journal provided a brief description in January of 1976; when it rejoined the WMA in 1977 and began to play an active role, the AMA publicized and praised the declaration. The declaration had a ripple effect, with additional groups noticing, publicizing, and endorsing it over the years. In 1987, *Surgical Neurology* declared that, as an international journal, it should take a strong position against torture. It suggested that the most important function of the declaration (which it published in full) was "to serve as a reminder to governments and to the world community that physicians are staunchly opposed to the cruel treatment of human beings."

Member associations of the WMA and individual physicians found occasion to invoke the declaration in refusing to associate themselves with abusive practices. Once the Pinochet regime allowed doctors to form a medical association with some autonomy, the Chilean Medical Association strongly condemned the physicians who were accessories to torture. The Uruguayan Medical Association cited the Declaration of Tokyo as well as United Nations documents in censuring two physicians, one of whom was an association member.

The Declaration of Tokyo was followed by related action of other professional organizations. The World Psychiatric Association, for example, unanimously adopted the Declaration of Hawaii (1977) condemning the political use of psychiatry. There were also echoes in the human rights community. Amnesty International stated in its annual report in 1976 that the WMA's action demonstrated that "There is no doubt that NGOs [nongovernmental organizations] can play and are playing an invaluable role in promoting international law and guidelines to prevent torture."

One group of critics implied that the declaration goes too far. Raj Jandoo, a forensic scientist, complained that the principles were too abstract; they fail "to appreciate the extreme situations that some doctors must endure in countries where repressive measures exist." Such criticisms were partially responsible for United Nations members' conclusion that the Tokyo Declaration was not enough, and that the United Nations should adopt a supplementary set of ethical principles.

In December of 1982, the United Nations General Assembly acted. Its principles were based on the WMA's declaration but also incorporated the concerns of Amnesty International and other groups. The U.N. principles applied to all health personnel, whereas the Tokyo Declaration applied only to physicians. WMA leaders voiced concern about language that might absolve a military or police doctor who was present during torture. A 1978 draft of the United Nations principles would have instructed physicians "obliged by force to contravene certain aspects of these principles" to "reduce to the minimum the harmful effects" of their maltreatment.

Although it would be dubious speculation to attribute physicians' increasing consciousness about human rights to the WMA declaration, it is certain that this consciousness led in some cases to the exposure of torture. For example, police surgeons in Northern Ireland provided documentation of ostensibly "self-inflicted" injuries that revealed a pattern of abuse. New physicians groups investigate and report on human rights conditions, among them Physicians for Human Rights (a U.S. group) and the French Medecin sans Frontieres (Doctors Without Borders).

The WMA has continued to address human rights issues. In response to the first execution by intravenous injection, carried out in Oklahoma, Secretary-General André Wynen issued a press release declaring that "no physician should be required to be an active participant" and that "acting as an executioner is not the practice of medicine." The thirty-fourth World Medical Assembly held in Lisbon, Portugal, in 1981 passed a Resolution on Physician Participation in Capital Punishment endorsing the press release and adding stronger language, that "it is unethical for physicians to participate in capital punishment." Certification of death, however, could be performed ethically.

There are certainly limits to the WMA's influence. Many physicians are unaware of its existence, preferring to participate in national medical associations if at all. The association candidly acknowledges what it calls "a lamentable lack of awareness among the profession itself about the nature of the WMA's work." The 1990's brought hopes for change within the WMA and elsewhere. Soviet and East European physicians welcomed opportunites to participate in such international organizations. The WMA hoped to induce its former sections to return, hoping that a return to its former size might provide greater financial stability and added impact for its declarations, among them the Declaration of Tokyo.

Bibliography

Amnesty International. *Codes of Professional Ethics.* 2d ed. London: Author, 1984. This pamphlet includes the text of the Declaration of Tokyo, a WMA resolution on physician participation in capital punishment, and other codes. Thoughtful introductory essays by Alfred Heijder and Herman van Geuns. No reference features.

British Medical Association. *The Medical Profession and Human Rights: Handbook for a Changing Agenda.* New York: Palgrave, 2001. Thorough, well-researched account of the role of doctors and medical professionals in acts of abuse, torture, and human rights violations. Bibliography and index.

Gordon, Neve, and Ruchama Marton, eds. *Torture: Human Rights, Medical Ethics and the Case of Israel.* Highlands, N.J.: Zed Books, 1995. An examination of the reported torture of Palestinian prisoners and the role of medical ethics codes in stopping it. Appendices and index.

McLean, Sheila. *Old Law, New Medicine: Medical Ethics and Human Rights.* New York: New York University Press, 1999. Scholarly examination of the implications of medical policies on human rights. Includes bibliographical references and index.

Stover, Eric, and Elena O. Nightingale, eds. *The Breaking of Bodies and Minds: Torture, Psychiatric Abuse, and the Health Professions.* New York: W. H. Freeman, 1985. Excellent reader. Essays address cases in which medical professionals have been perpetrators and victims of human rights abuses. The essay by Stover and Michael Nelson, "Medical Action Against Torture," describes the efforts of the WMA and other organizations. Useful appendices include ethical codes and a list of organizations. Index; bibliography organized by category.

World Medical Association. *Handbook of Declarations.* London: Author, 1985. This pamphlet contains a brief description of the WMA and English, French, and Spanish texts of its declarations up to its date of publication. Declarations on general ethical principles and capital punishment are of special interest. No reference features.

World Medical Journal. The World Medical Association's semimonthly publication. Includes reports from the secretary-general and articles covering WMA congresses and declarations. Interactions with the World Health Organization and national medical associations are described from the WMA perspective.

Arthur Blaser

United Nations Issues Declaration Against Torture

Category of event: Health and medical rights; international norms; prisoners' rights
Time: December 9, 1975
Locale: United Nations, New York City

> *The United Nations' declaration against torture and other cruel, inhuman, or degrading treatment of accused persons led to a number of conventions on human rights*

Principal personages:

ELEANOR ROOSEVELT (1884-1962), the chair and the moving spirit of the Human Rights Commission of the United Nations that promulgated the 1948 Universal Declaration of Human Rights

ANDREI SAKHAROV (1921-1989), a Russian theoretical physicist and human rights activist, recipient of the 1975 Nobel Peace Prize

NELSON MANDELA (1918-   ), a black South African political leader who was sentenced to life imprisonment in 1964 for his political activities against apartheid

Summary of Event

Prior to World War II, nations rarely were willing to allow foreign interference regarding public officials' treatment of their own citizens. This attitude changed quickly after the war. The revised attitude, a new international outlook, was connected with the horrors committed by the Axis Powers.

The idea of human rights as having a global or universal application goes back many centuries. The concept of human rights sprouted from a philosophy that speculated about the purpose of government and the worth of the individual person. Human rights were predicated on the belief that the human being existed for the good of himself and that government was established to protect certain innate or natural rights of the individual. Theology, especially in the West, gave credibility to the church's argument of the infinite significance of human beings as creations by and for God. The central objective of human rights was to assign a set of rules to clarify the relationship between government and the individual. Most explanations of this relationship held that individuals had specific obligations to government or the state, and government, in turn, had an equal, if not more compelling, duty to defend the inalienable rights of the individual.

History shows two major periods in which human rights made important headway in the West and eventually engulfed at least the imagination of non-Western states and intellectuals. The initial wave had its emergence in the seventeenth century and its finale in the late eighteenth century. English, French, and American thinkers such as John Locke, Voltaire, and James Madison claimed that human beings were imbued with fundamental rights that came from God or from Nature and that such rights were to be respected by government and could be invoked by the people as justification for revolution against a harsh government. The Lockean concept is seen most profoundly in the American Declaration of Independence (1776) and in the French Declaration of the Rights of Man and the Citizen (1789). Natural rights as basic civil rights were incorporated into the constitutions of a considerable number of countries.

The second eruption of human rights concern and agitation occurred in the 1930's. It grew out of revulsion against genocide and massive violations of the rights of accused persons by totalitarian regimes. The concept of human rights was strengthened by the defeat of totalitarian countries by the United States and its allies. The inhuman treatment of millions of people by the Nazis prompted the founders of the United Nations at the Conference of San Francisco in 1945 to place priority on the formulation of a declaration on fundamental human rights. The charter of the new United Nations required the enactment of appropriate declarations and conventions to safeguard human rights. It was unclear how diverse nations, democracies and communist nations alike, could agree on an international bill of rights.

In 1946, President Harry S. Truman appointed Eleanor Roosevelt, the widow of president Franklin D. Roosevelt, to lead the United States' delegation to the United Nations Commission on Human Rights. She became chair of the commission and guided its proceedings through unstable political waters. Roosevelt understood that the two superpowers viewed human rights differently; her job would be to blend the differences into an acceptable international bill of rights. The United States wanted a bill stressing political freedom, free speech, and freedom from cruel and unusual punishment, while the Soviets and their allies wanted to underscore economic freedoms such as the right to a decent standard of living, adequate housing, and affordable food.

The drafting and adoption process of the Commission on Human Rights took two years. On the night of December 10, 1948, in Paris, the Universal Declaration of Human Rights was approved by the General Assembly. The Universal Declaration was only a recommendation and did not bind nations to its lofty principles. The communists' economic freedoms were prominently set in the declaration: "Everyone has the right to a standard of living adequate for the health and well-being of himself and of his family, including food, clothing, housing and medical care." The declaration also offered protection from arbitrary arrest, detention, or exile, but "arbitrary" was not defined. This was only a beginning; the Universal Declaration, if it were to have genuine meaning, needed to be backed up with international treaties and enforcement agencies.

It took more than twenty years to reach that end. In 1966, the General Assembly accepted draft texts of two treaties as the definitive basis for an International Bill of Rights, the International Covenant on Civil and Political Rights and the International Covenant on Economic, Social, and Cultural Rights. Another decade passed before the two covenants entered into force in 1976. More than eighty nations have become signatories of those treaties.

In addition to these two treaties, known as the International Bill of Rights, several other international norms were established by the United Nations. One grouping has the status of recommendation, instructing nations what is right to do in respect to the treatment of their citizens. The second grouping is that of binding treaties.

Conventions or treaties are legally binding and thus require a large amount of time to draft and enact by the U.N. General Assembly. A declaration simply announces a principle or norm of what the international community considers to be appropriate behavior within certain contexts. Nevertheless, the declarations are essential in understanding the conventions, which require nations to observe and enforce the edicts of the United Nations. Accession to conventions by states is not always clear and their enforcement is unsure. Some conventions grew quickly and logically from declarations, such as the convention against genocide. Others were more laborious. The declaration against torture falls into that category.

The Declaration on the Protection of All Persons from Being Subjected to Torture and Other Cruel, Inhuman or Degrading Treatment or Punishment was a major triumph for the United Nations, as it struck at the internal norms of the nation-state. It demanded that public officials renounce and thoroughly reject what many people believe to be an innate instinct of the human species—to inflict pain on those persons who violate taboos and norms of the soci-

André Sakharov, whose protests against Soviet human rights abuses helped bring him a Nobel Peace Prize in 1975. (© The Nobel Foundation)

ety. The declaration exactingly defines torture, for example, as "intentionally inflicted by or at the instigation of a public official on a person for such purposes as obtaining from him or a third person information or confession." Torture, the declaration states, is an offense to human dignity; not even a public emergency can be used by public officials to justify torture. States must take requisite measures to prevent torture, and torture in all states is to be regarded as an offense against their criminal laws. Alleged victims of torture are given the right to impartial examination, and victims of torture will have redress at law. Any information gained from torture may not be used as evidence against any person.

The twelve articles of the declaration on torture contain reasonable guidelines for governments to monitor their own public officials. The U.N. convention on torture, following in 1984, gave grit to the convictions declared in the 1975 declaration.

Impact of Event

Ironically, in the same year as the U.N. General Assembly's declaration against torture, Andrei Sakharov, the father of the Soviet hydrogen bomb, received the Nobel Peace Prize for his advocacy of human rights and subsequent exile to Gorky. Sakharov had come to realize the monstrosity of his invention and had worked with deep conviction and passion for peace and protection of political critics of the Soviet government. He called compatriots to demand political equality and the right of the Soviet people to make choices. Nelson R. Mandela, a black political activist in South Africa, was sentenced, at the Rivonia trial in 1964, to life imprisonment for antigovernment activities. Mandela described himself as an African patriot who was working for the establishment of a nonracial democracy. There was little notice of Mandela's original imprisonment. Later events outside South Africa, specifically in New York City at the United Nations, focused a spotlight on the plights of Nelson Mandela and other prisoners of conscience during the course of the next twenty-five years.

The U.N. Declaration on the Protection of All Persons from Being Subjected to Torture and Other Cruel, Inhuman or Degrading Treatment or Punishment led to various other declarations on human rights and to a number of treaties. The impact of these pronouncements and treaties is immeasurable. They established a global norm for proper treatment of accused persons and actually led to the liberation of certain political prisoners. Both Sakharov and Mandela benefited from the international condemnation of cruel, inhuman, and degrading treatment of dissidents. Sakharov and Mandela were not only set at liberty by the governments of their respective countries, the Soviet Union and the Republic of South Africa, but also permitted to assume well-defined and prominent roles in the political institutions that they had previously attempted to reform.

Persistent pressure, through the declarations and treaties on human rights promulgated by the United Nations and its member states, had a surprising impact on communist countries concerning the way their governments treated accused persons and in democratizing their political processes. The most pivotal effect was on the Soviet Union itself, an effect shown by Mikhail Gorbachev's declaration of his policy of *glasnost* in 1985. With the dissolution of the Soviet Union into a loose grouping of independent states in 1991-1992, a third period of human rights seemed to be starting.

Bibliography

Amnesty International Report on Torture. New York: Farrar, Straus and Giroux, 1975. An excellent account of the history of torture. Western societies often practiced their much-acclaimed values, demonstrating respect for the rights of the individual, but torture has been common during times of war or social stress.

Bailey, George. *The Making of Andrei Sakharov.* New York: Penguin Books, 1988. A solid account of the factors shaping Sakharov's passion for peace and proper treatment of prisoners of conscience. Sakharov's personal courage is majestic and justifies the cliché that one man can make a difference.

Burgers, Herman, and Hans Danelius. *The United Nations Convention Against Torture: A Handbook on the Convention Against Torture and Other Cruel, Inhuman, or Degrading Treatment or Punishment.* London: Martinus Nijhoff, 1988. This is a comprehensive treatise on human rights since World War II. Especially useful for scholars and general readers who want to understand the major efforts of the United Nations to establish a global standard for treatment of accused persons by public officials.

Glendon, Mary Ann. *A World Made New: Eleanor Roosevelt and the Universal Declaration of Human Rights.* New York: Random House, 2001. Explores the history of the declaration and Roosevelt's role in its adoption.

Lauren, Paul Gordon. *The Evolution of International Human Rights: Visions Seen.* Philadelphia: University of Pennsylvania Press, 1998. This scholarly book was written for the fiftieth anniversary of the Universal Declaration of Human Rights.

Rodley, Nigel S. *The Treatment of Prisoners Under International Law.* New York: Oxford University Press, 1987. Describes the efforts of the United Nations and other intergovernmental organizations to eliminate torture and other mistreatments by governments. The brutal treatment of peoples by the Nazis gave rise to an international agreement to improve the human condition throughout the world.

Claude Hargrove

Argentina Conducts "Dirty War" Against Leftists

Category of event: Atrocities and war crimes; political freedom
Time: 1976-1979
Locale: Argentina

> *For three years, the Argentine military government fought a "dirty war" against left-wing terrorism, sweeping those suspected of "subversion" off the streets and out of their homes*

Principal personages:

JUAN PERÓN (1895-1974), the populist president of Argentina from 1946 to 1955 and again from 1973 until his death in 1974

JACOBO TIMERMAN (1923-1999), a prominent Jewish publisher of an Argentine newspaper which criticized the military regime

RAÚL ALFONSÍN (1926-   ), the president of Argentina from 1983 to 1989, appointed the Commission on the Disappeared (CONDEP)

Summary of Event

From 1976 to 1979, the Argentine military government conducted a relentless campaign against left-wing guerrillas. The military believed that the only way to defeat communism was to wage a "dirty war" which severed the insurgents from the population and excised them from the nation. Military death squads roamed the streets, picking up suspects and whisking them off to secret military installations where they were often beaten, tortured, and disposed of without a word, let alone a trial. No written records of the whereabouts of the *desaparecidos* ("the disappeared") were kept by the military *junta*, adding uncertainty to a culture of fear which gripped the nation.

The roots of the "dirty war" can be traced to the dominant figure of twentieth century Argentina, Juan Domingo Perón. The populist Perón curried the favor of the nation's working classes during his first nine-year stint as president (1946-1955). His ideology was ambiguous enough to appeal to different social classes. As long as the state-directed economy performed well, Perón was able to hold his seemingly contradictory coalition together, but when the nation's economy soured during his second term, the increasingly dictatorial Perón created scapegoats out of the Roman Catholic Church and the military. The strategy backfired, and he was ousted by a military coup in 1955.

Although Perón was forced to leave Argentina, his movement, *Peronismo*, was never really defeated. From exile in General Francisco Franco's Spain, Perón plotted his return. Successive military regimes employed various strategies to destroy his movement, such as purging sympathizers from the bureaucracy and outlawing his Justicialist party or permitting Peronist participation in national elections only to annul the results of the elections when the Peronists proved too successful. A new generation of Peronist youth challenged the establishment.

On occasion, the military responded by turning the government over to civilian politicians, and at times it staged coups and resorted to repression to quell unrest. Urban guerrillas opposed the seemingly endless succession of ineffectual regimes, targeting prominent politicians and influential businesspeople for kidnappings and ransom. Neither the military nor the civilian governments that governed during the unstable period between 1955 and 1973 proved capable of managing the Argentine economy, let alone the social peace.

Perón believed that if his movement were to succeed, he had to mobilize the masses. He ambiguously gave his support from exile to both the young revolutionaries of the far left and the labor unions that remembered his populist regime fondly. There was a revolutionary left, led by elements both within the Peronist movement (for example, *Los Montoneros*) and outside it (most notably, *El Ejército Revolucionario Popular,* or ERP). Although these groups did not share a common ideology, they were committed to traumatizing the nation by committing violent acts against those they had identified as oppressors: the military and the police, along with their collaborators, capitalist entrepreneurs.

The military leadership, steeped in the anticommunist ideology of the Cold War, saw these insurgents as a threat to national security. The guerrillas had helped create an atmosphere in which it was possible for the military leadership to insist that nothing short of a policy of extermination was sufficient to rid society of left-wing violence. The military responded by organizing and permitting the formation of right-wing death squads to retaliate against guerrilla groups. By 1973, the country was on the verge of anarchy. In a last-gasp measure, the military government permitted Juan Perón, now aging and infirm, to return from exile and participate in the upcoming elections.

Perón received an impressive 62 percent of the vote, a reflection of the electorate's desire for a fresh approach to Argentina's problems. Upon his return,

After eighteen years in exile, former Argentine president Juan Perón returned to power in 1973 but died the following year. (Library of Congress)

Perón made it clear that he would not tolerate left-wing insurgency. He cracked down on the Marxist ERP and his own movement's *Montoneros*. His conservative approach delighted the military and its constituency, but it alienated many members of the Peronist youth, who had looked upon the Argentine president as a leader committed to meaningful reform. In July, 1974, Perón died, leaving the presidency in the hands of his third wife, Isabelita, a former cabaret dancer. Argentina slipped into chaos as the economy careened out of control. Inflation reached 700 percent by early 1976. Señora Perón's spiritual adviser organized death squads, most notably the Argentine Anti-Communist Alliance (AAA), against *Montoneros*, Jews, and suspected leftists. The guerrillas continued their deliberately provocative attacks, with an estimated ten thousand Argentines actively involved with the insurgents. From bank robberies and ransomings, the guerrillas had built a formidable war chest of approximately $150 million. During the last month of Señora Perón's rule, *La Opinión*, a Buenos Aires daily newspaper, estimated that there was a political killing every five hours and a bomb attack every three. The question became when the military would take power, not if.

Argentina's best-predicted coup took place in March, 1976. The military *junta* gave itself sweeping powers. Congress was dismissed, the Supreme Court was replaced with military appointees, and the *junta* took command of the universities. Although the Argentine *junta* borrowed the tactic of "disappearances" from the Brazilian military, which had used it ruthlessly during the 1960's, the Argentine generals refined the practice. By not placing suspects under official arrest, they left no legal trail. *Los desaparecidos* were victims in a deliberate tactic designed to terrorize the country.

Suspects were taken from their homes and offices to detention centers, and their homes were ransacked and looted. Most of the disappeared lived the rest of their lives in the detention centers, blindfolded, forbidden to talk to one another, hungry, and living in filth. The military employed electric shocks, rape, near-drownings, and constant beatings, not only to discover information, for very few had knowledge of left-wing activities, but also to break the prisoners psychologically and spiritually. Most of those who somehow survived the torture were killed. When disposal of the bodies presented a problem, the military simply buried the dead in mass unmarked graves or loaded the prisoners into military planes, flew them over the Atlantic, and then threw them out. Some were drugged or killed beforehand, but others were alive and conscious when they left the plane.

The generals also implemented a war against certain ideas. The military sought to create an "appropriate" culture based on the fight against communism, simple patriotic values, the family, and Christianity. The persecution of journalists, the use of terror to silence educators, artists, and writers, and the widespread blacklisting of individuals all resembled Nazi Germany. At the University of Buenos Aires alone, more than fifteen hundred professors were replaced by military supporters. The military contended that they were only redressing the balance in public education, as university politics had become dominated by left-wing ideologies which supported revolutionary activities.

Curricula were altered. Political science, sociology, and psychology were suspect because they were heavily dependent on foreign influences and had been much favored by left-wing students and academics. Although John Wayne was a particular favorite of the *junta*, many American movies were banned. The music of Bob Dylan, Joan Baez, and the Beatles was forbidden on the airwaves. Books idealizing the Nazi regime in Germany went back into print in Buenos Aires. Mass public book burnings took place as the writings of Mao Zedong, V. I. Lenin, and Che Guevara were singled out for immolation. Citizens burned their own books to eliminate anything that might get them in trouble. Sex education books were banned, reflecting the strong puritanical mores of the regime.

The military regime also felt an obligation to defeat communism internationally. To this end, they helped militaries in Peru, Chile, and Paraguay in their struggle against leftist movements. In addition, the Argentines gave members of Somoza's Nicaraguan National Guard sanctuary in their Managua, Nicaragua, embassy after the victory of the Sandinistas in July, 1979. They further aided the ex-National Guardsmen by setting up a training school to organize the first "contras," or counter revolutionaries, who opposed the Sandinista regime. Although the military campaign destroyed the guerrilla movement, it prompted outrage and resistance both within and outside Argentina. U.S. president Jimmy Carter was an outspoken opponent of the military government, eventually cutting military and economic aid to the regime.

Resistance to the military sweeps came from one unexpected source. A group of fourteen mothers who had lost their sons petitioned the military-controlled judiciary for writs of *habeas corpus* in 1977. When their pleas fell on deaf ears, they went to the Plaza de Mayo in downtown Buenos Aires, armed with only their identity cards, and directly challenged the military to return their loved ones. The mothers returned each Thursday to the square. The protest movement grew and became a political statement on behalf of all of *los desaparecidos*. At first, the military ignored the protests, but when foreign reporters publicized the demonstrations, the government cracked down. The movement was infiltrated by the military, some organizers were harassed and arrested, others were driven off the streets, and finally twelve mothers were "disappeared."

Another case which showered international attention on *los desaparecidos* was the Jacobo Timerman affair. Timerman had founded a prominent Buenos

Aires newspaper, *La Opinión*. The paper expressed muted disapproval of the military regime, as Timerman was worried that publicity of any individual case might likely lead to that person's death. Timerman was "disappeared" and taken to a detention center. The negative publicity generated by an international campaign probably saved Timerman's life. He was released and sent into exile, where he penned a powerful account of his capture and treatment in the detention center.

Impact of Event

The worst of the repression had ended by 1979. The guerrillas had been decimated and the regime was in complete control. If the military proved successful in quashing the insurrection, however, it did not prove as diligent in righting Argentina's troubled economy. Rising indebtedness, hyperinflation, and a worldwide recession in 1980-1981 combined to shake national confidence in the military's ability to rule the nation. A disastrous military decision to invade the Falkland Islands (or as they are called in Argentina, Las Malvinas) in the spring of 1982 proved to be the final straw. In 1983, the military, now discredited, turned the government over to civilian politicians.

Elections were held in 1983, and Raúl Alfonsín won the presidency. Alfonsín was one of the few politicians who had spoken out publicly against the repression during the dirty war. During his campaign, he made two promises to the nation: He would investigate the disappearances and prosecute those responsible. He appointed a Commission on the Disappeared (CONDEP) with full powers to investigate and report.

The identities of 8,960 citizens who had disappeared were conclusively established. CONDEP stated that twenty thousand Argentines were arrested during military rule, and many of them were tortured or raped. Two million had fled the country to escape the possibility of death or imprisonment. The great majority of the disappeared were young adults, usually educated and politically aware. CONDEP concluded that the great majority were kidnapped during the first two years of the *junta*'s rule and then murdered in 1978, when the international call for information about *los desaparecidos* reached its height.

CONDEP's report fulfilled Alfonsín's first promise to investigate the tragedy. Next, a series of trials was held to prosecute past officials for criminal acts. For Alfonsín, it was essential that the process vindicate not only justice but also the Argentine legal system. After so many illegal acts, Argentina, if it was to persevere as a nation, would have to come to terms with its past through the rule of law. Alfonsín ordered the arrest of all nine generals who formed the three ruling *juntas* from 1976 to 1983. The new government passed a comprehensive statute which dealt with the issue of criminal responsibility.

The nine commanders went on trial on April 22, 1985. The highly publicized proceedings lasted five months. Although capital punishment was permissible for these offenses, the government prosecutor asked for life imprisonment for five of the nine defendants and lesser sentences for the rest. Two of the generals were given life sentences—Jorge Videla and Emilio Massera, commanders of the army and navy, respectively. Four others were acquitted, although three of the four were later convicted by separate military tribunals and sentenced to prison.

Some citizens were outraged by the court's decisions, and many wanted much tougher sentences. The court's policy of variable sentences was important for several reasons. It showed that the judiciary was politically independent of the government, which had called for heavier sentences. In other words, the trials were an exercise in due process, not political vengeance. More important, it made clear that there are degrees of guilt in crimes against humanity. The trials of junior officers were more troublesome. Drawing the line between following orders and taking responsibility proved more difficult for the judiciary. Although five hundred other members of the military were formally charged, few were ever brought to trial. Political considerations weighed heavily on Alfonsín and his successor, Carlos Saúl Menem. An attack on the military was regarded in some quarters as divisive and politically unwise, since the armed forces were needed to maintain the peace and prop up the fledgling civilian government. A number of attempted coups during Alfonsín's and Menem's terms graphically demonstrated how tenuous democracy was in Argentina. In 1989, Menem passed a series of general pardons which in effect dismissed the charges pending against all those who were tried and sentenced under the Alfonsín regime for their participation in the dirty war.

Bibliography

Argentina Comisión Nacional Sobre la Desaparición de Personas. *Nunca Más: The Report of the Argentine National Commission on the Disappeared.* New York: Farrar, Straus & Giroux, 1986. An abridged version, translated into English, of the CONDEP report that detailed the Argentine dirty war. The commission conducted thousands of interviews with eyewitnesses to produce this exhaustive analysis of these atrocities.

Feitlowitz, Marguerite. *A Lexicon of Terror: Argentina and the Legacies of Torture.* Oxford University Press, 1998. An analysis of life under this oppressive regime. Features descriptions of what prisoners had to endure in concentration camps.

Lewis, Paul H. *Guerrillas and Generals: The Dirty War in Argentina.* Westport, Conn.: Praeger, 2001. An examination of the causes of the dirty war. A balanced and exhaustive study of this period in Argentina's history.

Rock, David. *Argentina, 1516-1982: From Spanish Colonization to the Falklands War.* Berkeley: University of California Press, 1985. A solid scholarly survey of Argentine history which provides a thoughtful background to the dirty war.

Simpson, John, and Jana Bennett. *The Disappeared and the Mothers of the Plaza.* New York: St. Martin's Press, 1985. A hard-hitting journalistic account of the military government's policies, written by two British Broadcasting Corporation reporters. Solid investigative reporting is combined with obvious empathy for the victims of the military regime.

Valenzuela, Luisa. *Other Weapons.* Hanover, N.H.: Ediciones del Norte, 1990. A collection of revealing short stories, by one of Argentina's most prominent writers, dealing with a society coming to grips with the dirty war.

Verbitsky, Horacio. *The Flight: Confessions of an Argentine Dirty Warrior.* Translated by Esther Allen. New York: New Press, 1996. A memoir by a participant in the dirty war.

Allen Wells

IRA Prisoner Dies After Hunger Strike

Category of event: Health and medical rights; prisoners' rights
Time: February, 1976
Locale: Wakefield Prison, West Yorkshire, England

> *In an attempt to obtain special political status from the British government, IRA member Francis Stagg undertook a fast that led to his death*

Principal personages:
FRANCIS STAGG (1941-1976), a resident of Coventry, England, who was imprisoned in 1973 for IRA activities
ROY JENKINS (1920-   ), a Labour Party politician and British home secretary
HAROLD WILSON (1916-1995), the Labour Party leader and prime minister of Great Britain
LIAM COSGRAVE (1920-   ), the prime minister of the Irish Republic

Summary of Event

During the twentieth century, few problems strained the British political and judicial systems more than the demands of Irish nationalism. Decades of agitation, followed by a civil war, finally produced the uneasy compromise of 1922 that granted most of the island virtual independence but allowed six counties in Ulster to remain part of the British system as the province of Northern Ireland. This province, dominated by Protestants, obtained its own parliament at Stormont and exercised considerable control over Northern Ireland's internal affairs. For decades, the Protestant establishment systematically used this power to discriminate against the Roman Catholic minority in matters such as jobs, housing, and political representation.

Militants, chiefly represented by the Irish Republican Army (IRA), never reconciled themselves to the concept of a divided Ireland and periodically resorted to acts of terrorism and violence in Northern Ireland, the Irish Republic, and Britain in order to achieve their dream of a united Ireland free of any British control. The situation became particularly explosive in 1968 with the birth of a Catholic Irish civil rights movement in Ulster, patterned in many respects on the contemporary struggle for justice of African Americans in the

503

United States. The marches and demonstrations inevitably sparked violence by both Protestant and Catholic extremists and resulted in British troops being sent to the troubled province in 1969 to try to restore order and protect the civilian population.

In response to the tumult throughout Ulster, the IRA split into two factions. The more moderate wing, known as the Official IRA, expressed willingness to work with the parliaments in Belfast, Dublin, and London to achieve a political solution. The militant wing, infused with idealistic nationalism and a leftist political agenda, repudiated compromise and pledged allegiance to the traditional program of physical force to expel the British presence. Throughout the 1970's, this group, known as the Provisional IRA, or Provos, continued a campaign of bombings, assassinations, and other violent acts that reduced Northern Ireland to chaos and created serious problems for the British government regarding the proper treatment and status of IRA prisoners.

In an attempt to break the back of the IRA, in August, 1971, the government of Northern Ireland introduced internment without trial. By the end of the year, more than fifteen hundred suspects had been arrested. This failed to crush the IRA and succeeded only in alienating a larger proportion of the Catholic population, who saw internment as a discriminatory measure that violated basic civil rights. Perceiving themselves to be political prisoners rather than criminals, IRA inmates demanded special status, which essentially meant that they could wear civilian clothes, refuse penal labor, and have free association with other such internees. In order to obtain special status, several IRA prisoners in 1972 resorted to hunger strikes, a traditional weapon used by Irish nationalists to draw attention to their demands. With several such prisoners near death, the government of Prime Minister Edward Heath, which had recently abolished the Stormont Parliament and assumed direct control over the province, granted special status to those found guilty of politically motivated crimes.

The issue of special status did not limit itself solely to Northern Ireland. Four years later the Labour government of Harold Wilson found itself confronting yet another hunger strike, this time by an Irish prisoner in an English jail. The thirty-four-year-old prisoner was Francis Stagg, a native of the Irish Republic who had lived in Coventry, England, since 1959, where he had been a bus driver. Coventry has a large Irish population, and Stagg became involved in local IRA activities. An English court, after his arrest in 1973, sentenced Stagg to ten years in prison for conspiring with others to attack targets in Coventry and for participating in the management of the local IRA unit. In February, 1975, he was transferred to Wakefield Prison in West Yorkshire to serve the remainder of his sentence. In December, for the fourth time since his incarceration, Stagg embarked upon a hunger strike, demanding that the government transfer him to a prison in Northern Ireland, where he would automatically enjoy special political status.

When confronted with such an act of defiance, authorities had three basic options: concede to the demands, resort to force feeding, or allow the hunger striker to die. Previous British governments had shown no consistency in their response. Delours and Marion Price, two sisters imprisoned in London for car bombings in 1973, began a hunger strike during which they were force fed for 206 days before the government agreed to their demand to be transferred to Armagh prison in Ulster. In June, 1974, however, twenty-four-year-old IRA member Michael Gaughan, jailed in England for robbing a London bank, died after a sixty-five-day fast, his demand for transfer having been rejected. The following month Labour Home Secretary Roy Jenkins announced an official policy for dealing with hunger strikers. In the future, they would not be force fed and would be allowed to die unless they asked for medical intervention.

In embarking upon his strike in December, 1975, Stagg was thereby challenging the government to abandon its stated policy. Two days after he began his fast, he received official warning of the consequences of his actions, including the grim reminder that his condition would be allowed to deteriorate unless he specifically asked for medical intervention. On December 19, officials transferred him to the prison hospital, where he received medical supervision and advice, but no forceful steps were taken to prevent the inevitable grievous consequences of his actions.

Throughout the following weeks authorities made food readily available to Stagg, which he repeatedly refused. He was allowed virtually unlimited visits from family and friends. Although remaining steadfast in its refusal to transfer him to a prison in Northern Ireland, the government did indicate it would be sympathetic to a transfer to a penitentiary closer to his wife in Coventry. Stagg rejected this since it did not grant him recognition as a political prisoner.

As death grew imminent, Home Secretary Jenkins reiterated that the government would not give in to blackmail. The government hoped that the leadership of the Provisional IRA would call off the hunger strike, as it had done in January, 1973, when it decided that Chief of Staff San McStiofian's fifty-seven-day fast was serving no productive purpose. This time, however, no such order was forthcoming.

Six relatives, four British members of Parliament, the Auxiliary Bishop of Leeds, and one representative of the IRA's political wing visited Stagg during his final days. The young prisoner remained steadfast in his determination to continue his strike. On February 7, he dictated his will, requesting an IRA funeral with full military honors in his native Ireland. He died on February 12, sixty-one days after beginning his fast. According to his wife Bridie, his final words were, "Peace with everyone." Two days later, an official inquest ruled that Stagg's death was a suicide resulting from cardiac atrophy associated with malnutrition.

The Provos seized upon Stagg's death as an opportunity to stage a grand military funeral honoring their latest martyr. They planned an elaborate 180-mile march from Dublin to a cemetery in County Mayo. The government of Irish prime minister Liam Cosgrave had no intention of permitting such a demonstration by an organization which was illegal in the Irish Republic as well as in the United Kingdom. The Irish government diverted the plane carrying Stagg's body to Shannon airport and refused to release the body until the IRA agreed to take it quietly to County Mayo for interment. Over seven thousand people attended the funeral on February 22. IRA supporters threw stones at some of the eight hundred Irish police gathered to prevent disorder. As his IRA colleagues fired an illegal volley over his grave, Francis Stagg was laid to rest a mere forty yards from the grave of fellow hunger striker Michael Gaughan.

Impact of Event

Provisional IRA leaders had threatened violent retaliation should Stagg be allowed to die, and both British and Irish authorities braced for a wave of deadly reprisals. The British government placed full-page ads in Belfast's leading Catholic newspaper explaining its refusal to accede to Stagg's demands, pointing out that he had been sentenced by a British court for offenses committed in Britain and that he had no official ties with Northern Ireland.

Nevertheless, Stagg's death escalated the level of violence and political tension in Northern Ireland, the Irish Republic, and Britain. The day after his demise, London police defused a bomb at the crowded Oxford Circus underground station, and the same day bomb attacks occurred in Dublin at several department stores and a prominent hotel. The IRA later claimed credit for two explosions in the heart of London on February 22.

The deadliest violence, however, occurred in Ulster, some of it engineered by the Provisionals and some of it resulting from spontaneous rage by the Catholic citizenry. Riots erupted in Belfast and Londonderry, and by February 15 authorities estimated that arsonists and mobs had destroyed property valued at more than £5 million. More than twenty bombs wrecked homes and shops in Northern Ireland in the week following Stagg's death, and eleven people lost their lives. By August, as a result of escalating violence by the IRA and Protestant extremists, more than two hundred had died.

Continuing its no-compromise policy, the British government implemented a previously announced plan to abolish all future special political status for prisoners, effective March 1, 1976. Following the assassination of the British ambassador to Dublin, the Irish government declared a state of emergency and passed strenuous antiterrorist measures, giving the army power to search, arrest, and detain suspects.

The deaths of three young children in Belfast in August, 1976, gave birth to a peace movement led by Betty Williams and Mairead Corrigan. They organized massive demonstrations demanding an end to the violence and garnered more than three hundred thousand signatures on a peace petition by 1977. Hopes that this movement could end the bitter divisions proved illusory.

Five years after Francis Stagg's death, Bobby Sands became the thirteenth Irish nationalist in the twentieth century to starve himself to death, as he vainly attempted to intimidate the Conservative government of Prime Minister Margaret Thatcher into reinstituting special political status for IRA prisoners. Nine other young Irishmen followed him during 1981. The IRA finally called off the campaign late in the year.

Francis Stagg's sacrifice failed to end British rule over Northern Ireland and resulted in no significant change in the way the British handled political prisoners. It did reflect a long-standing belief that hunger strikes could influence public opinion and ultimately force a change in government policies. Such actions had been practiced not only by Irish nationalists but also by individuals as diverse as the British suffragists before World War I and Mohandas Gandhi in India. The 1976 hunger strike was but another example of an attempt to use prisoners to obtain political goals. William McKee, once the main IRA leader in Belfast, had proclaimed, "This war will be won in the prisons." Francis Stagg's 1976 death was yet another fatality reflecting this mentality.

Bibliography

Bartlett, Jonathan, ed. *Northern Ireland.* New York: H. W. Wilson, 1983. This book includes reprints of articles, chapters from books, and speeches that relate to the Irish dilemma. Section 2 contains six articles dealing with the background and nature of various hunger strikes. Includes a bibliography.

Bell, J. Bowyer. *The Gun in Politics: An Analysis of Irish Political Conflict, 1916-1986.* New Brunswick, N.J.: Transaction Books, 1987. Provides worthwhile information on the IRA. Parts 3 and 4 focus on the Ulster troubles related to the issues of terrorism and violence. Includes a bibliographic essay that surveys major works dealing with the Irish issue.

_____. _The IRA, 1968-2000: Analysis of a Secret Army._ Portland, Oreg.: Frank Cass, 2000. An examination of the function, structure, and evolution of the IRA over a period of more than thirty years.

Boyce, David George. _The Irish Question and British Politics, 1868-1986._ New York: St. Martin's Press, 1988. The fourth chapter covers the period 1950-1986 and provides useful information on the political climate of the era and how the Northern Ireland issue affected each major party's decision-making process. Bibliography and index.

Coogan, Tim Pat. _On the Blanket: The H-Block Story._ Dublin: Ward River Press, 1980. Although its main focus is on conditions of political prisoners in Northern Ireland in the late 1970's and early 1980's, Part I of this monograph by an Irish nationalist provides a useful background into the mentality and motivations of IRA prisoners. It also relates their treatment to basic human rights issues.

Flackes, W. D. _Northern Ireland: A Political Directory, 1968-1979._ New York: St. Martin's Press, 1980. Sets the hunger strike in perspective of its era and shows its consequences upon events. Provides a useful chronology of key events and brief biographical sketches of many of the main individuals involved. Also includes a useful directory of names and organizations.

Holland, Jack. _Too Long a Sacrifice: Life and Death in Northern Ireland Since 1969._ New York: Dodd, Mead, 1981. This moving account of the Irish troubles during the 1970's, written by a journalist who is a Belfast native, takes an essentially unbiased approach to the conflict and expertly shows the root causes of Catholic grievances. Chapter 6, "Martyrs," examines the IRA's tactics and motives. Includes a useful annotated glossary of key organizations and an index.

Hull, Roger H. _The Irish Triangle: Conflict in Northern Ireland._ Princeton, N.J.: Princeton University Press, 1976. This monograph, published in the year of Stagg's death, examines the conflict from three perspectives, those of London, Dublin, and Belfast. It provides a scholarly approach to the problems with an analysis of possible solutions. Particularly useful bibliography.

O'Malley, Padraig. _The Uncivil Wars: Ireland Today._ Boston: Beacon Press, 1990. This updated version of a 1983 work by an Irish-born scholar provides a comprehensive analysis of the principal parties and ideologies involved in the Irish conflict. The seventh chapter focuses upon the IRA and the issue of hunger strikes. Includes an index and a bibliography.

Tom L. Auffenberg

South African Government Suppresses Soweto Student Rebellion

Category of event: Atrocities and war crimes; political freedom; revolutions
and rebellions
Time: June 16, 1976
Locale: Johannesburg, South Africa

> *The Soweto Riots of 1976 changed the fundamental relationship between the Afrikaner-dominated regime and the African majority*

Principal personages:

BALTHAZAR JOHANNES (JOHN) VORSTER (1915-1983), the prime minister of
the Republic of South Africa at the time of the Soweto rebellion
JAMES T. KRUGER (1917-   ), the minister of justice under the Vorster regime
DESMOND TUTU (1931-   ), an African national religious and political
leader
DANIEL SECHABO MONTSITSI (1956-   ), a member of the Soweto Eleven
put on trial in the aftermath of Soweto
MAFISON MAROBE (1957-   ), a member of the Soweto Eleven put on trial in
the aftermath of Soweto

Summary of Event

On June 16, 1976, ten thousand African school children in the segregated
public schools of South Africa openly protested against a new regime policy
which required instruction in Afrikaans, the Dutch language of the white minority that controlled government institutions. Afrikaans is the language of
Dutch Afrikaners, who along with the British settled the tip of southern Africa
and eventually colonized the indigenous African population in what is known
today as South Africa.

The Soweto protest was, in part, the outgrowth of more than three hundred
laws passed by the white regime which subjected black Africans to inferior status in every aspect of life from cradle to grave. The black majority suffered
from poverty, unemployment, underemployment, poor health care, segregated housing, and lack of suffrage. White children had eight times as much
money spent on their education as did black children and had only one-third

the number of students in a typical classroom. Laws treating the races differently were known by the euphemism "apartheid," which is a Dutch word meaning "separate development." The name Soweto is actually an acronym which stands for Southwest Township, a sprawling black ghetto on the outskirts of Johannesburg which housed more than one million poor Africans in 1976.

Soweto leaders, including the Very Reverend Desmond Tutu, a national figure, warned political and legal authorities that the township, with a high level of alienation, particularly among its youth, represented a powder keg that could explode at any time. Manie Mulder, chair of the West Rand Bantu Administration Board that governed Soweto, scoffed at the idea, arguing that Soweto's black citizens were perfectly content. In 1974, use of Afrikaans became a political issue before the board that would further divide people by generation, race, and political ideology.

The protest in Soweto began nonviolently with the carrying of placards protesting the language of Afrikaans in classrooms. Students attempted to march to Soweto's largest stadium for a rally, singing and chanting black nationalist and liberation songs. Sowetoians already knew two languages, their own ethnic group's and English. To have Afrikaans, not only a difficult language but a language associated with oppression, forced on students represented the proverbial straw that broke the camel's back. Interpretations differ as to whether the police (which ironically were mostly black, with white supervisors) or students initiated hostilities. As the confrontation unfolded, police used tear gas followed by open gunfire. The students responded with rocks and stones. The students, joined by older teens and young adults, attacked, overturned, and burned police cars, trains, and buses, and set fire to government property and buildings. They attacked and killed two whites. South Africa had never witnessed this level of black rage.

The evening of the first night of the uprising, Minister of Justice James T. Kruger appealed to Sowetoians for calm and asked them to help police do their job. Prime Minister John Vorster was put in an embarrassing position, since the uprising took place on the eve of his meeting with U.S. secretary of state Henry Kissinger. Nevertheless, several days after hostilities began, Vorster warned that the state would use whatever force was necessary to put down the rebellion. Vorster, in a special message to the all-white parliament, argued that the violence was not spontaneous and was meant to polarize the races. Kruger made similar arguments before parliament, claiming that police were not using excessive force, and stating that the presence of young Africans in their twenties suggested that the riots were organized. Evidence uncovered later shows that some of the violence may have been organized, since telephone calls to authorities often preceded violence and the same nationalist placards and slogans were seen in different parts of the country.

The protests and violence spread to other black townships around the country as well as to mostly white and mostly black colleges and universities, one of the latter on the coast of the Indian Ocean, 350 miles from Johannesburg. White students, in a show of support, fought bloody battles with police on campuses as well as in the streets of Johannesburg and Cape Town. In the end, more than six hundred blacks were shot and killed by the police in the Soweto area alone. In the country as a whole, it is estimated that the number of blacks killed may have reached several thousand and that several thousand more may have fled the country to take up arms with the African National Congress, the outlawed black guerrilla organization fighting to overthrow the apartheid regime. Hundreds more were arrested and detained, including Winnie Mandela, wife of Nelson Mandela, the world renowned leader of the African National Congress (ANC). It is hard to develop an accurate count of those killed since the regime was sensitive to international opinion that could influence foreign capital and investment and thus would understate the totals.

The Soweto uprising did not end with the state's suppression of the Soweto rebellion against the language of Afrikaans. A number of blacks were put on trial, with proceedings beginning in July, 1978. The leaders of the uprising who were not killed or who had not fled the country to prevent their prosecution and possible persecution by the state came to be known as the "Soweto Eleven." These eleven were made up of one female and ten males. The defendants were Susan Sibongile Mthembu, Wilson Welile Chief Twala, Daniel Sechabo Montsitsi, Seth Sandile Mazibuko, Mafison Marobe, Jefferson Khotso Wansi Lengane, Ernest Edwin Thabo Ndabeni, Kennedy Kgotsietsile Mogami, Reginald Teboho Mngomezulu, Michael Sello Khiba, and George Nkosinati Yami Twala. These students ranged from sixteen to twenty-one years of age and were charged with sedition.

The state concentrated on two of the eleven defendants, Montsitsi and Marobe. These two were older, more mature, more intellectually sophisticated, and unimpressed by the power of the state regime to determine their fate. In addition, Marobe was known to have connections with the ANC, the organization most hated by the state. Montsitsi was brutally beaten a number of times by state security agents before the trial in an attempt to change his attitude. The state set out to prove that the Soweto Eleven were older, organized instigators and that conditions in Soweto really were not that bad for blacks. The Soweto Eleven contended that the rebellion was a spontaneous event provoked by the police and the poverty-stricken conditions of blacks. Ten of the eleven were eventually convicted of various charges emanating from the Soweto uprising. Nine of the eleven drew suspended sentences. Montsitsi and Marobe, the two primary targets of the prosecution, drew four- and three-year prison terms, respectively.

Impact of Event

The Soweto rebellion continued for months, and many blacks were killed before it was crushed. This incident contributed to South Africa's legacy of racism and oppression in international circles. Additional sanctions were instituted by Western countries as a result. In the past, the regime had put down black rebellions almost instantaneously with brutal shows of force. This was the case in the Sharpeville Massacre in 1960. More than five thousand unarmed black men, women, and children had protested in front of a police station against carrying of passbooks, or internal passports. The police responded without warning with deadly force, shooting at point-blank range. Seventy-two blacks were killed, most shot in the back as they attempted to flee from the barrage of gunfire. Hundreds were wounded.

Soweto is considered a turning point in the black revolution in South Africa to overthrow the system of apartheid and white minority rule. After Soweto, guerrilla and revolutionary activities against the apartheid regime intensified. From the ashes of the Soweto conflict arose the Black Consciousness movement, composed of a number of student organizations committed to self-help and liberation as well as condemnation of the older generation of moderate blacks. By the early 1980's, the regime had begun to institute a number of political reforms aimed at reducing international criticism, attracting greater foreign investment, and dividing the indigenous Asian and colored populace from the black majority.

One of these reforms was the creation of a tricameral legislature. Whites, Asians, and coloreds would have their own chambers, but with the white chamber having veto power over all legislation approved by the other houses. Under this reform, the black majority, 68 percent of the total population in South Africa, still would not have national representation. Lacking representation, blacks had no mechanism to voice their grievances. Black protests against the so-called reforms were the spark for President Pieter Botha to declare a state of emergency in 1985, in which the military and police killed and wounded thousands of protesters and imprisoned thousands more with neither charge nor trial. A second state of emergency was declared as antiapartheid protests, many nonviolent, continued. Thousands were killed or imprisoned.

By 1986, the U.S. Congress had responded by passing the Comprehensive Anti-Apartheid Act, imposing severe sanctions for the racial atrocities and human rights violations against the black majority. The European Commonwealth and the European Economic Community each also imposed a variety of economic sanctions in the aftermath of the violent suppression.

South Africa continued to undergo reform, including removal of most of the apartheid laws that ensured cruel and unusual treatment of blacks. These reforms are widely attributed to sanctions by other countries, which had a devastating effect on the South African economy.

Bibliography

Carroll, Raymond, Peter Younghusband, and Scott Sullivan. "From Sharpeville to Soweto." *Newsweek* 87 (June 28, 1976): 32-34. The title of this article is misleading. It does not chronicle events from Sharpeville, in 1960, to Soweto, in 1976. Rather, it discusses the issues, personalities, and events related to the Soweto rebellion and focuses on relations with the United States in the aftermath of the uprising.

Glaser, Clive. *Bo-tsotsi: The Youth Gangs of Soweto, 1935-1976.* Portsmouth, N.H.: Heinemann, 2000. Includes a chapter on Soweto gangs and the rise of student politics. Includes a bibliography and an index.

Johnson, Paul. "The Race for South Africa." In *At Issue: Politics in the World Arena*, edited by Steven L. Spiegel. 5th ed. New York: St. Martin's Press, 1988. This chapter analyzes the debate regarding sanctions against South Africa in light of apartheid policies. Concludes by arguing that it would be best for the United States to impose sanctions before a black government takes over and develops a hostile attitude toward the West.

Rubin, Leslie, and Brian Weinstein. *Introduction to African Politics: A Continental Approach.* New York: Praeger, 1974. Although this work is somewhat dated, the sixth chapter focuses on Southern Africa, the roots of apartheid, African resistance to it, and the regime's reaction to the resistance. The authors reach nine major conclusions based on increasing resistance to apartheid and economic pressures by foreign governments for societal change and equality in South Africa.

Seegers, Annette M. "South African Liberation: Touchstone of African Solidarity." In *African Security Issues: Sovereignty, Stability, and Solidarity,* edited by Bruce E. Arlinghaus. Boulder, Colo.: Westview Press, 1984. This chapter investigates the history of the armed struggle against South Africa by other black African nations and explains the impact of this struggle on the regime's changing domestic and foreign policies against the African neighbors. The author focuses on organized efforts against apartheid.

"The Soweto Uprising: A Soul-Cry of Rage." *Time* 75 (June 28, 1976): 29-34. This article examines the origins, issues, and events associated with the Soweto rebellion and discusses the international ramifications of the domestic turmoil, particularly concerning the United States and the former British colony known as Rhodesia (now Zimbabwe).

Zartman, William I. *Ripe for Resolution: Conflict and Intervention in Africa.* New York: Oxford University Press, 1989. This work is divided into six major chapters on war and prospects for peace in the major regions of Africa. Chapter 5 is of particular interest, focusing on the prospects for independence for Namibia, a colony of South Africa in 1989, and the weaknesses and strengths in the negotiation process between the United States and South Africa.

Mfanya Donald Tryman

South African Government Kills Biko

Category of event: Atrocities and war crimes; health and medical rights;
prisoners' rights
Time: 1977
Locale: South Africa

> *Detained under the Terrorism Act, Stephen Bantu Biko became the forty-sixth polit-
> ical detainee to die in the custody of the security police*

Principal personages:
STEPHEN BIKO (1947-1977), a fighter against apartheid and a leader of the
 Black Consciousness movement
PIETER GOOSEN, the chief of security police in the Eastern Cape
JAMES T. KRUGER (1917-　　), the minister of justice, police, and prisons
MARTHINUS PRINS, the chief magistrate of Pretoria, who presided at the in-
 quest into Biko's death
BALTHAZAR JOHANNES (JOHN) VORSTER (1915-1983), the prime minister of
 South Africa

Summary of Event

Apartheid, the policy of institutionalized racial domination and exploitation imposed in South Africa, was denounced by the United Nations as a flagrant violation of the U.N. Charter and of the Universal Declaration of Human Rights. Apartheid caused immense suffering and the forced removal of
millions of Africans from their homes. Its enforcement entailed ruthless repression and the denial of basic human and political rights. Apartheid, based
on fundamental premises of racial superiority and separation, became the official ideology of South Africa in 1948 with the electoral victory of the Nationalist Party. The apartheid system persisted into the 1990's, and only in 1991 did
President Frederik Willem de Klerk begin to dismantle it. In one of the great
political miracles of world history, all legal vestiges of apartheid were removed
from South Africa by 1994, and the country had a new constitution with some
of the strongest protections of human rights in the world.

Prior to the apartheid system, the history of South Africa from the beginning of European colonialism in 1652 had been one of deepening racial op-

515

pression and economic exploitation. The result of this history is a situation in which the approximately 5.5 million white South Africans (out of a 1990 total population of about 34 million) owned 87 percent of the land. The political system totally excluded the 25 million black South Africans and afforded very limited participation to the three million "Coloureds" and one million Asians. The legal and economic systems were designed to control the movement and exploit the labor of the black majority. A repressive "police state" security structure quashed black resistance.

Resistance by the black African majority was a constant feature of South African history. Increasingly in the twentieth century, allies were found among the white, Coloured, and Asian populations of the country. Most prominent among the twentieth century black resistance movements were the African National Congress (ANC), the Pan-Africanist Congress (PAC), the Black Consciousness movement (BCM), and the United Democratic Front (UDF). The leaders of these movements, including Nelson Mandela of the ANC, Robert Sobukwe of the PAC, and Stephen Biko of the BCM, all suffered repression by the South African state. In Biko's case, the state not only detained and restricted his movements on many occasions but also ultimately killed him while he was in detention.

Stephen Bantu Biko was born in King William's Town, Cape Province, on December 18, 1947. After a high school career interrupted by reprisals for his political activism, he began medical studies at the University of Natal in 1966. Two years later, he helped found and became the first president of the South African Student Organization (SASO), established to provide a voice of liberation for black students and the black community and to propagate the emergent philosophy of Black Consciousness. In 1971, Biko helped found the Black People's Convention (BPC) as an umbrella organization for the growing Black Consciousness movement. Because of his activism, Biko was expelled from medical school, and in 1972, along with other SASO and BPC officers, was "banned" by the state. The banning order forced his removal from membership in SASO, BPC, and the other community self-help programs and activist organizations with which he was associated; prohibited him from attending gatherings of three or more people and from writing for publication or being quoted; and confined him to King William's Town for five years. The banning was intended to bring an end to Biko's political activities; however, he continued to establish community programs and to develop and articulate Black Consciousness. Biko's national and international stature grew, and in 1976 he was elected honorary president of the Black People's Convention. He was arrested and detained many times between 1974 and August, 1977, accused of breaking the terms of his banning order or undermining the security of the state. He was always cleared of such charges, and during his life he was never convicted of any crime.

At the heart of Biko's activism was the philosophy of Black Consciousness, a philosophy with roots in African nationalism, pan-Africanism, and liberation theology. At its core, Black Consciousness is both a philosophy of psychological emancipation, self-assertion, racial pride, and dignity and also an ideology for combating the legal, economic, political, and physical repression intrinsic to the apartheid system. The need to free black South Africans of their entrenched inferiority complex, mental emancipation, was seen as a prerequisite for political emancipation. The goal of Black Consciousness was not artificial integration among the races in South Africa but instead true humanity, devoid of racist solidarities and power politics. Biko declared, "We are looking forward to a nonracial, just, and egalitarian society in which color, creed, and race shall form no point of reference."

Central to the political practice of Black Consciousness were the rejection of white liberal domination of the antiapartheid organizations and the establishment of community-based self-help and mass agitation programs involving the rededication of black intellectuals to the black community. SASO, BPC, the Black Community Programs, and the Zimele Trust Fund, devoted to community development via housing, health, and literacy programs, were concrete manifestations of this philosophy and practice. The commitment to nonviolence was another key element of Black Consciousness. There was a deliberate effort by the Black Consciousness movement to avoid being banned by the state. The movement wanted to fill the gap in internal, legal black politics that had existed since the banning of the ANC and the PAC in 1960, after the Sharpeville Massacre.

Biko was arrested for the last time on August 18, 1977, in Grahamstown. He was detained under the provisions of the Terrorism Act of 1967, which permitted the police to arrest without a warrant anyone suspected of terrorist activities or having knowledge concerning such activities. Detained persons could be held incommunicado for as long as the commissioner of police or minister of justice deemed necessary. Biko's arrest in Grahamstown meant that he was in violation of the terms of his banning, which restricted him to King William's Town. Biko was kept in isolation, naked and manacled, for twenty days. On September 6, he was moved to the Security Police Headquarters in Port Elizabeth, and was interrogated. Sometime on September 6 or September 7, Biko received blows to the head, causing brain damage and ultimately his death on September 12. The day before he died, Biko had been driven seven hundred miles in the back of a police van, from Port Elizabeth to Pretoria Prison Hospital.

Biko was the forty-sixth person to die in detention under South Africa's security laws. These deaths dated back to September, 1963. Twenty-three of these deaths of political detainees occurred in the eighteen-month period from March, 1976, to September, 1977. Official explanations for these deaths include "natural causes," "suicide by hanging," "fell out of seventh floor window," "slipped in shower," and "slipped down the stairs." Many other political prisoners died while detained under nonsecurity laws.

The South African minister of justice, police, and prisons, James Kruger, initially announced that Biko had died as the result of a seven-day hunger strike, and that Biko had been examined regularly by a team of doctors, who found nothing physically wrong with him. This explanation was disbelieved universally. Biko was a big, strong man who would not have died of starvation in one week. In addition, Biko previously had told Donald Woods, the editor of the *Daily Despatch*, that if it ever were announced that he had died as a result of a hunger strike, it would be a lie—he would never engage in such a futile action.

While Kruger was telling delegates of the Nationalist Party that "I'm not pleased, nor am I sorry; Biko's death leaves me cold," the world diplomatic corps and media voiced their doubts and called for an official investigation. U.S. senator Dick Clark, who had met with Biko, declared that Biko's "death represents a loss not only to the blacks of South Africa . . . but to all . . . who believed that through responsible and talented leaders like Biko, there still remained a chance for peaceful racial accommodation." Criticizing the "pattern of outright racial oppression conducted by an authoritarian state," Senator Clark called for an impartial inquiry into Biko's death. U.S. secretary of state Cyrus Vance similarly called for a full investigation, declaring that Biko "must be regarded as another victim of the apartheid system and the South African security legislation which supports that system."

Within South Africa, similar disbelief at the official explanation and concerns for the future of the country were voiced. The *Financial Mail* called Biko an inspiration to his generation. The reaction of black South Africans was summed up by Soweto community leader Nthatho Motlanda at a memorial service: "I say boldly to you and to the whole world that we accuse Mr. Vorster and his government of killing Steve Biko. . . . There is no greater force in this world than an idea whose time has arrived, and this idea is Black Consciousness, which is going to free the black man from the shackles of white imperialism, white slavery, and white oppression."

The autopsy carried out on Biko by two state pathologists and a doctor representing the victim's family revealed the cause of death to be severe brain damage resulting from a blow to the forehead. The autopsy report destroyed any credibility that the official hunger-strike explanation may have had. Kruger recanted this explanation and acknowledged "irregularities" in police handling of the case.

Impact of Event

On November 14, 1977, an official inquest into Biko's death began, presided over by Marthinus Prins, the chief magistrate of Pretoria. The inquest lasted three weeks. Despite numerous contradictions in the testimony of the police and the doctors who "attended" Biko, Magistrate Prins concluded that Biko died as the result of head injuries suffered in a scuffle with police during the interrogation, and that "the available evidence does not prove that death was brought about by an act or omission involving an offense by any person." *Newsweek* described the inquest as a charade. Hodding Carter III, the U.S. State Department spokesman, said "We are shocked by the verdict."

More than ten thousand people attended Biko's funeral, including diplomats from thirteen Western countries. The 1976 Soweto student uprisings had focused world attention on South Africa. Biko's death reinforced the growing international outcry against apartheid and strengthened calls for comprehensive economic sanctions and an arms embargo against the state. In the immediate aftermath of Biko's death, the United Nations Security Council imposed a mandatory arms embargo against South Africa. Foreign investment decreased drastically, and major Western multinational corporations began to divest themselves of their South African subsidiaries. International banks severely limited new loans to South Africa.

The South African state responded in typical manner to the wave of public grief and anger occasioned by Biko's death. Police opened fire at a memorial service in Soweto, killing one youth and wounding several others. Twelve hundred university students were arrested at the University of Fort Hare for holding a gathering to mourn Biko. The Nationalist Party called a snap election to reinforce its mandate from the white-only electorate, and Prime Minister Vorster warned foreign critics against "meddling" in South Africa's internal affairs.

Repressive governments imprison and kill those of their critics they cannot silence. Biko was one such critic. As Nobel Peace Prize winner Desmond Tutu said on the tenth anniversary of Biko's death, "Steve's fate shows clearly that you can silence a person with a banning order, harass him, torture him.... Yes, you can kill him, but you will never destroy his ideas." The system of apartheid has had many victims—millions of exploited workers, farmers forced off their lands, miseducated school children, jailed trade union leaders, banned intellectuals, and imprisoned and murdered political activists. Each generation, however, took up the struggle against apartheid and produced its own martyrs for the cause of human justice. A realization that apartheid must eventually fall perhaps prompted Frederik de Klerk finally to begin dismantling the system and move the country toward full democracy not based on race.

Bibliography

Bernstein, Hilda. *No. 46: Steve Biko.* London: International Defence and Aid Fund, 1978. Recounts in detail the testimony presented at the inquest into the death of Stephen Biko, the forty-sixth person to die in security police detention in South Africa. Provides valuable insights into the workings of the legal, political, and security structures designed to sustain apartheid and quash critics.

Biko, Steve. *Steve Biko: Black Consciousness in South Africa.* Edited by Millard Arnold. New York: Random House, 1978. An extensive account of the testimony for the defense given by Biko at the 1976 terrorism trial of nine activists from the South African Student Organization and the Black People's Convention. In what was his last public appearance, Biko detailed the rationale, history, and substance of Black Consciousness.

Fatton, Robert. *Black Consciousness in South Africa.* Albany: State University of New York Press, 1986. An analysis of ideological resistance to white supremacy (apartheid) in South Africa. Locates Black Consciousness among the various historical strands of African nationalism and traces the organizational and ideological development of the Black Consciousness movement.

Graybill, Lyn S. *Religion and Resistance Politics in South Africa.* Westport, Conn.: Praeger, 1995. Features a chapter on Biko and the Black Consciousness movement. Bibliography and index.

Juckes, Tim J. *Opposition in South Africa: The Leadership of Z.K. Matthews, Nelson Mandela, and Stephen Biko.* Westport, Conn.: Praeger, 1995. An account of the political growth of the three activists and their effect on social developments within South Africa. Includes a select bibliography and an index.

Motlhabi, Mokgethi. *The Theory and Practice of Black Resistance to Apartheid.* Johannesburg: Skotaville, 1984. Evaluates the histories, goals, ideologies, and activities of the African National Congress, the Pan-Africanist Congress, and the Black Consciousness movement within a framework of norms grounded in Christian ethics. Concludes that the lack of "principled action programs" explains the failure of the three national liberation organizations to bring an end to apartheid.

Woods, Donald. *Biko.* New York: Vintage Books, 1979. Seeks to explain what in Biko's life and death made him so remarkable. This work, intended as a personal tribute to Biko from a close friend and written in secret because of the threat of imprisonment, provides an intimate view of Biko's life, commitments, and activities. The work also provides an informed critique of the South African "police state" from the perspective of one of the country's leading journalists.

Hashim Gibrill

Zia Establishes Martial Law in Pakistan

Category of event: Civil rights; political freedom
Time: 1977
Locale: Pakistan

> *Martial law in Pakistan set the framework for serious abuses of the rights of citizens and political detainees, creating international outrage*

Principal personages:

GENERAL MOHAMMAD ZIA-UL-HAQ (1924-1988), the chief of staff of the Pakistani army, established martial law after he deposed the civilian government and declared himself president

BENAZIR BHUTTO (1953-   ), the daughter of Zulfikar Ali Bhutto, the deposed prime minister of Pakistan

NUSRAT BHUTTO (1932-   ), the widow of Zulfikar Ali Bhutto

KHWAJA KHAIRUDDIN, the secretary general of the Movement for the Restoration of Democracy (MRD); persisted in protesting martial law despite numerous arrests and detentions

MALIK QASIM, the chairman of the MRD who openly accused the Zia government of fabricating charges against the MRD to justify arrests

Summary of Event

On July 5, 1977, General Mohammad Zia-ul-Haq, chief of staff of the Pakistani army, deposed the civilian government of Prime Minister Zulfikar Ali Bhutto in a military coup and established martial law throughout Pakistan, declaring himself president and chief martial law administrator. Under martial law, fundamental human rights as specified in the Universal Declaration of Human Rights and other internationally recognized agreements were violated frequently. These abuses were widely publicized, especially by Amnesty International and by the Human Rights Society of Pakistan. The report of this latter Pakistani society on the condition and treatment of political detainees played a major role in strengthening indigenous groups which took a stand against the abuses of Zia's regime. Opposition was particularly intense concerning Zia's desire to establish a new political system "true to Islamic principles." Zia's efforts at Islamization were intended not only to reduce alien influence but also to liquidate the sophisticated, cosmopolitan elite that had dominated Pakistan since its beginning. A disproportionate number of political detainees whose rights were abrogated were members of this elite.

General Zia suspended the fundamental rights guaranteed by Pakistan's four-year-old constitution, including freedoms of speech, assembly, association, and movement, and security of citizens against arbitrary arrest and detention. In spite of public promises to hold fair elections, Zia maintained martial law and imprisoned thousands of political opponents in order to consolidate his power. Zia greatly expanded the jurisdiction of military courts at the expense of civilian courts, virtually destroying the latter system. The majority of defendants tried for political offenses were tried by summary military courts, established by Martial Law Order Number 4 of 1977 and given extraordinary powers to impose severe penalties following trials lacking even the most rudimentary elements of procedural fairness. Punishments, according to Islamic law, included death, amputation, life imprisonment, flogging, and confiscation of property. Under the Provisional Constitution Order (PCO) promulgated on March 14, 1981, no higher court could review or challenge the actions of the martial law authorities or the decisions of the military courts. The PCO suspended all orders made by the superior courts pertaining to decisions of military courts and declared null and void all other decisions addressing the legality of the military government. Article 17 of the PCO provided that judges of the supreme and high courts of Pakistan could not continue to hold their offices unless they swore an oath to abide by the PCO. Some justices of the high courts of Punjab and Baluchistan defied the military regime by overturning military court decisions. The PCO forced those judges who were committed to upholding the 1973 constitution to resign. Nineteen supreme court and provincial high court justices lost their seats on the bench for refusing to take the oath required by the PCO. After these dismissals, judges were appointed only to "acting justice" status, facilitating their removal. Pakistani lawyers of the time stressed that before Zia seized power, no matter how erratic or arbitrary government action was, one always had the opportunity to appeal one's case or to seek a writ of mandamus or habeas corpus when a lower court or government official acted improperly.

Ordinary Pakistani citizens virtually were prohibited from participating in the political process, since Zia banned all political parties and activities and imposed press censorship. Human rights violations escalated in the early 1980's, at the same time the United States, under President Ronald Reagan, was providing a $3.2 billion military and economic assistance program to Pakistan.

Arrests under preventive detention provisions were frequent in the early

Pakistani president Mohammad Zia-ul-Haq during a visit to the Pakistani community in Sacramento, California, in 1982. (Sacramento Ethnic Survey Collection)

1980's. Under martial law, hundreds of politicians, political party workers, lawyers, students, trade unionists, and others were arrested and rearrested on numerous trumped-up charges or on the basis of no charge at all. These arrests generally took place either under the Maintenance of Public Order Ordinance or under Martial Law Order (MLO) Number 78. The latter provided for indefinite detention without the prisoner being informed of the reason for arrest.

Detainees were held for periods ranging from several days to several years, in spite of the provision that such detainees were to be held for a maximum of ninety days at a time, renewable for a total of one year. Even periods of short detention were associated with a sustained cycle of arrest, release, and rearrest. During detention, torture of prisoners during interrogation was commonplace and severe, including beating, often while the prisoner was suspended from the ceiling. Methods of torture also included applying electric shocks, burning the body with cigarettes, pulling out hairs, subjecting prisoners to continuous loud noise, and depriving prisoners of food and sleep for long periods. People were arrested without their families being notified and were often held incommunicado in solitary confinement. The Human Rights Society of Pakistan reported that seven political detainees died while in captivity during 1982. The United States Department of State counted eleven deaths.

Political detainees held after the 1983 protests organized by the umbrella opposition alliance, the Movement for the Restoration of Democracy (MRD), were held without formal charges or trials. In February of 1983, the MRD decided to hold a "political prisoner's day" in Lahore, but its meeting was interrupted by the police, who took attendees into custody. The MRD persisted in demanding a return to civilian government and an end to the arbitrary system of martial law. The Zia regime made a practice of keeping opposition leaders under detention. Lawyers in particular came under attack during Zia's reign of terror because they continued to argue for the reinstatement of civil law and courts.

Among the police and army agencies named as responsible for the arrest, interrogation, and torture of political prisoners were the Inter-Services Intelligence, the joint intelligence unit of the three armed forces, under the control of the federal government; the Field Intelligence Unit, an army intelligence agency regularly cited as conducting arrests; the Special Branch attached to the provincial police; and the Federal Intelligence Agency. Of particular cruelty was the use of flogging to punish political detainees. During the 1977-1981 period, hundreds of political prisoners were flogged, prisoners accused of nonviolent crimes. In addition, the death penalty was imposed on a great number of political prisoners. As of March, 1982, it was reported that 1,350 prisoners in Punjab were under sentence of death.

Impact of Event

The publication of reports by Amnesty International, the Human Rights Society of Pakistan, and the Lawyers Committee for International Human Rights in the early 1980's signaled a growing movement within both Pakistan and the international community to stand up against abuses of human rights being perpetrated under Zia's martial law regime. The reports put pressure on Zia to call elections by 1985. The reports also put pressure on the Reagan administration to make U.S. assistance conditional upon the reinstatement of civil law in Pakistan. Reports of brutality and violation of rights ultimately led to the demise of Zia's regime and to the political victory of Benazir Bhutto.

The open publicity of the human rights violations created an international context within which Zia's major opponents could maneuver more effectively. One of the major groups included the politicized intelligentsia, especially lawyers. The bar associations, particularly vexed at Zia's imposition of Islamic law, organized numerous demonstrations in defiance of martial law. The lawyers were especially concerned that Zia's institution of courts of "qadis," or Islamic clerics who would administer justice on the basis of Islamic codes, would eliminate lawyers trained in English common law and destroy the independence of the judicial system. They continued to obtain international support against Zia and to oppose all of his legal reforms. The All-Pakistan Lawyers Convention met in Lahore in October, 1982, with the stated purpose of criticizing the government program. In spite of numerous arrests, the lawyers continued to be some of the most outspoken opponents of the government. The Punjabi bar association demanded the withdrawal of the Provisional Constitutional Order of 1981 and the repeal of all laws, orders, and regulations which barred or curtailed the jurisdiction of the superior courts. They observed a symbolic two hour strike protesting the military *junta*'s denial of civil liberties and the discarding of the rule of law.

The politicization of the intelligentsia entered a new phase as Malik Qasim, chairman of the MRD, accused the government of fabricating a case against the movement in order to justify arresting members. Qasim declared that thousands of MRD supporters had been arrested and were wasting away in prison. More and more professional associations declared that they would no longer remain apolitical and began openly to renounce the Zia government, further pressuring both Zia and his international allies, such as the United States, to begin to show some semblance of justice.

Bibliography

Amnesty International USA. *Pakistan Violations of Human Rights.* New York: Author, 1985. This report summarizes the human rights violations taking place in Pakistan in the early 1980's, including the treatment of political detainees.

Arif, K. M. *Khaki Shadows: Pakistan 1947-1997.* Karachi: Oxford University Press, 2001. Written by a retired general with a position in the martial law regimes, the text focuses on the dominant role of the army in the political arena in Pakistan

_____. *Working with Zia: Pakistan Power Politics, 1977-1988.* Karachi: Oxford University Press, 1995. An insider's account (Arif was Zia's chief of staff for seven years) of the Zia regime.

Burki, Shahid Javed. *Pakistan: A Nation in the Making.* Boulder, Colo.: Westview Press, 1986. Provides a comprehensive account of the development of Pakistan, including the events which took place under Zia's martial law.

Greenberg, Deborah M. *Justice in Pakistan.* New York: Lawyers Committee for International Human Rights, 1983. This report summarizes the abuses which took place in Pakistan under the military rule of Zia, especially during the period of 1981-1983, which was particularly notorious.

Naqvi, Jamal, Shaukat Ali, and Farz Ali. *Inside Pakistan.* New Delhi: Patriot Publishers, 1986. This book is a Marxist analysis of the ruling elite in Pakistan and the "revolution" of the people seeking basic human rights.

Nyrop, Richard, ed. *Pakistan: A Country Study.* 5th ed. Washington, D.C.: Headquarters, Department of the Army, 1984. This book, written to brief foreign service officers assigned to Pakistan, has a detailed chapter on the development of politics in Pakistan and the regime of Zia, including events leading up to the establishment of martial law and events putting pressure on Zia to rescind this law.

Raza, Rafi. *Zulfikar Ali Bhutto and Pakistan, 1967-1977.* New York: Oxford University Press, 1997. An examination of Bhutto's career.

Talbot, Ian. *Pakistan: A Modern History.* New York: St. Martin's Press, 1998. An analysis of the problems that have besieged this country since 1947. Provides an examination of the political careers of Zia-ul-Haq, Zulfikar Ali Bhutto, and Benazir Bhutto.

Randal J. Thompson

Soviet Citizen Group Investigates Political Abuses of Psychiatry

Category of event: Civil rights; health and medical rights
Time: 1977-1981
Locale: Moscow, Soviet Union

> *Concern about the increasing use of psychiatry for political purposes led a small group of concerned Soviet citizens to form a working commission to monitor and publicize such practices*

Principal personages:

ALEXANDER PODRABINEK (1953-   ), a paramedic who helped form the commission

ANATOLY KORYAGIN (1938-   ), a psychiatrist and consultant to the commission from 1979 until his arrest in February, 1981

VYACHESLAV BAKHMIN (1947-   ), a computer specialist working in a government research institute who cofounded the commission

FELIX SEREBROV (1930-   ), a self-educated worker and cofounder of the commission

ALEXANDER VOLOSHANOVICH, the commission's first psychiatric consultant

LEONID ILICH BREZHNEV (1906-1982), the Soviet leader whose government initially tolerated, then suppressed, groups like the working commission

ANDREI SNEZHNEVSKY (1904-1987), the director of the Soviet Institute of Psychiatry in Moscow whose theories suggested treatment of political dissidents

Summary of Event

Under Leonid Brezhnev, many political, religious, ethnic, and professional groups dissented from Soviet policy. Brezhnev's government used a wide range of tactics in dealing with this opposition, among them toleration, co-optation, harassment, exile, and imprisonment. The Working Commission for the Investigation of the Use of Psychiatry for Political Purposes was founded by Vyacheslav Bakhmin, Irina Kaplun, Alexander Podrabinek, Felix Serebrov, and Dzhemma Kvachevskaya. It was affiliated with Moscow's Helsinki Watch Group and worked closely with General Pyotr Grigorenko, a dissenter who had been involuntarily committed for psychiatric care. The working commission proclaimed the intention of working within the Soviet legal system and of effecting Soviet commitments to the Final Act of the Conference on Security and Cooperation in Europe (the Helsinki Agreement of 1975). It routinely sent copies of its bulletin to the Procuracy (legal officials) and health ministry. Although the commission proclaimed that it was nonpolitical, the government considered it to be a political danger; the government claimed that organs of the Communist Party could guarantee human rights and that independent monitoring groups would undermine the role of the Party. By focusing on those illegally detained, the commission acknowledged that psychiatric detention is sometimes justified and that some dissidents might be mentally ill. The commission's objection was that neither proper legal nor psychiatric procedures were employed.

The working commission was always a small group. Its largest membership was five, with others serving as consultants. The expertise of its members varied. It included industrial workers and health workers but also drew on psychiatrists and lawyers, some working anonymously to avoid losing their jobs. Those without psychiatric backgrounds had intense curiosities. The accuracy and detail of commission reports impressed leaders of the world psychiatric community.

The commission took on three tasks: to publicize and win the release of individuals illegally and forcibly detained in mental hospitals, to aid such people and their families, and to improve the conditions in mental hospitals. The commission focused public attention on Soviet psychiatric practices. Political dissidents were frequently subjected to psychiatric examinations and hundreds were interned in psychiatric institutions. Drugs were often forcibly administered, and many patients were sent to hospitals in remote areas of the country. Dissidents were frequently diagnosed as schizophrenic, based on writings of Andrei Snezhnevsky implying that nonconformity and antisocial behavior required treatment. Working commission cofounder Alexander Podrabinek argued that Snezhnevsky and his associates were not sincere in their claims. Podrabinek claimed to know of only one psychiatrist who honestly regarded dissidents incarcerated in special psychiatric hospitals as mentally ill.

Commission members used a variety of tactics. They visited psychiatric hospitals and gathered data on patients and the treatment they received. They wrote to psychiatrists on commission stationery about particular patients. This sometimes resulted in improved treatment, because of the impression that the commission was a state-sanctioned body. They offered advice to citizens who risked commitment to a psychiatric hospital. They issued more than one hundred statements and appeals. The commission's *Information Bulletin* circulated secretly in the Soviet Union and openly in the West. Excerpts from the *Information Bulletin* were summarized in the *Chronicle of Current Events*, the Soviet human rights movement's journal. Radio listeners were acquainted with the commission's work through Western stations' Russian-language broadcasts. The commission regularly requested additional information about listed individuals so that it could update or, if necessary, correct its reports.

The commission gained respect internationally, as well as in the Soviet human rights community. Amnesty International called a draft of Alexander Podrabinek's book, *Punitive Medicine* (1980), an important new source of information and understanding and helped to disseminate it. Amnesty produced a twenty-five-page summary of the draft for distribution to psychiatrists attending the 1973 World Psychiatric Congress, a sexennial meeting sponsored by the World Psychiatric Association (WPA), in Honolulu. That congress unanimously passed a set of ethical guidelines, the Declaration of Hawaii; it narrowly passed a resolution specifically criticizing Soviet psychiatry.

The Soviet delegation to the World Psychiatric Congress voted in favor of the Declaration of Hawaii. The working commission sought to demonstrate that psychiatrists regularly violated its guidelines. An analysis in the commission's *Information Bulletin* compared the declaration's standard requiring psychiatrists to keep their patients well informed with the Moscow region's form used in ordering civil commitment. That form categorically forbade the sharing of any information contained in the order with the patient or the patient's relatives.

The commission was an organized effort to carry on the work of such dissidents as Vladimir Bukovsky, who sent extensive information about Soviet psychiatric abuse to the West in 1971. Bukovsky's information was the basis for initial queries into Soviet practices at the World Psychiatric Congress. The commission was one of several Soviet groups advocating ostracism of Soviet psychiatrists at the 1977 Congress. Western psychiatrists did act, but slowly, and were reluctant to impose a total boycott.

The commission encouraged Western governments to protest Soviet psychiatric practices at meetings of the United Nations and of the Conference on Security and Cooperation in Europe. Along with the Moscow Human Rights Committee, it provided reliable data and analyses of abuses. American and Western European committees worked in common cause with the commission. The International Association on Political Uses of Psychiatry, the Working Group on the Internment of Dissenters in Mental Hospitals, the

Vladimir Bukovsky Foundation, the International Podrabinek Fund, and a host of other groups publicized psychiatric abuses.

Until the commission's demise, its members kept professional associations apprised of new developments. Two months after the Honolulu Congress, it reported to the WPA on five new forcible commitments to mental hospitals. Five months later, it appealed to national sections of the WPA, complaining of WPA in action. Bakhmin urged, in a 1979 letter to the American Psychiatric Association, that psychiatrists not keep quiet and pretend the problem does not exist. Soviet hospital and government officials, as well as representatives of the All-Union Scientific Society of Neuropathologists and Psychiatrists, routinely denied working commission members' requests for information. The commission was, though, credited with occasional successes by independent observers. For example, the Serbsky Institute, a Moscow psychiatric institution, acknowledged detainees' legal right to receive parcels.

Impact of Event

The working commission, as one of many forces agitating for an end to human rights violations, increased public awareness of psychiatric abuse in the Soviet Union. Although its members were imprisoned or exiled, and government persecution led to the group's demise, its members' goals were eventually achieved.

Commission members were subjected to repression. The Soviet government and many Soviet psychiatrists attempted to dismiss its efforts as slanderous and unscholarly. Late in 1977, Serebrov was charged with falsifying his labor documents and sentenced to a year's imprisonment. Podrabinek's writings, reconstructed in *Punitive Medicine*, were confiscated. He was "administratively detained" for two weeks in April, 1977, then jailed in May, 1978. The reported charge was "dissemination of fabrications known to be false which defame the Soviet state and social system."

The Soviet government's practice of "punitive medicine" and its actions against dissidents who challenged such practices would intensify, then diminish. In October, 1978, the official psychiatric organization set up its own commission to investigate cases presented by working commission consultant Alexander Voloshanovich. Its operations seemed designed to mollify foreign critics rather than to reform psychiatry. The working commission's bulletin reported that at one meeting, all Voloshanovich's references to specific violations of the directives of the ministry of health were ignored. Voloshanovich concluded that the hidden intent was to discredit him personally and to deprecate the results of his examinations.

The harassment of working commission members and consultants continued. Voloshanovich emigrated in 1980. A court labeled activities of his successor, Anatoly Koryagin, incompatible with the calling of a Soviet scientist and took away his doctoral degree. Bakhmin was jailed, as were two other members, on charges of slander. By 1981, all of the working commission members were imprisoned or had emigrated. The harshest sentence, seven years of labor camp and five of exile, was reserved for Koryagin. This was likely designed to deter other psychiatrists from following his example. Imprisonment did not stop Koryagin, who smuggled letters out of prison camps, urging the world psychiatric community to remember the plight of Soviet psychiatric prisoners.

The outcry from Western governments and nongovernmental organizations changed the nature of psychiatric repression. It diminished in major cities but continued in remote areas. As the working commission and other monitors became more sophisticated, so too did the Soviet government. The government learned to use a range of sanctions, some of them criminal but others supposedly therapeutic. The government could control access to information about sentencing procedures and about the punishments.

There is evidence that the commission made a difference in individual cases. In some cases, commission intervention was followed by the authorities' decision not to intern a dissenter. In other cases, commission intervention was followed by changes in treatment; in still others the result was sentencing to a labor camp or exile rather than detention in a special psychiatric hospital.

Most national and international psychiatrists' associations came to share the commission's perspective. By 1983, most national sections of the WPA were ready to isolate and ostracize the Soviet section. The Soviets withdrew, complaining that the WPA had been turned into a tool of the forces, among them the U.S. State Department, using psychiatry for their own political goals. Anatoly Koryagin, still in a Soviet labor camp, was given honorary membership in the WPA.

Almost four years after the commission's demise, Mikhail Gorbachev rose to power and popularized the theme of *glasnost,* or openness. Procedures for psychiatric internment were changed, and Soviet officials acknowledged past abuses. Human rights activists greeted the changes with cautious approval. Some questioned whether they went far enough to change deeply rooted practices of leaders in the psychiatric profession, hospital administrators, and government officials. Andrei Sakharov gave the working commission, along with the Moscow Human Rights Committee and allies in the West, much of the credit for new legal safeguards but cautioned that "the assistance of Western psychiatrists is needed to halt psychiatric repression completely."

Bibliography

Alexeyeva, Ludmilla. *Soviet Dissent: Contemporary Movements for National, Religious, and Human Rights.* Middletown, Conn.: Wesleyan University Press, 1987. Excellent, detailed description of a plethora of movements. The working commission is discussed as part of the human rights movement and distinguished from nationalist and religious forms of dissent. Photographs, index, and extensive notes.

Bloch, Sidney, and Peter Reddaway. *Soviet Psychiatric Abuse: The Shadow over World Psychiatry.* Boulder, Colo.: Westview Press, 1984. Chapter 3 offers a sympathetic description and analysis of the commission's efforts. Appendices include letters by Bakhmin and Koryagin and a Soviet defense to allegations of psychiatric abuse. Index.

Chronicle of Current Events. This is the major periodical covering the Soviet human rights movement, published in translation by Amnesty International. Includes regular coverage of the activities, harassment, arrests, imprisonment, and exile of working commission members.

Podrabinek, Alexander. *Punitive Medicine.* Ann Arbor, Mich.: Karoma Publishers, 1980. A classic account of Soviet psychiatric abuses by a leading commission member. Appendices include legislation and administration regulations on hospitalization and treatment of the mentally ill. Indexed.

Rubenstein, Joshua. *Soviet Dissidents: Their Struggle for Human Rights.* Boston: Beacon Press, 1985. A well-written description of the varied human rights activities of Soviet dissidents. Addressed to a general readership. Good bibliography and index.

Smith, Theresa C. *No Asylum: State Psychiatric Repression in the Former USSR.* New York: New York University Press, 1996. Scholarly account of the abuse of psychiatry in punishing political dissent. Bibliography and indexes.

Van Voren, Robert, ed. *Koryagin: A Man Struggling for Human Dignity.* Amsterdam: Second World Press, 1987. A tribute to the Soviet psychiatrist and working commission consultant. Includes excerpts from Koryagin's trial and contributions from Koryagin and Voloshanovich. Foreword by Dutch members of Parliament who nominated Koryagin for the Nobel Peace Prize. Photographs and appendices. No index or bibliography.

Wynn, Allan. *Notes of a Non-Conspirator: Working with Russian Dissidents.* London: Andre Deutsch, 1987. A physician's tale of his, and the British Working Group on the Internment of Dissenters in Mental Hospitals', efforts to call attention to Soviet abuses. The role of the Soviet working commission and other groups is described. Indexed.

Arthur Blaser

Soviets Crack Down on Moscow's Helsinki Watch Group

Category of event: Civil rights; international norms; political freedom
Time: February-March, 1977
Locale: Moscow, Soviet Union

> *After dissidents had engaged in public protest for two years against Soviet violations of the Helsinki Accords on human rights, authorities had the protesters arrested*

Principal personages:

ANATOLY SHCHARANSKY (1948-   ), a prominent Soviet dissident, a founder of the Helsinki Watch Group in Moscow, and a Jewish "refusenik"

YURI ORLOV (1924-   ), a founder of Helsinki Watch in Moscow

ALEKSANDR GINZBURG (1936-   ), a dissident author and a founder of Helsinki Watch in Moscow

LEONID ILICH BREZHNEV (1906-1982), the General Secretary of the Communist Party and leader of the Soviet government

Summary of Event

After the death of Joseph Stalin in 1953, the Soviet Union, under Nikita Khrushchev and Leonid Brezhnev, sought international accommodation with the West while still trying to maintain strict control over politics and economics at home. One of the Kremlin's major goals was Western recognition of the border changes that Soviet leaders had made after World War II. Western leaders were reluctant to recognize these and insisted on linking any recognition to improvement in human rights in the Soviet Union.

Khrushchev had introduced a brief period of liberalization in the Soviet Union with his de-Stalinization campaign in 1956. In Western eyes, this had not gone far enough. It was limited to partial relaxation in the social and cultural areas; noncommunist economic and political activity still remained strictly forbidden. Furthermore, when the Communist Party's Central Committee suddenly dismissed Khrushchev from power in 1964, Brezhnev became the leader of an even stricter regime.

Nevertheless, Soviet leaders still wanted a period of "peaceful coexistence" with the West and the recognition of postwar borders. In the early 1970's, the spirit of détente promised a new age in relations between Moscow and the West. On Moscow's urging, European and North American leaders convened the Conference on Security and Cooperation in Europe, which held a series of meetings from 1973 to 1975 to discuss détente, the recognition of existing borders, and, at the insistence of the West, the guarantee of fundamental human rights—the so-called "Basket 3" issues. Representatives from all European countries, the United States, and Canada received invitations. Only the hard-line isolationist communist government in Albania refused to attend. The last session met in Helsinki, Finland. In August, 1975, the heads of state of all the attending countries signed the nonbinding Helsinki Final Act, popularly called the "Helsinki Accords."

The accords recognized most of the border changes Moscow wanted but also provided for international cooperation in humanitarian, cultural, and economic endeavors and required the signatories to guarantee a whole series of political and civil rights. These rights included the freedom of information—specifically the right of citizens to receive and read foreign newspapers and to listen to foreign broadcasts—and the right to travel and to migrate. The "Basket 1" agreement on international boundaries and security, however, provided for noninterference in a country's internal affairs by other countries. Thus, the Soviets continued to suppress many civil liberties. They refused to allow free emigration; noncommunist newspapers were generally unavailable, although the hotels in Moscow and Leningrad catering to Western tourists sold a few copies of such periodicals as the *International Herald Tribune*, and the jamming of Western radio broadcasts also continued. When Western diplomats complained about violations of the Basket 3 stipulations of the accords, the Kremlin replied that the Basket 1 agreement protected the Soviet Union's internal affairs.

On May 12, 1976, eleven Muscovites formed the first Helsinki Watch Group in the Soviet Union to monitor the government's fulfillment of the accords. Among the members were Anatoly Shcharansky and Vitaly Rubin. Shcharansky and Rubin were already well known as outspoken critics of the Soviet policy of refusing to allow Jews to migrate to Israel; the policy had been one of the reasons that Western leaders had insisted on including freedom of migration on the agenda at Helsinki. Shcharansky, a brilliant scientist, was the spokesperson for the so-called "refuseniks," Soviet Jews who requested and were refused exit visas. In fact, the government often punished the refuseniks with loss of employment or arrest. Many around the world had taken up their cause, and in the United States congressional leaders were linking their plight to the economic agreements between Washington and Moscow that the Kremlin desired. Other members of the Helsinki Watch Group in Moscow included Yuri Orlov, another scientist, Aleksandr Ginzburg, a writer, and Elena Bonner, the wife of the world-renowned physicist Andrei Sakharov, one of the country's most prominent dissidents. Sakharov, however, who avoided joining organizations himself, did not become a member of Helsinki Watch, although he gave it public and private support. Orlov and Bonner had previously helped to found the Moscow committee of Amnesty International.

Soviet authorities brought official and unofficial pressure to bear upon members of the Moscow Helsinki Watch Group. Because of the prominence of the issue of Jewish emigration, Shcharansky was particularly subject to attack. He was fired from his job and denied a living permit for Moscow. The scientist moved to a village near the capital and found private work as a tutor of English and physics in order to avoid imprisonment as an unemployed parasite. (Under Soviet law, "parasitism" applied to persons without work, but in practice the authorities used it as a political weapon against dissidents.) Shcharansky also acted as an interpreter, and prominent visitors to the Soviet Union familiar with and sympathetic to his case, including a number of American congressmen, sought him out for employment. He also worked as an interpreter for Sakharov and gave Orlov English lessons. Sakharov employed Ginzburg, as well, as a secretary.

From May, 1976, to February, 1977, the Helsinki Watch Group prepared sixteen reports on the state of human rights in the Soviet Union. One report dealt with prisoners of conscience subjected to "physical and moral torments, genuine torture by means of hunger, in combination with hard physical labour." Other reports stated that the authorities continued to persecute political prisoners even after release, that political prisoners suffered abuse in psychiatric hospitals, and that the police harassed Pentecostal Christians and Jews who applied for emigration to Israel. A report of June, 1976, dwelled on the separation of Jewish families applying for emigration. In conclusion, the Helsinki Watch Group stated that Moscow had no intention of fulfilling its human rights obligations under the Helsinki treaty. The group sent these reports to the Soviet authorities, and when there was no reply they released them to the Western press. The *Los Angeles Times*, in particular, published a number of the group's statements.

In August, 1976, at a press conference that the Helsinki Watch Group convened, the group commented on the application of the Helsinki Accords to Jews applying to emigrate. Although the group specifically invited Moscow journalists, only Western reporters attended. The group claimed that the government was not only hindering emigration to Israel but also harassing the refuseniks by taking away their telephone service and intercepting their mail. In November, Shcharansky, in his capacity as a member of the Helsinki Watch Group, publicized in the West a government press release regarding the banning of a number of Jewish cultural events and institutions in violation of both the Helsinki Accords and the Soviet constitution. He appealed for reestablishment of Jewish theaters and schools.

By January, 1977, the Soviet authorities, disturbed by the adverse Western publicity, decided that their policy of trying to ignore the Moscow Helsinki Watch Group was not working. They began a concentrated effort of harassment of the group leaders and systematically searched their apartments for evidence of criminal activity. On January 22, 1977, Soviet television showed a documentary, *Traders of Souls*, denouncing Soviet refuseniks as traitors in league with an international anti-Soviet Zionist conspiracy based in Israel and the United States. Shcharansky was one of several Jews shown in the film and mentioned by name. In the following days, various Moscow newspapers published a series of anti-Zionist articles. Although only Shcharansky and Rubin among the Helsinki Watch Group's members were Jews, the government and the press implicated the group as collaborators. On February 3, Soviet secret police arrested Aleksandr Ginzburg, one of the leaders of the group. Ginzburg's mother was Jewish, but he himself was a practicing Christian. A few days later, authorities arrested Orlov, also a non-Jew, and on March 15 they arrested Shcharansky.

Impact of Event

The arrests of Ginzburg, Orlov, and Shcharansky did not have an immediate impact on the human and civil rights situation in the Soviet Union. The adverse publicity abroad, however, allowed the West to put further pressure on Moscow for a liberalization program based on the promises of the Helsinki Accords. A Helsinki review conference was convened in Belgrade in July, 1977. Western leaders brought up the cases of the arrested "prisoners of Zion" (Jewish refuseniks also arrested in the raids of early 1977) and the leaders of the Helsinki Watch Group, but to no avail.

The trials of Shcharansky, Orlov, and Ginzburg took place in the spring and summer of 1978, more than a year after their arrests, during which period they remained incarcerated. The government accused the three of espionage and antistate activity. Although the latter charge was technically true under the laws of the Soviet Union, which forbade citizens to criticize the state, government, or Communist Party abroad, the defendants argued that this law itself was contrary to rights guaranteed under the Soviet constitution and the Helsinki Accords. The charge of espionage, claiming that the three gave state secrets to foreign journalists, was clearly false. As expected, the tribunal found the three guilty and gave them harsh sentences: Orlov, seven years in prison; Ginzburg, eight; and Shcharansky, thirteen.

Negotiations for their release and permission for emigration were the subject of many talks between Soviet and Western authorities. President Jimmy Carter brought the matter up at a summit meeting in 1979 and successfully attained the release of Ginzburg as part of an exchange of five Soviet prisoners for two espionage agents being held by Washington. Ginzburg then immediately emigrated to the United States. Shcharansky and Orlov, however, remained in prison, and their fate continued to receive world attention.

In the meantime, the Helsinki Watch Group still functioned, issuing reports detailing the ongoing violations of Soviet human rights. The authorities paid no attention to the reports but continued the harassment and arrest of Watch Group members. In 1982, only three of the group's nineteen members remained in Moscow. The others sat in prison, were exiled within the Soviet Union, or had left the group in despair. Thus frustrated in its work, the Moscow Helsinki Watch Group dissolved itself.

In December, 1979, the Soviet Union invaded Afghanistan, and the gap between Moscow and the West widened even further. International questions took precedence over Basket 3 issues. In 1982, Brezhnev died, and Yuri Andropov replaced him as leader of the Soviet Union. The latter introduced a modicum of liberalization in some of his policies in order to improve relations with the West. These, however, were the early years of the presidency of Ronald Reagan, who wished to make no accommodations to what he called the "Evil Empire"; moreover, Andropov's liberalization still held little hope for Soviet political prisoners. Shcharansky and Orlov remained in prison even though Shcharansky was nominated for the Nobel Peace Prize. Another Helsinki review conference met in Madrid in 1983. The West brought up once more the cases of Shcharanksy, Orlov, and the other prisoners and refuseniks. Andropov had died shortly before the conference, however, and a caretaker government under Konstantin Chernenko ruled in Moscow. Nothing definite could be settled, but there appeared to be some hope for the future. In 1985, Chernenko died, and Mikhail Gorbachev replaced him. Gorbachev began a process of change in the Soviet Union that included both economic and human rights reform. Within a year, both Shcharansky and Orlov were released from prison and allowed to emigrate from the Soviet Union.

Bibliography

Alekseeva, Liudmila, and Paul Goldberg. *The Thaw Generation: Coming of Age in the Post-Stalin Era.* Pittsburgh, Pa.: University of Pittsburgh Press, 1993. This book, written by a member of the Helsinki Watch Group, is a fascinating personal account of the dissident movement. Illustrated, with bibliography and index.

Gilbert, Martin. *Shcharansky: Hero of Our Time.* New York: Viking, 1986. An excellent biography of Shcharansky emphasizing his role as a Jewish leader in the Soviet Union and his struggle to emigrate to Israel. Also contains details of the Moscow Helsinki Watch Group and discusses the fate of other members. Appendices list the fate of other prisoners of Zion and statistics on Soviet emigration to Israel. Undocumented. Index, bibliography, illustrations, and a map.

Goldberg, Paul. *The Final Act: The Dramatic, Revealing Story of the Moscow Helsinki Watch Group.* New York: William Morrow, 1988. A detailed history of the Helsinki Watch Group including the fate of its members, the reports that it made, and the harassment it received. Illustrated, documented, and indexed.

The Jerusalem Post. Anatoly and Avital Shcharansky: The Journey Home. San Diego: Harcourt Brace Jovanovich, 1986. A joint biography of Shcharansky and his wife, emphasizing their efforts to get to Israel. Avital Shcharansky received permission to emigrate while Anatoly was in prison and played a major role in bringing attention to his plight in the West. Illustrated. No bibliography, index, or documentation.

Orlov, Yuri. *Dangerous Thoughts: Memoirs of a Russian Life.* Translated by Thomas P. Whitney. New York: William Morrow, 1991. Orlov's memoirs and his analysis of the role of dissident opposition in the Soviet Union in bringing about change in human rights. A valuable primary source.

Podrabinek, Alexander. *Punitive Medicine.* Ann Arbor, Mich.: Karoma, 1980. An indictment of the Soviet use of psychiatric hospitals and treatment for dealing with prisoners of conscience. Contains a foreword by Aleksandr Ginzburg. Illustrated and documented.

Shcharansky, Anatoly. *Fear No Evil.* Translated by Stefani Hoffman. New York: Random House, 1988. Shcharansky's autobiography from the time of his arrest until his release and emigration. Presents details of his contacts with the West as well as his role in the Jewish emigration movement and the Helsinki Watch Group. Very valuable as a primary source. Index and illustrations.

Shcharansky, Avital, with Ilana Ben-Josef. *Next Year in Jerusalem.* Translated by

Stefani Hoffman. New York: William Morrow, 1979. Shcharansky's wife's own story of her efforts to free her husband. Valuable as a primary source; she includes copies of correspondence with Anatoly and world leaders. Illustrated.

U.S. House of Representatives. Commission on Security and Cooperation in Europe. Ninety-Ninth Congress, Second Session. *Documents on the Helsinki Monitoring Groups in the U.S.S.R. and Lithuania (1976-1986)*. Vol 1. Washington, D.C.: Government Printing Office, 1986. A collection of documents reporting violations of the Helsinki Accords by Soviet authorities. Some of the documents are from the Moscow Helsinki Watch Group.

Frederick B. Chary

Dissident Writer Mihajlov Is Released from Prison

Category of event: Political freedom; prisoners' rights
Time: November 24, 1977
Locale: Sremska Mitrovica Prison, near Belgrade, Yugoslavia

> *After years of intermittent captivity and international notoriety in the struggle for political freedom, Yugoslav writer Mihajlo Mihajlov was freed under a general amnesty*

Principal personages:

MIHAJLO MIHAJLOV (1934-   ), a Yugoslav writer and dissident

TITO (1892-1980), the creator and president of the republic of Yugoslavia

JIMMY CARTER (1924-   ), the thirty-ninth president of the United States (1977-1981)

MILOVAN DJILAS (1911-1995), a Yugoslav dissident and writer, formerly a government official

LEONID ILICH BREZHNEV (1906-1982), the president of the Soviet Union and Communist Party secretary-general

Summary of Event

Josip Broz, widely known by his military code name "Tito," gained the support of England and Russia in 1943. After World War II, he was chosen to head the newly formed federal republic of Yugoslavia, comprising the republics of Croatia, Serbia, Slovenia, Montenegro, Bosnia-Herzegovina, and Macedonia. The nation fell generally within the orbit of the Soviet Union, but in 1948 Tito asserted a more independent course in the formation of foreign policy and internal affairs. Tito, considered a renegade within the communist-socialist world, watched as the Soviet Union cracked down on liberal policies in its satellites—Hungary in 1956, Czechoslovakia in 1968—and managed to tread a thin line between serving his own national goals and placating his neighbor to the east.

The fear of Soviet domination was not Tito's only concern. The six distinct republics of the federation had their own languages, cultures, and, more important, feelings of nationalism. Tito had embarked the nation on a unique economic plan, less explicitly socialist and more devoted to "self-management" of enterprises under the socialist umbrella. Tito proclaimed nonalignment and was a leader in the Non-aligned Movement of the early 1960's. Yugoslavia's independent political and economic stance allowed the government to deal with the specific challenges of its ethnic diversity and geographical situation, standing between the Eastern and Western blocs and commanding a four-hundred-mile seacoast on the Adriatic and, by extension, the Mediterranean Seas. During modern Yugoslavia's first three decades, the constitution was changed four times, in 1946, 1953, 1963, and 1974.

Like the other Soviet-influenced regimes, Yugoslavia under Tito did not tolerate opposition parties or vociferous criticism of government policy. Milovan Djilas, a close friend of Tito, was a dissident who had been a partisan leader during World War II. He had served as vice president in the early years of the republic but was demoted, harassed, and imprisoned when he began to question and criticize Tito's course for the nation. His example provided Yugoslavia with a vivid image of the precariousness of its political freedom.

One citizen keenly aware of that situation was Mihajlo Mihajlov. Born on September 26, 1934, in Pančevo, a city near Belgrade, to Russian émigré parents, Mihajlov was an authority on Russian language and literature. He worked as a translator, writer, and lecturer, and in December, 1963, at the age of 29, was elected Assistant Professor of Russian Literature and Language on the Philosophy Faculty at the Zadar branch of the University of Zagreb. Through his position, he had the opportunity to travel, and in the summer of 1964 he spent five weeks in the Soviet Union on an exchange program. While in Moscow and Leningrad, Mihajlov met with prominent Soviet writers and learned about Soviet social and political life. Upon his return, Mihajlov wrote a travelogue describing his impressions of Russian literary trends. The piece, which appeared in the January and February, 1965, issues of the Belgrade monthly *Delo*, included references to the labor camps established under Vladimir Ilyich Lenin, ballads of camp life, conversations with literary figures, and charges of genocide under Joseph Stalin.

In Yugoslavia in 1965, three dangerous topics were ethnic distinctions and nationalistic tendencies among the six republics, the possibility of establishing a multi-party system, and criticism of Soviet influence or policy. At a meeting with public prosecutors on February 11, 1965, Tito denounced Mihajlov and called for seizure of *Delo*. On March 4, after a formal protest from the Soviet ambassador, Mihajlov was arrested. On March 27, he was dismissed from the university, and on April 23, he was tried in Zadar for making false charges against a friendly government and for distribution of his banned articles. At the time, the PEN Club, the international writers' organization, was having a conference in Slovenia and heard of the case. Mihajlov wrote and personally delivered to the press an open letter to Tito protesting his Soviet-style repression. Adverse publicity and protests from PEN and others led the Supreme Court of Croatia, on April 29, to give Mihajlov a five-month suspended sentence.

Mihajlov's appeal was denied. He found himself with no job and no passport, supported by his wife's modest salary as a proofreader. He wrote articles for *New Leader* magazine in New York, and, in a relatively liberalized period in the summer of 1966, took the legal steps necessary to begin an opposition journal, *Slobodni Glas* (voice of freedom), as a seed for an opposition party.

Mihajlov was arrested again for his publications abroad. On August 22 and September 1, 1966, Tito delivered speeches denouncing him and his colleagues as foreign agents. Mihajlov was sentenced to a year in prison at his second trial, in September. In April of 1967, he was brought from prison to Belgrade to be tried for circulating his articles to his friends. He was sentenced to another forty-two months, seven of which he spent in solitary confinement.

Upon release on March 4, 1970, Mihajlov was barred from publishing in Yugoslavia or leaving the country to accept lecturing positions at Western universities. Over the next four years, he published dozens of articles in foreign periodicals such as *The New York Times, New Leader,* and *Posev,* a strident anti-Soviet, Russian-language journal published by Soviet exiles in Frankfurt, West Germany.

In 1974, Tito was eighty-three years old, and concern was growing over the issue of succession. A new campaign was initiated to suppress ideological opposition, and in October Mihajlov was arrested again. On the eve of his trial in the city of Novi Sad, Tito denounced him in a nationwide broadcast. Facing judges who were all Communist Party members, Mihajlov openly condemned the one-party system. His lawyer was Jovan Barovic, the premier civil rights advocate who also represented Djilas, Vladimir Dapcevic, and other prominent dissidents. In February of 1975, Mihajlov was convicted of disseminating hostile propaganda and associating with foreign émigré groups. He was sentenced to seven years imprisonment with hard labor.

In December of 1974, Djilas came out in the international press in Mihajlov's support. In March of 1975, *Newsweek* reported that the Soviets considered Mihajlov as a primary enemy. World attention, however, turned to human rights violations. In 1975, thirty-five nations signed the charter of the Conference on Security and Cooperation in Helsinki, Finland. This charter contained provisions regarding human and civil rights. The United States center of PEN fought for two years on Mihajlov's behalf, with letters and petitions. With increased publicity, his case garnered the attention of Helsinki Accord watchdog organizations. In 1976, Jimmy Carter was elected president of the United States and initiated an American foreign policy based on human rights (though he remained silent regarding Mihajlov). The East-West Commission on Security and Cooperation was to meet in Belgrade in late 1977 to discuss implementation of the Helsinki Accords.

Meanwhile, Mihajlov endured prison life. He saw in Carter's election hope for political prisoners under repressive regimes. He was deprived of books, a radio, and a typewriter, and forbidden to associate with other political prisoners. He waged three hunger strikes protesting the conditions of his imprisonment. During his second hunger strike, in 1976, he was transferred to a different prison and force-fed. On December 10, 1976, he stopped eating for the third time; seven weeks later, on January 17, 1977, his wife, Milica, personally delivered a note to Vice President Vidoje Zarkovic asking for Mihajlov's transfer to a hospital. He had lost forty pounds and was, as reported in *The New York Times*, seriously ill. His demands were finally met, and he ended his strike.

With incessant international pressure on Mihajlov's behalf and the Belgrade human rights conference focusing attention on Yugoslavia, Tito declared, in honor of Yugoslavia's National Day (November 29, 1977), a general amnesty that would affect 723 prisoners. On November 24, 1977, Mihajlov was released from prison, having served half of his sentence.

Impact of Event

The release of Mihajlov from prison in 1977 had both tangible and symbolic repercussions on both personal and global levels. In personal terms, Mihajlov's release gave him a new beginning in life at the age of forty-three. In 1974, denied a passport to leave the country for foreign teaching engagements, he had addressed a plea to Tito: "Either enable me to live normally in this country, or allow me to leave the country." Three years later, his request was granted. He received a passport and made his first visit to the United States, where his mother and sister had already emigrated, in the summer of 1978. During the following year, he delivered lectures throughout the United States, Europe, and parts of Asia. Throughout the 1980's, Mihajlov accepted the positions at Western universities which he had had to turn down in years past. He held visiting professorships at Yale University, the University of Virginia, Ohio State University, the University of Siegen in Germany, and the University of Glasgow in Scotland. He joined dozens of organizations focusing on literature, international affairs, and human rights, including the French and

American Centers of PEN and the International Helsinki Group Committee for the Free World. More important, Mihajlov began writing and speaking without restriction, with free and full access to the world intellectual community and the publishing and broadcasting industries. He received numerous awards, including the International League for Human Rights Award in 1978 and the Ford Foundation Award for the Humanities in 1980. His release from prison gave to the world a powerful and uncompromising voice in the struggle for freedom and human rights.

On a larger scale, Mihajlov's release had great symbolic importance. His case had become a cause célèbre; he had come to represent for many observers the repression practiced by regimes in both the Soviet satellite nations and, given Yugoslavia's unique identity, the nonaligned nations of the Third World as well. Immediately following the amnesty, President Jimmy Carter expressed praise for Tito's decision and the progress it represented. Mihajlov's freedom accentuated the continued plight of other political prisoners, and more attention was focused on such cases as the imprisonment of Soviet dissidents Yuri Orlov, Anatoly Shcharansky, Alexander Ginsburg, and Viktor Petkus for monitoring violations of the Helsinki Accords.

It must be noted, however, that the impact of Mihajlov's release was, to a certain degree, illusory. Mihajlov's notoriety, and that of such figures as lawyer Djuro Djurovic, retired judge Franc Miklavcic, and Croatian nationalist Marko Veselica, provided Tito with impressive media coverage and gave the general amnesty magnitude. Not immediately apparent, however, was that many of the 723 prisoners affected by the amnesty were not freed and that less than one-third were political prisoners. Tito had seized the moment, highlighted by the international conference in Belgrade, to suggest a general and permanent liberalization.

As Mihajlov himself cynically noted, apparent relaxation in communist nations was often a tactic that would be followed by a wave of renewed repression. In August, 1979, Yugoslav authorities issued a warrant for Mihajlov's arrest, discouraging him from returning to his native land. When Djilas moved in the following month to launch a mimeographed journal entitled *Casovnik* (clock), featuring substantial contributions from Mihajlov, the government immediately stopped the publication as subversive propaganda. Six years later, the writings of Djilas and Mihajlov were still among the categories of material proscribed for publication in newspapers.

Nevertheless, the 1980's brought dramatic changes throughout Europe. The Soviet policy of *glasnost* (openness), the reunification of Germany, and the political democratization of the satellite nations changed the political face of Europe. While Yugoslavia welcomed the relaxation of Soviet pressure and much-needed political and economic reform, with openness came internal troubles. Toward the end of the 1980's and in the early 1990's, the general liberalization and the examples set in the independence-minded Soviet Baltic and Caucasian republics revived the specter of ethnic tension and nationalist separatism in Yugoslavia, endangering the precarious federation that Tito had created.

Bibliography

Beloff, Nora. *Tito's Flawed Legacy: Yugoslavia and the West Since 1939*. Boulder, Colo.: Westview Press, 1985. This book gives the most slanted approach on this list—anti-Tito but not specifically pro-American. Beloff is well informed and aims her analysis of Yugoslav history at persuading American readers to shift American policy.

Carter, April. *Democratic Reform in Yugoslavia: The Changing Role of the Party*. Princeton, N.J.: Princeton University Press, 1982. This is an exhaustive academic study focused specifically on the Yugoslav Communist Party in the decade 1961-1971. The appendix gives a broad statistical profile of the party.

Clissold, Stephen. *Djilas: The Progress of a Revolutionary*. New York: Universe Books, 1983. This is a well-documented biography of one of the two most fascinating figures of modern Yugoslavia. Clissold maintains a balanced tone and avoids excessive praise; his narrative is smooth and lively.

Djilas, Milovan. *Conversations with Stalin*. Translated by Michael B. Petrovich. New York: Harcourt, Brace & World, 1962. Written during a short period of freedom between political imprisonments, this book covers the eventful years 1943-1961. It gives a good sense of Djilas's fluctuating political position, his personal feelings, and his hopes for the future.

Doder, Dusko. *The Yugoslavs*. New York: Random House, 1978. Doder, a Yugoslav-American journalist, provides a personalized survey of Yugoslav life, culture, and attitudes. Includes portraits of leaders, intellectuals, and dissidents, and material from interviews of thousands of Yugoslavs, including Djilas.

Mihajlov, Mihajlo. *Underground Notes*. Translated by Maria Mihajlov Ivusic and Christopher W. Ivusic. Kansas City, Kans.: Sheed Andrews & McMeel, 1976. This book consists of nineteen essays on literary and political topics written between 1972 and 1975. Mihajlov is erudite and articulate, and these essays express his strong religious faith and his hope for a reconciliation of Christianity with socialism.

Pavlowitch, Stevan K. *Tito—Yugoslavia's Great Dictator: A Reassessment.* Columbus: Ohio State University Press, 1992. Balanced biography of the influential leader. Illustrated, with bibliography and index.

Ramet, Sabrina P. *Balkan Babel: The Disintegration of Yugoslavia from the Death of Tito to the Fall of Milosevic.* 4th ed. Boulder, Colo.: Westview Press, 2002. Ramet, a political science professor, provides a revised and updated look at the political history of Yugoslavia. Supplemented with maps, bibliography and index.

Rusinow, Dennison. *The Yugoslav Experiment, 1948-1974.* Berkeley: University of California Press, 1977. Rusinow's long personal involvement in the Adriatic region informs this detailed history, which focuses on political developments and the major figures and events that caused them. The book is easy to read though at times overly speculative.

West, Richard. *Tito: And the Rise and Fall of Yugoslavia.* New York: Carroll & Graf, 1995. Survey of the history of Yugoslavia under Tito. Includes maps, bibliography and index.

Barry Mann

Guatemalan Death Squads Target Indigenous Indians

Category of event: Atrocities and war crimes; indigenous peoples' rights
Time: 1978-1985
Locale: Western highland departments of Guatemala

> *Indian reform demands brought violent responses from the army and allied unofficial death squads, leading some Indians to join guerrilla forces and others to flee into exile*

Principal personages:

ROMEO LUCAS GARCÍA (1925-   ), a general and elected president (1978-1982) under whom death squads flourished

EFRAÍN RÍOS MONTT (1926-   ), a general who took power in a 1982 military coup

OSCAR HUMBERTO MEJÍA VÍCTORES (1930-   ), led the 1983 military overthrow of Ríos Montt and presided over the transition to civilian administration

POPE JOHN PAUL II (1920-   ), the Roman Catholic leader who criticized army mistreatment of Guatemalan Indians

PRÓSPERO PEÑADOS DEL BARRIO (1926-   ), the archbishop of the Roman Catholic Church in Guatemala

Summary of Event

Since the sixteenth-century Spanish conquest of the Americas, relations between indigenous peoples and the mixed-race descendants of the conquerors have been volatile. Land and human resources which once were controlled by indigenous peoples became spoils for the conquerors, denying many Indians access to socioeconomic rights. In Guatemala, the political arrangements heavily favored the interests of the mixed-race *ladino* population. Throughout most of the modern era, military figures presided over this political system in which the generally poor indigenous people were excluded from effective participation. Between 1978 and 1985, indigenous peoples and reform advocates in the *ladino* community challenged this system through both peaceful and violent means. Comprehensive and violent suppression of this challenge by the Guatemalan army and its civilian allies was accomplished by gross violation

548

of Indians' civil rights, by use of internationally banned torture, and by breaking up Indian social and political organizations.

Political instability has long been the norm in Guatemala. In the late 1960's in Eastern Guatemala, several thousand *ladino* peasants perished when guerrilla insurgents were suppressed by army units and allied death squads. The acute violence of 1978 to 1985 decimated non-Indian unions, cooperatives, and reform advocates among the general *ladino* population, but the greatest element in the tragic Guatemalan political violence from 1978 to 1985 was its focus on the indigenous or Indian population.

Grievances over denial of Indians' socioeconomic rights set the stage for confrontation. By the mid-1970's, under pressure from population growth and economic change, many indigenous communities had begun to assert themselves, demanding in diverse ways that their interests be respected. More than five hundred cooperatives had been formed to enable members to pool resources more effectively to compete in the marketplace. Others had formed Christian "basic communities" within which literacy was taught and religious texts read for the purpose of enabling members to work together to change conditions and advance social justice. Essentially, this grassroots activity focused on economic grievances. In 1978, indigenous life expectancy (forty-four years) lagged fifteen years behind that of *ladinos*, Indian incomes were barely 58 percent of that of *ladinos*, and Indian infant mortality was 70 percent higher than for *ladinos*. In a society where 82 percent of all children experienced some form of malnutrition, Indian children were most likely to go hungry.

Some among the indigenous had been strongly influenced by Roman Catholic activists. The key political movement of modern Latin American Catholicism, the Christian Democrat Party (DCG), however, had little influence in Guatemala until the 1985 election of its leader, Vinicio Cerezo Arévalo, as president. In the 1978 to 1985 period, more than three hundred DCG activists and leaders were assassinated. Catholic activists in the indigenous community increasingly were driven to adopt nonelectoral tactics to bring pressure for change.

Signs that military rulers had opted to repress Indian protests became visible in May, 1978. Indians from the Panzos municipality, Alta Verapaz department, joined about eight hundred others and marched to present petitions objecting to army seizures of nearby Indian lands to local government officials. More than one hundred perished when army troops opened fire on the marchers. After this Panzos massacre, Defense Minister Otto Speigler publicly blamed clerics for Indian unrest; the Catholic missionary who led the marchers was deported. Detailed death lists naming others soon appeared, and proarmy political parties called on the people to judge communists, who were said to include religious people. These were not idle threats. One month after the Panzos massacre, activist priest Father Hermógenes López was murdered. He was the first of more than a dozen priests to die between 1978 and 1985.

Both religious rights and rights to free association clearly were under attack. Leaders of Indian cooperatives, Catholic basic communities, and other organizations were victimized. Members of these Indian self-help organizations were frequently targeted by death lists, violently abducted by anonymous armed men, or killed outright. Thousands of Indian children were orphaned as populations of whole villages fled into the mountains to avoid army massacres. Fear broadened and intensified as guerrillas committed reprisals against Indians who collaborated with army authorities. Once tranquil, the highlands became killing fields with tortured and dismembered corpses littering paths and highways.

The Roman Catholic Church and its followers were especially hard hit by army and allied "death squad" atrocities. As the violence peaked in 1981 and 1982, Catholic Father Stanley Rother, a missionary committed to organizing assistance to the orphaned Indians near picturesque Lake Atitlan, Okarche, was murdered in his church sanctuary. The Catholic bishop of adjacent El Quiché department fled the region as many church properties were confiscated or desecrated by the army. In such a situation, without the moderating guidance of ordained clerics, some victimized Indians sought revenge.

Other Indian activists, inspired by the apparent successes of revolutionaries in nearby Nicaragua and El Salvador, voluntarily chose to join offshoots of existing armed guerrilla groups which had appeared in 1961. Most who turned to guerrilla violence did so after relatives or neighbors fell victim to soldiers or private proarmy death squads. Four separate guerrilla forces recruited angry survivors and savagely killed favored targets (landlords, local officials, and army officers). By 1981, the guerrilla and counterinsurgency violence had polarized the nation as most Indian areas fell into near civil war. Action was most intense in El Quiché, Huehuetenango, Sololá, Alta Verapaz, San Marcos, and several other largely Indian departments. Rates of assassinations, wholesale massacres, and guerrilla violence rose there between 1978 and 1982. Other Indian departments, such as Totonicapán and Chiquirnula, remained virtually free of a guerrilla presence and also suffered fewer incidents of army and death squad violence.

Abductions and killings directed against the Indians divided army commanders after Pope John Paul II sharply criticized military rulers during a 1983 visit to the nation. This tension contributed to the overthrow of

Protestant dictator and general Efraín Ríos Montt by Catholic officers in August, 1983. After coup leader General Oscar Humberto Mejía Víctores ended secret trials and public executions, the official Catholic voice remained in opposition to all forms of brutality, continuing to call for social reforms. In well-publicized papal letters and through numerous criticisms aired by the Guatemalan Bishops' Conference, especially those by its chair, Archbishop Próspero Peñados del Barrio, the church demanded that human rights be respected.

Military rulers formally relinquished control to the Cerezo administration in January, 1986. By then, seventy-five thousand Guatemalans of both major ethnic groups had perished and more than thirty-eight thousand others had been kidnapped and were feared dead. By any measure, the events of 1978 to 1985 were the most intensely violent in all of Guatemalan history.

Impact of Event

Disruption of normal life in Guatemala's indigenous areas was comprehensive, went well beyond that endured by nearly all non-Indian communities, and left a large imprint on the nation. Of more than four hundred villages destroyed in the army counterinsurgency campaign, nearly all were in indigenous areas. In several cases, whole communities were annihilated in the process: For example, at the San Francisco plantation, Nentón municipality, Huehuetenango department (near the Mexican border), more than 350 people were massacred by the army in late July, 1982. Many of the distinct Indian subcultures so decimated no longer exist.

The events of 1978 to 1985 significantly affected public attitudes. Even among civilian government officials, distrust came to reign. A disgusted Vice President Francisco Villagrán (who later resigned and fled into exile) in 1982 stated: "There are no political prisoners in Guatemala—only political murders." Fear of the army remained widespread throughout the 1980's and formed a serious barrier to realization of the human right to free association, especially in the Western highlands. Army occupation of large areas of El Quiché, Huehuetenango, Alta Verapaz, San Marcos, and Sololá departments continued for more than a decade and transformed Indian society. Civil defense patrols substantially restricted rights to travel freely and to work outside government supervision. These organizations also undermined traditional authority in Indian communities, sowing suspicion and creating dependency on nearby military administrators. After the greatest guerrilla threat ebbed, remaining rural military bases undermined civilian officials' authority and inhibited realization of Indians' rights to self-government and to free movement within the nation.

The events also created large numbers of displaced persons, further eroding the distinctive indigenous cultures. In 1982, the Bishops' Conference of
the Guatemalan Roman Catholic Church stated that nearly one-seventh of the
national population had been displaced from their home areas, including
more than one hundred thousand who had fled Guatemala for Mexican sanctuary. Tensions between the Guatemalan army and these exiles exacerbated
foreign relations, producing minor skirmishes between the nations, and led to
United Nations assistance to the refugees. These migrations were sympatheti-
cally chronicled in the film *El Norte* (1984). In some cases a semblance of a new
community evolved, as was the experience of Kanjobal Indians from San
Miguel Acatán municipality, Huehuetenango department, who reconstituted
a Guatemalan community in the United States at Indiantown, Florida. For
most Guatemalan Indians, the violence shattered a world, and the civilian governments of Guatemala since then have failed to recreate it.

The events of 1978-1985 had great impacts on the whole Guatemalan social
and political system, not only on the indigenous peoples. Army victory, pursued without reservation or negotiation, had been achieved by 1985. The brutal excesses involved in the victory, however, had exhausted the army and had
repulsed the public. Systematic use of human rights violations to eliminate
both armed and peaceful challengers carried high costs. With legality in tat-
ters, corruption had flourished, alienating much of the Guatemalan business
community. International isolation in response to human rights abuses produced cuts in foreign aid, complicating economic recovery. These and other
factors in 1985 and 1986 led ruling generals to abandon governmental offices
they had held for nearly thirty years.

Electoral participation was unusually high as common people, Indian and
ladino, exercised long-denied rights to self-government, choosing reformer
Cerezo to lead them. Momentum toward realization of socioeconomic rights
through reform policies under his civilian Christian Democrat administration, however, waned after two unsuccessful military coup attempts in 1988
and 1989. Neither the 1986-1991 Cerezo administration nor its more conservative Serrano successor proved fully able to end political violence, though
army massacres virtually ceased and overall casualty levels from assassinations
and kidnappings fell. Civilian administrations also initiated peace negotiations with the guerrilla movements in 1987 as part of the Arias Peace Plan for
Central America.

Bibliography

Bizarro Ujpán, Ignacio. *Campesino: The Diary of a Guatemalan Indian.* Translated and edited by James D. Sexton. Tuscon: University of Arizona Press, 1985. A fascinating oral history of Indian life in villages around Lake Atitlan, 1977-1984. Balances leftist bias in the Menchú volume listed below. Includes excellent explanatory notes by Sexton; completely indexed with thorough references.

Bowen, Gordon L. "U.S. Approaches to Guatemalan State Terrorism, 1977-1986." In *Terrible Beyond Endurance? The Foreign Policy of State Terrorism*, edited by Michael Stohl. Westport, Conn.: Greenwood Press, 1988. In fifty pages, presents a thorough analysis of Guatemalan violence and the varied U.S. role during the Carter and Reagan presidencies. Contrasts sharply with Jonas in tone and interpretation. Indexed, extensive documentation.

Davis, Shelton, and Julie Hodson. *Witnesses to Political Violence in Guatemala.* Boston, Mass.: Oxfam America, 1983. A valuable short (fifty-four pages) collection of dozens of transcribed first-person accounts of carnage in the Guatemalan highlands between 1978 and 1982. Includes testimonials from refugees, aid workers, priests, and others. No reference features.

Delli Sante, Angela. *Nightmare or Reality: Guatemala in the 1980s.* Amsterdam: Thala Publishers, 1996. A well-researched work on the history of the "dark decade" of civil war and state terrorism. The central focus of the book is on the displacement of thousands who escaped the violence in Guatemala.

Grandin, Greg. *The Blood of Guatemala: A History of Race and Nation.* Durham, N.C.: Duke University Press, 2000. A revealing look at the history of the struggles between the indigenous Indians and Mayan elites.

Jonas, Susanne. *The Battle for Guatemala: Rebels, Death Squads, and U.S. Power.* Boulder, Colo.: Westview Press, 1991. A leading Guatemalan analyst among leftist American academics takes an interdisciplinary approach to interpret a crisis which is viewed as continuing. Extensive documentation; indexed.

Menchú, Rigoberta. *I, Rigoberta Menchú, an Indian Woman of Guatemala.* London: Verso, 1984. First-person testimonial of a Guatemalan Indian woman's childhood and family life during violence and radicalization. Jarring, graphic in places. Without documentation, but events described have been authenticated in Amnesty International and other reliable reports. Glossary of Indian terms.

Taylor, Clark. *Return of Guatemala's Refugees: Reweaving the Torn.* Philadelphia: Temple University Press, 1998. An examination of refugees after their return to their homeland. Includes a bibliography and an index.

Gordon L. Bowen

European Court of Human Rights Rules on Mistreatment of Prisoners

Category of event: International norms; prisoners' rights
Time: January 18, 1978
Locale: Strasbourg, France

> *The European Court of Human Rights found the United Kingdom guilty of the mistreatment of prisoners in Northern Ireland*

Principal personages:

JACK LYNCH (1917-1999), the prime minister of the Republic of Ireland (1966-1973 and 1977-1979)
LIAM COSGRAVE (1920-   ), the prime minister of the Republic of Ireland (1973-1977)
EDWARD HEATH (1916-   ), the British prime minister (1970-1974)

Summary of Event

The situation in Northern Ireland had engendered abuses of human rights since the creation of the province in 1922. When, after a two-year war with the British, the Irish Free State was created, Northern Ireland was not included. With a majority population of Protestants who preferred union with Great Britain, the province was retained within the United Kingdom. This left one-third of the population as Roman Catholic Nationalists, who preferred to be part of the Irish Free State. Tension and violence marked the politics of the province for decades.

The government of Northern Ireland in 1922 passed the Civil Authorities (Special Powers) Act, which indirectly encouraged police harassment and oppression of the Roman Catholic minority since it removed most citizen protections against arrest, detainment without warrant, interrogation, searches, and the like. A British commission reported in 1969 that the Special Powers Act had caused widespread resentment among Catholics. A tradition of police repression grew, especially against Catholics and the Irish Republican Army (IRA), the organization most committed to removing Northern Ireland from British rule. In 1968 and 1969, civil rights marches triggered an outburst by the Royal Ulster Constabulary (RUC), the police of Ulster, which in turn led to mob violence. In August of 1969, the British government sent in troops to keep order. Within eighteen months, British Army activities—house searches, arrests, and interrogations—were as offensive to the Catholic minority community as those of the RUC. A renewed IRA engaged in violent attacks against the police and army.

In August of 1971, the Northern Ireland government invoked the internment provision of the Special Powers Act. In cooperation with the British Army, approximately 350 suspected IRA members were arrested without warrant and detained without limit. At the end of six months, about twenty-four hundred had been interned and about sixteen hundred had been released after interrogation. Evidence began to accumulate that these prisoners were being subjected to brutal treatment in order to obtain information from them. This was consistent with the Army policy of acquiring as much information as possible about the inhabitants of Republican areas.

The principal charges were against five techniques that included the use of hooding. The prisoners, at all times other than interrogation periods, wore heavy black bags over their heads, causing an extreme sense of isolation. Another charge was that of subjecting prisoners to intense noise, such as that of a high-pressure drill or steam escaping, at all times other than interrogation, causing psychological disorientation. These conditions were coupled with a deprivation of sleep for two and three days at a time and deprivation of food for the same period, causing intense stress and physical weakness. Finally, prisoners were forced to stand on their toes, leaning against a wall, with their hands above their heads and legs spread apart, for days at a time, despite the periodic collapse of the prisoners. Patrick Shivers, for example, was held for eight days in 1971 and was subjected to beatings, wall standing, hooding, and lack of sleep. He feared for his sanity, and his body ended up shaking uncontrollably.

Allegations about the techniques were widespread, and the British government appointed a committee under Sir Edmund Compton to investigate the practices. The committee report, issued in November of 1971, indicated that the practices were taught to the RUC by the English Intelligence Center in April of 1971 and that their use was authorized "at a high level." After discounting allegations of even more serious abuses—beatings, dog attacks, and the like—the report concluded that the interrogation techniques were "ill-treatment" but not "physical brutality," as the committee understood the term. The response to the Compton report was critical skepticism among the British and complete rejection by the Catholic community, which saw the report as a whitewash.

Another committee was appointed that year, and it reported in March of 1972. The majority report held that the treatment of prisoners was justified on moral grounds. The minority report disagreed, but the minority and majority reports concurred that some of the techniques were illegal under domestic British law. When this report was issued, Prime Minister Edward Heath declared that the five techniques would be discontinued as aids to interrogation.

The government of the Republic of Ireland, under Prime Minister Jack Lynch, decided that the results of the Compton report warranted bringing the evidence to the European Commission on Human Rights in December of 1971 and March of 1972. The Irish government was motivated by what it saw as insufficient response to the explosion of violence in Northern Ireland and the treatment of the minority community. The Irish government asserted that the maltreatment of prisoners constituted a violation of Article 3 of the European Convention on Human Rights on the part of the United Kingdom. The Irish government sought a finding that torture and inhuman treatment had been used on prisoners. The Irish government also maintained that internment was

After a committee issued a report criticizing certain techniques—such as hooding— used to interrogate Irish prisoners in 1972, British prime minister Edward Heath announced that the government would stop using the objectionable techniques. (Library of Congress)

a violation of Article 5 of the convention, which protects the right to liberty and security of a person, and also Article 6, which protects the right to a fair trial. The manner in which internment was carried out, directed almost exclusively against Catholics, was also held to be a violation of Article 14, which forbids racial or religious discrimination.

In 1976, the European Commission on Human Rights considered evidence based upon 228 cases from 1971 to 1974 and heard 118 witnesses. The commission report, issued in 1976, accepted the British position that instituting internment was necessary under the conditions in Northern Ireland at the time and thus was not discriminatory. The commission held, however, that the treatment of prisoners did violate Article 3 and that the treatment of prisoners constituted torture. The British government again disavowed the use of the techniques and paid out more than $320,000 in damages to prisoners. The Irish government, under Prime Minister Liam Cosgrave, then brought the case to the European Court of Human Rights in March of 1976 to seek a confirmation of the commission's findings and the punishment of those responsible.

In January of 1978, the court issued its judgment. On the key matter of the torture of prisoners, it did not go as far as the European Commission's judgment. The court accepted that the five techniques created fear, humiliation, and debasement and thus constituted inhuman and degrading treatment. The court, however, saw torture as a particularly cruel and "aggravated" form of inhuman treatment. The techniques used by the security forces in Northern Ireland were held by a vote of sixteen to one not to be "torture" under Article 3 of the European Convention on Human Rights. The British judge, in fact, did not even see the five techniques as cruel and inhuman. Finally, the court concluded it did not have the power to direct the British to bring criminal charges against those responsible.

The court went on to agree with the commission that the British did deprive citizens of their liberty outside of the judicial process but allowed that the larger issue of special powers for the RUC and judiciary were justified by presence of a terrorist threat. The type and character of the laws used to combat terrorism were the responsibility of the British, and the court accepted their necessity. The court also addressed the question of whether RUC and army actions, directed at the IRA and Catholics, constituted a form of discrimination. The judges concluded, along with the commission, that the British government had tried to eliminate a formidable terrorist organization, the IRA, and that such a goal was not discriminatory. The means of achieving it, in addition, were not viewed as disproportionate.

Impact of Event

The revelations of the Irish case before the commission were embarrassing to the British government. When the commission found that the methods used constituted torture, the fact that they had been authorized officially in the first place and then accepted by the Compton commission was less than flattering to British security policy in Northern Ireland. When the Irish government proceeded to take the findings to the European Court of Human Rights in 1976, as it was entitled to do, the British government reacted with anger, as the five techniques had by then been discontinued. London believed that to continue the case was a deliberate insult to the United Kingdom. In fact, the case was often cited by those critical of British human rights policy in Northern Ireland.

The British government had not contested, in the case before the European Court, the European Commission's report that the five techniques constituted torture. In 1972 and again in 1977, the British government vowed that the techniques would not be used in interrogation. The practice of internment was stopped in 1975. The Irish government's case would seem to have been effective in curbing the abuses. In fact, however, subsequent reports indicated that the abuse of prisoners continued. In 1977, thirty defense lawyers in the juryless court system wrote the secretary of state for Northern Ireland that ill-treatment of prisoners was a common practice used to extract confessions. In 1978, Amnesty International issued a report indicating continued regular maltreatment of prisoners and calling for an investigation. Amnesty also called for a review of the special police powers, citing the arrest, interrogation, and conviction of a retarded man who could not have formulated the confession he supposedly gave. The media attention given to the Amnesty report and the European Court's decision in 1978 prompted the British government to appoint the Bennett Commission to study the issue. Its report called for restrictions on ill-treatment of prisoners and new rules for interrogation. The evidence of maltreatment, however, continued to accumulate. Two RUC doctors resigned because they believed that the injuries they were treating were caused by police abuse during interrogation.

The pattern continued of arrest on suspicion without a warrant, followed by brutal interrogation to obtain a confession, and then use of the confession to obtain a conviction. A vast majority of convictions (85 percent) for terrorist crimes came from confessions. The fact that the five specific techniques cited in the European Court's decision were no longer used does not ameliorate the fact that RUC abuses to obtain confessions from Catholics were not halted by the European Court in 1978.

The precedent of challenging security practices in Northern Ireland through European institutions was set by the 1978 case. Four Republican prisoners in the Maze Prison brought their case to the European Commission on Human Rights, arguing that the conditions of their imprisonment constituted inhuman and degrading treatment. The commission in 1980 rejected their claim and said that they were not entitled to be treated as political prisoners. Other cases concerning Northern Ireland have been brought to the commission since 1971. The protection of human rights decided in the 1978 case apparently encouraged the use of both the court and the commission.

Bibliography

Arnold, Bruce. *Jack Lynch: A Hero in Crisis.* Dublin: Merlin Publishing, 2001. Examines the career of the prime minister of Ireland during a troubling time.

Coogan, Tim P. *On the Blanket: The H-Block Story.* Dublin: Ward River Press, 1980. The mistreatment of prisoners in Northern Ireland began before August of 1971 and continued after the period that the European court examined (1971-1975). Coogan's book covers the genesis of the human rights issue in Northern Ireland and the period of internment. Covers in great detail the status of prisoners in Northern Ireland that led to their blanket protest and eventually to the hunger strike of 1981, in which Bobby Sands and nine others died.

McGuffin, J. *Internment.* Tralee, Ireland: Anvil Books, 1973. Written at the time that the internment policy was in practice. McGuffin compiled stories and evidence from those interned. Although emotionally charged, the book reveals the practices upon which the European Court decision of 1978 was based.

Walsh, Dermot. *The Use and Abuse of Emergency Legislation in Northern Ireland.* London: Cobden Trust, 1983. This detailed treatment of the emergency legislation pertaining to Northern Ireland includes the Prevention of Terrorism Acts promulgated in both London and Belfast as well as the older Special Powers Act and the Emergency Provisions (Northern Ireland) Act of 1973. The European Court's decision is also covered. Walsh argues that the European Court decision did not change the practice of mistreatment of prisoners but only eliminated certain techniques. The book takes the position that no legislation in the criminal justice area is going to solve the political conflict in Northern Ireland.

Weston, Burns H., Richard A. Falk, and Anthony A. D'Amato, eds. *International Law and World Order.* St. Paul, Minn.: West, 1980. Pages 516 to 533 have key excerpts from the European Court of Human Rights decision of January 18, 1978. The decision is quite involved, as the court considers matters concerning the justification of the United Kingdom for the Emergency Provisions Act of 1973, the degree to which the British cooperated with the investigation, and the discriminatory character of the actions of the RUC under the articles of the European Convention on Human Rights. This valuable summary focuses on the key judgments and the reasons for them.

Richard B. Finnegan

China Promises to Correct Abuses of Citizens' Rights

Category of event: Civil rights; political freedom
Time: Spring, 1978
Locale: Beijing, People's Republic of China

> *Post-Mao Chinese communist officials encouraged Chinese citizens to publicize their grievances against the government in a short-lived democracy movement*

Principal personages:

DENG XIAOPING (1904-1997), the power behind the post-Mao political and economic reforms in China, although not occupying a major government post

PENG ZHEN (1902-1997), the former mayor of Beijing, persecuted during the Cultural Revolution; one of the Deng reformers who encouraged the "Beijing Spring"

WEI JINGSHENG (1950-   ), a member of the Chinese Human Rights Alliance sentenced to fifteen years in prison; one of the editors of *Explorations*

FU YUEHUA, a leader of Beijing demonstrations against hunger and oppression; the first Beijing Spring leader arrested

Summary of Event

After the death of Chinese Communist Party Chairman Mao Zedong, many Party leaders, under the leadership of then Vice-Premier and veteran party cadre Deng Xiaoping, called for a major break from past political and economic practices. In the political arena, the reformers called for the rebuilding of the legal system, for redressing the wrongs committed since 1957 against Chinese of all political persuasions, and for ridding the Chinese Communist Party of the influence of the so-called "Gang of Four"—Mao's wife, Jiang Qing, and three of her Cultural Revolution colleagues.

In the economic area, Chinese post-Mao reformers called for the economic "responsibility system" that would free both rural and urban economic institutions from overreliance on central control. Peasants would be able to leave the communes and lease farmland from the state. Factory managers would be responsible for running more efficient factories that sold goods to the market.

The economic and political reforms were, however, resisted by at least some of the Communist Party members who had joined the party during the previous twelve years, that is, since the beginning of the 1966 Cultural Revolution. As many as one-half of the party's members fell into this category. Reforms were also opposed by some of the older party members who still remembered Chairman Mao with fondness and who feared the subversive influence of new ideas. They particularly seemed to fear Chinese versions of liberal democracy.

In 1978, the leaders supporting Deng Xiaoping mobilized popular support to resist these attacks on reforms. They encouraged popular opposition to the Maoists and permitted people to air their grievances. The Cultural Revolution began to be characterized as the "Ten Lost Years," and former Red Guards were encouraged to write about their feelings in an outpouring of writings called the literature of "the wounded." Chinese from all walks of life were also encouraged to voice their criticisms of government policies during the Cultural Revolution using big character posters posted on the Democracy Wall in Beijing (and other cities), or in various unofficial publications. Leading publications included *Explorations, Beijing Spring, April Fifth Forum, Today,* and the *Masses' Reference News.* Leading organizations included the Chinese Human Rights League, the Enlightenment Society, and the Thaw Society. The unofficial publications, and the organizers and contributors to them, generally used their new freedoms to call for a "fifth modernization," that is, for democracy, in addition to the other four modernizations (agriculture, industry, science and technology, and military) that focused on economic development.

In March of 1978, a new constitution was promulgated that guaranteed many new democratic rights, what were called the "four freedoms" (the right to speak freely, to air views fully, to hold debates, and to put up wall posters). By the fall of 1978, about thirty-four thousand peasants had come to Beijing to publicize their problems and to seek redress from the authorities. In November, 1978, the Democracy Wall in Beijing became a rallying point for leaders of the democracy movement as well as petitioners to the government.

Deng called for the rehabilitation of many of China's political outcasts and sufferers from the previous twenty years. Among those whose verdicts were reversed were 110,000 people who had been imprisoned since 1957. Deng insisted on righting the records of many others who had died in prison or were persecuted to death. During this period, the newspapers were filled with belated obituaries.

In the area of intellectual activity, Deng moved the society from a situation of "politics in command" under former Communist Party Chairman Mao to one of seeking truth from facts and using practice as the sole criterion for testing truth. He followed these general statements in 1978 with specific support for popular expression of criticism and discontent. He condoned the setting up of the Democracy Wall, calling the posters there "a good thing" in November of 1978. Also in November of 1978, Deng reaffirmed that unofficial media would be permitted to flourish, as guaranteed by the new constitution. He noted that it was useful sometimes for the party to be urged along by the masses. It was even rumored that the unofficial journal *Beijing Spring* had Deng's tacit support.

The reaction of democracy movement participants in late 1978 was sometimes ecstatic. They wrote posters, composed articles, joined demonstrations, and made public statements. On November 29, 1978, a huge demonstration called for democracy and human rights, while cheering Deng Xiaoping and the late Chou Enlai. One excited man was reported to have told a foreigner, "You are witnessing the greatest thing to happen in China."

Unfortunately for Chinese human rights advocates, Deng Xiaoping began to react against the movement by January, 1979. He did this in part because the movement had served its political purpose of embarrassing Maoists and providing reformers with popular support, and now was no longer needed. Perhaps more important, Deng began to repress the democracy movement because it was beginning to call for substantial democratic reforms, reforms which could have led to the loss of the Chinese Communist Party's monopoly of power.

On January 18, 1979, Fu Yuehua became the first democracy movement leader to be arrested. On March 16, 1979, Deng, in a secret speech on the Sino-Vietnam War, warned that the democracy movement had "gone too far," and that it was not in the interest of "stability, unity, and the four modernizations."

The Communist Party in 1979 began to take steps to make arrests and detentions easier, steps that would rein in the democracy movement. The National People's Congress reissued regulations using a 1957 Stalinist law that permitted Chinese police to practice administrative detention of people for three years without charges or trial. This detention was intended to accomplish what was called "reeducation through labor."

Impact of Event

By December, 1979, wall posters on Democracy Wall in Beijing were banned. On January 1, 1980, Democracy Wall was officially closed, and on January 17, Deng announced that the right to put up wall posters and to exercise the "four freedoms" would be deleted from the new constitution because of "abuse." Many of the democracy movement leaders were arrested, and all the unofficial publications were either closed or voluntarily ceased publication.

In sum, the Beijing Spring lasted from March, 1978, to March, 1979. During that time, Chinese were encouraged by post-Mao reform leaders such as Deng Xiaoping to air their grievances and to seek redress from the government. The Beijing Spring also saw the beginnings of a number of unofficial prodemocracy magazines and the use of the Democracy Wall in Beijing.

Unfortunately, once the Cultural Revolution was repudiated (as evidenced by the Gang of Four trial in early 1980), Deng's economic reforms approved, and the Communist reform leadership consolidated, Deng no longer had a need for the democracy movement. He also feared this movement because the Beijing Spring leaders called for a democratization of the entire political structure, including free elections, a free press, and open criticism of the government. Beijing Spring leaders began to be arrested and were often given long sentences, ranging from two to fifteen years, and harsh treatment in prisons.

As with human rights movements in many countries, leaders paid a high price, including long prison terms and extremely harsh treatment, some of it documented by Amnesty International. At the same time, this movement and the democracy protests that have occurred since 1978 seem to have moved the country closer to a more democratic system. The leaders of the Beijing Spring, although in some cases still in prison, continued to be an inspiration to the leaders of democracy movements in 1984, in 1986, and at the 1989 Tiananmen Square demonstrations.

In terms of immediate consequences, the 1978-1979 year of freedoms moved the entire range of Chinese civil rights forward. Although there was some reversal in the immediate post-Beijing Spring period, and much suffering by its leaders, each generation of leaders' sacrifices have seemed to move forward the entire cause of democratic rights. The long-term consequence of these human rights movements is that it became harder for the Chinese government to repress without cause, or totally to repress, later democracy movements. After the democracy movement of 1989, there was even more Chinese support for the goal of a fifth modernization, democracy, even though few were willing to express it publicly.

Each new movement has received wider support, and each new movement has built upon the last. When the history of China's democracy movement is later written, the Beijing Spring movement of 1978 will most likely be seen as the opening shot in a struggle that will have taken many years, but will probably ultimately be successful, although at a high cost in human suffering.

Bibliography

Amnesty International. *China: Torture and Ill-Treatment of Prisoners.* New York: Amnesty International Publications, 1987. Describes the Chinese debate on the use of torture, the extent of torture and ill-treatment, and some of the reasons for torture. Outlines the legislation against torture as well as the official efforts to reduce torture. Also offers Amnesty International's conclusions and recommendations for changes that might reduce the practice of torture in the People's Republic of China.

Chan, Anita, Stanley Rosen, and Jonathan Unger, eds. *On Socialist Democracy and the Chinese Legal System: The Li Yizhe Debates.* Armonk, N.Y.: M. E. Sharpe, 1985. The 1974 writings of three former Red Guards that were to emerge during the democracy movement of 1978 as a major critique of Chinese bureaucracy and party dominance, as well as a call for democratic reforms. The book also traces the lives of the three authors from their 1975 exile to their 1977 imprisonment through their 1978 vindication during the period of the "reversal of verdicts." In 1981, one of the three was rearrested in the wake of the anti-Beijing Spring tide because of his continued calls for democracy.

Chang, David Wen-Wei. *China Under Deng Xiaoping: Political and Economic Reform.* New York: St. Martin's Press, 1988. A discussion of Deng Xiaoping's reforms that helps to place the Beijing Spring movement into historical context.

Evans, Richard. *Deng Xiaoping and the Making of Modern China.* New York: Viking Press, 1994. An examination of the life and career of one of the most important leaders of the post-Mao era.

Seymour, James, ed. *The Fifth Modernization: China's Human Rights Movement, 1978-1979.* Stanfordville, N.Y.: Human Rights Publishing Group, 1980. Translations of many of the most important documents posted on Democracy Wall or published in the various democracy movement publications. Also contains an introduction to and description of the 1978 Beijing Spring.

Svensson, Marina. *Debating Human Rights in China: A Conceptual and Political History.* Lanham, Md.: Rowman & Littlefield, 2002. A detailed account of the history of human rights in China. Contains a bibliography and an index.

Stephen C. Thomas

Iran Uses Executions to Establish New Order

Category of event: Atrocities and war crimes; religious freedom
Time: 1979-1985
Locale: Teheran, Iran

> *Iran under the rule of Ayatollah Ruhollah Khomeini had a poor record in human rights, including countless deaths of the young, underage children, political figures, and members of religious minorities, particularly of the Baha'i faith*

Principal personages:
AYATOLLAH RUHOLLAH KHOMEINI (1902-1989), the Islamic leader who took control of Iran and created a religious state
MOHAMMAD REZA SHAH PAHLAVI (1919-1980), the ruler of Iran (1941-1979)
SHAHPOOR BAKHTIAR (1916-1991), the ruler of Iran for thirty-nine days, after the shah's abdication

Summary of Events

Until 1979, Iran was under a monarchy headed by the self-styled shah, Reza, the son and successor of a minor officer who had sought to establish a new dynasty, the Aryan Pahlavis. The shah sought to modernize Iran as a Western state and establish it as a major regional power. The shah found it expedient to be conciliatory toward Israel and brutal toward his opponents, weeding them out systematically. This persecution, along with corruption and poor economic performance, led to urban unrest. By 1978, Iran was paralyzed, and the shah was forced to abdicate. A provisional government under Prime Minister Shahpoor Bakhtiar was installed. He was forced out of power and replaced by Medhi Bazargan. The government lasted only until November, when the clerics took over. Ayatollah Ruhollah Khomeini thus came to full power.

Systematic persecution followed. A secret list of enemies of the state was compiled. Ten to twenty thousand suspects were instructed not to leave the country. Arbitrary arrests followed investigations of the suspects. Those charged rarely received fair public trials. Revolutionary Guards began searching homes for liquor and pornographic materials, possession of which violated Islamic law.

By the end of 1979, the new regime had imprisoned more than fifteen thousand. Of these, seven hundred, all political and military figures prominent during the shah's reign, were executed summarily by firing squads. The remainder were judged to be counterrevolutionaries, seditious plotters, and persons violating Islamic ethics and codes of conduct—prostitutes, drug traffickers, homosexuals, suspected shah sympathizers, and seditious members of ethnic minorities in Kurdistan, Khuzestan, Baluchistan, and Azerbaijan.

In early 1980, the clerics moved a step further. They sought to legitimize the evolving theocracy. Elections were held for a new president and a clerically biased Parliament, the Majlis. Iran moved toward theocratic fundamentalism and became viscerally opposed to separation of church and state. Laws were promulgated making all aspects of private and public life subject to *Fiqh*, or Islamic jurisprudence. Individuals were no longer citizens of a secular state. They were part of the Ummah, a transnational fellowship dictating every aspect of human life. Iran was seen by the Western world as a blatant violator of basic secular tenets regarding human rights. Of these, the laws that were seen as most pernicious dealt with personal freedom and choice in matters of sexuality, public appearance, politics, and liturgical observance.

Women were required to appear modestly dressed in public, wearing the *chadoor,* or head veil. No exceptions were made for non-Muslim women. Secular divorce laws were replaced, and traditional Islamic family law was instituted. This law severely limited certain rights and privileges in matters of custody of children and initiation of divorce proceedings by women. Political participation by women was restricted, and women were limited effectively to one in their representation in the Majlis.

Homosexuality was banned. It was declared a moral depravity and a criminal offense. Public flogging was instituted for it and other moral offenses. Death by stoning was introduced, as was amputation of fingers as a measure of punitive deterrence in cases of theft. Revolutionary courts and the Guards were given considerable powers to use private initiative for the public moral good. They were to see that public and private behavior conformed to moral standards set by the new order.

Revolutionary guards searched, without warrants, private homes for anti-Islamic materials, political or pornographic. They searched homes suspected of "anti-Islamic" activities, including possession of liquor. Governmental acquiescence to this private initiative by the Guards opened opportunities for individuals to settle old scores, a process made easier by the lack of juridical standards ensuring due process to protect the accused. The burden of innocence was left with the accused. Political offenders were not given easy access to a legally constituted defense counsel, and admissions of guilt extracted under duress or torture were admissible proof. Torture was indeed used.

Opposition to the new Islamic order in most forms was deemed illegal, be it by individuals, expressed orally or in the press, or by anticlerical groups. One such group singled out for brutal attack by the clerics was the Mojahedeen-e-Khalq, a group of radical left-wing revolutionaries, three thousand of whom were executed by the end of 1982.

In April, 1980, universities were closed down. Left-wing elements were weeded out, and the universities were reopened under new Islamic guidelines. Similar purges were instigated and carried out in the public sector. Public-sector employment and admission to educational institutions were granted to individuals achieving satisfactory scores in tests of knowledge of Islam and its orthodoxy. These Islamic test requirements were dropped in the mid-1980's, but while they were in effect, they further increased discrimination against non-Muslim minorities.

By the end of 1982, according to some observers in Teheran, the new regime had executed more than ten thousand people, some summarily and others under brutal conditions. Perhaps the single most systematic violation of human rights, even by Islamic standards, occurred against religious minorities. As befitted a theocratic state, the constitution of 1980 recognized the legal rights of the *Ahl-e-Kitah* (the People of the Book, or Christians and Jews) and one other pre-Islamic religious group, the Zoroastrians. Representatives from these three minorities were granted seats in the newly formed Parliament, the Majlis. These three religious minorities were to be guaranteed protection of life and property under the law only as long as they complied with government regulations.

Armenians and non-Farsi-speaking religious minorities could not propagate religious instruction without severe restrictions, particularly instruction carried out in non-Farsi languages. To allow this, the authorities argued, was to allow the possibility of subversive activities among such minorities. Perhaps the greatest infringement to individual freedom of worship was to occur against Iranians of the Baha'i faith. Baha'is were charged with crimes against God and warring against God. At the revolution's onset, mobs had demolished Baha'i shrines in Shiraz. Revolutionary Guards had subsequently confiscated Baha'i properties and businesses. Vigilante groups continued to weed out known Baha'is. A few were singled out for summary trials and executions. The persecution intensified. In the new constitution, the Baha'is were specifically singled out and excluded as a protected religious minority. The Ayatollahs considered the Baha'i faith as heretical and the Baha'is, numbering about one-third of a million, as religious subversives. Thereafter, Baha'i social welfare organizations and businesses were banned. Public and private Baha'i worship was made illegal. Baha'is could no longer hold government jobs; employment in the private sector was also discouraged. Baha'i marriages were no longer recognized. Married Baha'i women were thus liable to persecution on grounds of immorality, that is to say, prostitution.

Impact of Event

The most dramatic impact of laws advocating the supremacy of theocracy over the rights of the individual was felt by religious minorities. Relations between the government and the religious minorities were fraught with tension and conflict, tensions which began manifesting themselves almost at the outset of the revolution. These tensions centered on Jews suspected of Zionist or seditious tendencies.

In the light of the regime's virulence toward Zionism, international Jewry, and Israel, many Jews became increasingly anxious and began leaving Iran. Some Jews were charged with harboring Zionist sympathies, a treasonable offense punishable by death. Ten of these suspected sympathizers were killed, accused of "warring against God" and "corruption of Earth." Subsequently, larger numbers of Jews fled Iran. The drive to leave intensified, particularly after a concerted raid led to several arrests. Among those arrested was a rabbi who was charged with helping Jews to flee Iran. Others were forced to make public anti-Israeli statements. The public recanting of one's faith or political sympathies in return for clemency for life or permission to work was not confined to Jews. Christians suffered similar discrimination and persecution. On the whole, however, Jews fared better than Christians. Unlike the Christians, predominantly of Armenian descent, Jews in Iran spoke Farsi. This helped ease tensions between them and the authorities.

The Baha'i leadership, fully aware of the regime's fundamental commitment to eradicate the faith as heresy, responded swiftly. It sought to comply with the new regulations. It disbanded the national association, but to no avail. The persecution continued and intensified. By September, 1980, seven Baha'i leaders had been executed. In December, 1981, eight more followed. The Baha'is, now rendered formally leaderless, became easy targets, ready to be plucked one by one. Members of the Baha'i national executive committee who sought to evade prosecution were all spotted, apprehended, and killed. Baha'is sought to prevent desecration of graves in their cemeteries, again to no avail. Baha'i cemeteries were, like Baha'i residences, easily earmarked.

Lesser-known Baha'is sought to avoid arrest by going into hiding. Some found refuge with friends of non-Baha'i faiths. Arrests, however, continued. Baha'is could not evade vigilante groups, spies, and Revolutionary Guards. More than 190 Baha'is were arrested following the prosecutor general's orders banning Baha'i worship. By December, 1985, 767 Baha'is were languishing in jail. Approximately 200 Baha'is had been killed since the outbreak of the Islamic revolution. Their plight continued, and Iran remained firmly entrenched in theocracy, committed to a new order, rid of heretics and secularist tendencies.

The human rights record of Iran from October, 1979, to the end of 1984 shows 6,108 accountably dead. One hundred thousand were killed during the Iran-Iraq War, many in their early teens. This sad record is a chilling manifestation of the potential harms stemming from purist normative doctrines.

Bibliography

Amnesty International. _Amnesty International Report._ London: Amnesty International Publications, 1979. This is an invaluable report on human rights violations. It outlines in detail the horrendous impact that the march of Iran from a secular state to a theocracy had on human rights. It is a must for anyone wanting a graphic documentation on the subject. Also see the next five annual reports published by Amnesty International documenting year by year the events that led to religious, political, and protheocratic persecutions.

Keddie, Nikki R. _Iran: Religion, Politics, and Society._ London: Frank Cass, 1980. Keddie has written extensively on Islam. This work is a broad survey on Iran, with ample information for the general reader as well as the informed.

Khomeini, Ruhollah. _Islam and Revolution: Writings and Declarations of Imam Khomeini._ Translated by Hamid Algar. Berkeley, Calif.: Mizan Press, 1981. A useful book worth dipping into to grasp the thoughts and the mind of the man who brought the shah to his knees.

MacKay, Sandra. _The Iranians: Persia, Islam, and the Soul of a Nation._ New York: Dutton, 1996. An informative text that examines Iran's old and new civilizations. Features a chapter on Khomeini and Mohammad Reza Shah.

Moin, Baqer. _Khomeini: Life of the Ayatollah._ New York: I. B. Tauris, 1999. An exploration of Khomeini's rise to power and an analysis of his life. Bibliography and index.

Mustafah Dhada

Pakistan Hangs Former Prime Minister Bhutto

Category of event: Atrocities and war crimes; political freedom
Time: April, 1979
Locale: Rawalpindi, Pakistan

> *Bhutto was executed by the government of General Zia ul-Haq after being found guilty of complicity in a political murder*

Principal personages:

ZULFIKAR ALI BHUTTO (1928-1979), the chief martial law administrator and president of Pakistan (1972-1977)

SHEIKH MUJIBUR RAHMAN (1922-1975), the leader of the Awami League party in East Pakistan and president of Bangladesh (1971-1973)

MOHAMMAD ZIA-UL-HAQ (1924-1988), the chief of the army staff, chief martial law administrator, and president of Pakistan (1977-1988)

AGHA MOHAMMAD YAHYA KHAN (1917-1986), the chief of the army staff, chief martial law administrator, and president of Pakistan (1969-1971)

Summary of Event

The career of Zulfikar Ali Bhutto and the significance of his ultimate fate can be understood and appreciated only within the broader context of Pakistan's political history. The most decisive factor in this history is the country's creation. Pakistan was born on August 14, 1947, when the British ended their two centuries of imperial rule over the Indian subcontinent and transferred governing authority to two countries, India and Pakistan. India inherited a political tradition and a culture that were millenia old. Pakistan, on the other hand, could lay claim to no prior existence as a separate country. It had come into being as the result of a separatist movement based upon the common identity and sense of minority status of the South Asian Muslim community. India, which declared itself to be a secular state, contained a majority Hindu population as well as many other communities, including millions of Muslims. Pakistan, in contrast, was intended to be a homeland for Muslims, which meant that its social and political institutions should be fashioned according to the dictates of Islam.

571

The combination of newly gained independence and the role of Islam created a difficult political environment within which Pakistan tried to develop politically. For nine years, Pakistan attempted to govern itself by means of a legal framework set down by the Government of India Act of 1935. This document had been enacted by the British to meet their imperial needs in governing India. Designing a constitutional framework befitting its distinctive needs and desires was frustrating for Pakistan. Institutions of government together with the rights, duties, and responsibilities of citizens were so intensely controversial that a constitution was not finally agreed to until 1956.

This proved to be an abortive effort, as the combination of Western political traditions and institutions and efforts to establish an Islamic state proved beyond the grasp of Pakistan's political leaders. The results of this experience were chronic political disorder and frequent direct intervention by the military into the political affairs of the country, a practice that has continually frustrated, and indeed inhibited, Pakistan's political development. The constitution of 1956 lasted only two years, and martial law was declared for the first time in 1958. The military regime, after reestablishing civil order, set about crafting a new constitution, one which would not borrow directly from European parliamentary experience under which voters directly chose their representatives. Instead, an indirect approach was chosen in which the political system was divided into layers and the representatives of each layer would choose the personnel of the next higher level.

This arrangement was introduced in the new constitution of 1962. This constitution, carefully crafted to suit the interests of the military and the bureaucracy, set Pakistan on a course of political development fully consistent with Western models of administrative organization but which, at the same time, gave only limited political and social freedoms to the citizenry. The new regime, under General Mohammad Ayub Khan, lasted for more than a decade. During this time, Pakistan became a close friend of and received considerable financial support from the United States. In the late 1960's, however, Ayub's government encountered increasing difficulties generated by the politically frustrated opposition. Those opposed to the government included not only those seeking more democracy and freedom but also advocates of a more vigorous Islamic approach to nation building. Opposition came to a head following the failure of Pakistan's military in its confrontation with India over Kashmir in 1965.

Among those opposing the regime was Zulfikar Ali Bhutto. Bhutto, scion of a wealthy family of landlords in the province of Sindh, came to hold an important place in politics in the late 1950's. During the period of Mohammad Ayub

Zulfikar Ali Bhutto. (Library of Congress)

Khan's rule, Bhutto was foreign minister. He eventually broke with Ayub and formed his own political party, the Pakistan People's Party (PPP).

The government's incapacity to deal with mounting disorder again brought out the army. Martial law was established for the second time, and Ayub was replaced by another general, Agha Mohammad Yahya Khan. Yahya Khan was committed to democratic elections to resolve fundamental constitutional issues, especially the relationship between the East and West wings of the country.

In the election of 1971, there were two major political parties. The Awami League, under the leadership of Sheik Mujibur Rahman, represented East Pakistan. In West Pakistan, although there were several parties, the largest and most powerful was Bhutto's PPP. The Awami League won a decisive majority in the National Assembly, capturing nearly all the seats allocated to the East wing. Bhuttos's PPP managed to gain only a majority of the seats allocated to the West wing.

In the negotiations leading to the meeting of the National Assembly, the Awami League demanded a new constitution that would give East Pakistan the political dominance to which it was entitled by virtue of its larger population. Efforts to control the agenda for determining a new constitution were viewed by Bhutto, and by most West Pakistanis, as tantamount to secession of the East wing. Bhutto refused to attend the meeting of the National Assembly on the grounds that the Awami League was unwilling to compromise. Yahya Khan's attempts to resolve the situation based on negotiations proved fruitless. On March 26, 1971, the army intervened in East Pakistan and civil war resulted. In December, India invaded East Pakistan and brought the conflict to an end. East Pakistan became Bangladesh, Yahya Khan was removed from power, and Bhutto assumed control of the government in a truncated Pakistan.

Bhutto had come to power at the time of Pakistan's most severe national and international crisis. The new government moved quickly to resolve many of the problems facing the country. Bhutto went to Simla and met with Indian leader Indira Gandhi. The negotiations gave a new and cooperative tone to India-Pakistan relations. Bhutto also set about drafting a new constitution that radically altered the direction of Pakistan's politics. This new constitution, introduced in 1973, expanded the political and economic opportunities of ordinary citizens. All educational institutions were nationalized in order to expand opportunities for low-income groups. Labor unions were encouraged and given enhanced legal standing. Restrictions on the press and political organizations were reduced. In taking these actions, Bhutto offended traditional political constituencies, especially Islamic fundamentalists and conservative elements in the military and the bureaucracy. Moreover, the less restrictive atmosphere encouraged opposition to the central government by some provincial groups, especially in Baluchistan.

Having raised expectations, the government found it increasingly difficult to meet public demands. Bhutto was no more successful than his predecessors had been in controlling communal rivalry. Pakistani politics have always been volatile, and street demonstrations are a way of life. Political opposition to the government became increasingly violent among diverse groups who were, for various reasons, frustrated with the government. Whipped up by Bhutto's enemies, especially among religious conservatives, this violence provided an invitation for the military once again to take political control.

The military, humiliated by its defeat by India in 1971, was never friendly toward Bhutto. In 1977, the army stepped in, placed Bhutto under house arrest, and "temporarily" suspended the constitution until order could be restored. Martial law administrator General Mohammad Zia-ul-Haq, who had been appointed by Bhutto and who had a reputation as a desk general and was thus politically safe, promised elections would be held as soon as possible. He declared that the military had no desire to remain in power a day longer than necessary.

One of Bhutto's problems was the accusation that he had been involved in a politically related murder in 1974. This charge provided the opportunity for General Zia to remove Bhutto from the political scene permanently. In December, 1978, Bhutto was convicted. In an effort to add to his political discredit, the government undertook a campaign detailing the misdeeds and oppressive practices of Bhutto's administration. It came as no surprise, since many of its members were Zia loyalists, when the conviction was upheld by Pakistan's Supreme Court in February, 1979. Despite public pleas from national leaders around the world, Zia remained resolute in his determination to end Bhutto's political career. Zia could not free Bhutto because of Bhutto's large and loyal following. Keeping Bhutto in jail for a long period of time was also impractical, as this would make him the symbol of military oppression. Zia concluded that for his own political future, the safest thing to do was to execute Bhutto and weather the storm of protest that would surely follow. Bhutto was hanged in the Rawalpindi jail on April 4, 1979.

Impact of Event

The immediate consequences of Bhutto's execution were public protests and demonstrations. The country was already under martial law, so the government needed little justification for suppressing political rights. Many members of Bhutto's Pakistan People's Party had been arrested before the execution, thus diminishing effective resistance to the government. Nevertheless, political violence continued for some time. The arrest of Bhutto and his subsequent execution, the imposition of martial law, and the suspension of the constitution compromised the political integrity of Pakistan. The arbitrary use of force had once again replaced the rule of law. The justification for this action—the doctrine of necessity—means that whenever the military considers it "necessary" it can nullify any law, including that of the constitution.

By executing Bhutto, General Zia removed the most immediate threat to his political control but created an enduring problem. Bhutto had become a martyr and served as the symbol of resistance to government oppression. It was this very resistance that the government used to justify continuing restrictions on political freedoms. When he first seized power in 1977, Zia had promised to restore constitutional government within a matter of months. He instead planned, even before executing Bhutto, to change the system under which the elections, scheduled for November, were to be conducted. In a gesture to fundamentalists, Muslims and non-Muslims were to vote separately. Zia declared that local elections would be held before the general election and on a nonpartisan basis. In August, he issued an ordinance narrowly restricting the ability of political parties to function. In October, he postponed the elections on the grounds that they would not yield positive results. Restoration of democracy, he said, would come eventually, although it might take years.

In the months to follow, martial law was tightened and civil liberties further restricted. Newspapers published issues with large blank spaces to protest censorship. The government accelerated its efforts to bring every activity and institution in the country into conformity with Islam, a process that raised questions about the social and political status of women. Banks were Islamized, which meant the elimination of interest. Instead, fees were charged for loans and depositors shared in the profits and losses of their bank. The legal system, inherited from the British, was to be reviewed and made consistent with Islamic law. Public entertainment, such as dancing, films, women's sports, Western music, and art, were either significantly proscribed or discouraged.

By the mid-1980's, opposition to Zia's rule was growing. Open resistance came in the form of the Movement for the Restoration of Democracy, established in 1981, but it was unsuccessful in changing the course of action under Zia. In 1988, the situation was dramatically altered when General Zia was killed in a plane crash. Elections were held very soon thereafter, in November. The PPP won a substantial victory and was restored to power. In a dramatic historical twist of fate, the new leader of the government of Pakistan was Bhutto's daughter Benazir. Not only was a Bhutto once again leading the government of Pakistan, but for the first time in the history of Islam, a woman had been elected to lead a predominantly Muslim country.

Bibliography
Burki, Shahid Javed. *Pakistan Under Bhutto.* New York: St. Martin's Press, 1980. This is a detailed study of the political transformation of Pakistan during the Bhutto years and includes material related to the problems that brought about Bhutto's downfall.
Hayes, Louis D. *The Crisis of Education in Pakistan.* Lahore, Pakistan: Vanguard Books, 1987. Several chapters in this book discuss the reforms introduced during the Bhutto period and evaluate their subsequent effects. Special reference to increased educational opportunities for lower-class citizens and for women. Also considered is the dismantling of many of these reforms under the Islamization program of general Zia.
Raza, Rafi. *Zulfikar Ali Bhutto and Pakistan, 1967-1977.* New York: Oxford University Press, 1997. An examination of Bhutto's career.
Sayeed, Khalid Bin. *Politics in Pakistan: The Nature and Direction of Change.* New

York: Praeger Special Studies, 1980. This is a standard work on Pakistan's political history. Coverage includes the rise and fall of Bhutto and the role of Islam in political and constitutional development. Detailed consideration of the military and its involvement in politics.

Talbot, Ian. *Pakistan: A Modern History.* New York: St. Martin's Press, 1998. An analysis of the problems that have besieged this country since 1947. Provides an examination of the political careers of Zia-ul-Haq, Zulfikar Ali Bhutto, and Benazir Bhutto.

Louis D. Hayes

Iranian Revolutionaries Hold Americans Hostage

Category of event: Atrocities and war crimes; prisoners' rights
Time: November 4, 1979-January 20, 1981
Locale: Teheran, Iran

> *The Iranian hostage crisis was the direct result of United States support of a regime whose flagrant violation of human rights precipitated the Iranian revolution*

Principal personages:

JIMMY CARTER (1924-   ), the thirty-ninth president of the United States (1977-1981)

AYATOLLAH RUHOLLAH KHOMEINI (1902-1989), an Islamic religious leader who became the chief political figure in Iran in 1979

MOHAMMAD REZA SHAH PAHLAVI (1919-1980), the shah of Iran from 1941 to 1980

CYRUS VANCE (1917-2002), the U.S. secretary of state (1977-1980)

Summary of Event

The anti-American sentiment that culminated in the seizure of the United States embassy in Teheran in 1977 had its roots in the 1953 overthrow of popular prime minister Mohammad Mosaddeq. Prior to that time, the United States had been praised by many Iranians as a liberating force that had protected them from the British and the Russians. After 1953, though, Iranians of all political persuasions began to condemn the United States as an oppressive exploiter that had allied itself with the imperialistic interests of Great Britain. The United States' support of the governing regime of Iran, which began with the rescue of Mohammad Reza Shah Pahlavi, solidified its reputation as an interventionist power in the eyes of many Iranian citizens. By the 1970's, the anti-American movement had become associated with the antimonarchical movement that had arisen as a response to the shah's oppressive policies.

The year 1977 set the stage for the Iranian revolution and the virtual severance of ties between Iran and the United States. First, the Iranian economy, which had experienced a boom between 1973 and 1975, began to plummet. The tremendous gap in the distribution of income between rural and urban people was aggravated by the fact that the peasants could not compete with imports that were being sold at subsidized prices. Because there was a shortage of skilled laborers, workers were imported from the Philippines, Korea, and the United States. In an effort to control spiraling inflation, the shah set up groups of inspectors who prowled through the bazaars looking for price gougers. Because most of the people who were arrested and exiled were the pillars of the traditional business community, the bazaar, which lay at the heart of the Iranian economy, was alienated. Even after the economy began to level off later in the year, the people were no better off because the corruption that had accompanied the boom in the early 1970's was firmly entrenched in the economic system. It is important to note that many people who had instigated the taking of bribes, the fraudulent land schemes, and the exorbitant commissions on contracts were the shah's family and his close associates.

The event that had the greatest impact on Iranian and American relations in 1977 was the revival of Islam. Throughout that year, young men and women in secondary schools, universities, and religious study centers engaged in dialogue concerning social and political matters. Women even began wearing the long black *chador* as a way of making a political statement. The resurgence of Islam as a powerful political force first became evident on October 9, 1977, when two dozen masked students at Teheran University burned buses and smashed windows to protest the integration of women on campus. During the following weeks, a number of religious demonstrations were held in the holy city of Qum. Iranians appeared to embrace Islam as a refuge from the tyranny of the shah's regime.

The year 1977 was also witness to the shah's "liberalization" program, called *musharikat*, which was developed as a response not only to the growing Islamic movement but also to President Jimmy Carter's human rights policy. On January 20, 1977, President Carter said in his inaugural address, "Our moral sense dictates a clear preference for those societies which share with us an abiding respect for individual human rights." Hoping to win continued military and financial support from the United States, the shah instituted the White Revolution, which was a reform program that focused on land reform and literacy. He also invited Amnesty International, the International Red Cross, and the International Commission of Jurists to investigate the social and political conditions in Iran.

The volatile situation in Iran was made even more so by Cyrus Vance's visit to Teheran in May, 1977, for the purpose of discussing the sale of 160 F-16 aircraft to Iran. After Vance's return, the United States tried to emphasize the progress that the shah had made in human rights, but most Iranians believed that the shah had improved conditions only a little and that he would regress once he had won favor in President Carter's eyes. The shah's critics pointed to the fact that only one political party, the shah's Rastakhiz party, was permitted in Iran. They also exposed the shah's tendency to categorize his opponents as either communists or reactionary clerics. Both types of opponents, the shah's critics claimed, were branded as "suffering from mental imbalance" and thrown into prison, where they were beaten and tortured.

Ironically, the efforts by the shah's police and the military to destroy the opposition in 1978 only served to strengthen it. A secret network of the Ayatollah Ruhollah Khomeini's followers, which had been in place ever since his exile in 1964, escalated its operation by distributing millions of dollars to the impoverished masses who were its constituents. On January 8, 1978, an event occurred that united the fragmented opposition forces. Following a verbal attack on Khomeini in the newspaper *Ittila'at* the day before, clerics and students staged a massive protest march in Qum. The police opened fire, killing two dozen people and wounding many more. Thereafter, antiregime demonstrations became commonplace; at least one was held every month from January, 1978, to February, 1979. At the end of the fourteen-month period, an estimated ten to twelve thousand persons were killed and another forty-five to fifty thousand were injured.

Anti-American sentiment, which had been growing along with the opposition movement, increased dramatically after the Black Friday massacre on September 8, 1978. The shah's soldiers had fired at the crowds in Jalah square, killing and wounding hundreds of unarmed men, women, and children. Two days later, President Carter called the shah and assured him that he still had the support of the United States. This phone call was construed by the Iranian people as an expression of the U.S. president's approval of the Jalah massacre. The Iranians' hostility toward the United States reached its peak when the shah was granted refuge in New York City on October 22, 1979, following the takeover of his country by the Ayatollah Khomeini on February 1.

The new era in Iranian-American relations of distrust and violence that was ushered in after the fall of the shah reached tragic proportions in November. On November 1, 1979, two million angry Iranians demonstrated in Teheran, shouting slogans such as "Death to America." On November 4, 1979, a group of nearly five hundred extremist students stormed the U.S. embassy in Teheran and initially took about ninety hostages, most of whom were embassy workers and about sixty of whom were U.S. citizens. The extremists vowed to hold the hostages until the United States returned the shah to Iran to stand trial.

For the next 444 days, the fifty-two Americans who remained as hostages (some hostages were released early) were subjected to the same sort of inhu-

Iranians demonstrating against the United States in front of the U.S. embassy in Te-heran shortly after the beginning of the hostage crisis. (Library of Congress)

mane treatment that the shah had been accused of by the revolutionaries. After being held in the embassy for twenty days, the hostages were bound, blindfolded, covered with blankets, and taken to a series of makeshift prisons. During a series of seemingly endless interrogations, they were beaten and humiliated by their captors. Except for a rare "feast" of hamburgers and sodas, their meals consisted of bread and tea in the morning, cold rice at lunch, and cold soup at night. The only exercise that they were permitted was an hour of running in place in the morning. After three months, the hostages were placed in small cells; during their incarceration, they were not permitted to communicate. Hostages who violated the rules were locked in cold, dark cubicles for as long as three days. Toward the end of their confinement, they were forced to stand before a mock firing squad. When the hostages were finally released on January 20, 1981, their emaciated and hollow-eyed appearance provided mute testimony to the suffering that they had endured during their brutal ordeal.

Impact of Event

The taking of hostages from the U.S. embassy in Teheran immediately received worldwide attention. Most of the nations of the world joined the

United States in condemning the actions of the Iranian revolutionaries. In 1983, a United Nations treaty took effect that called for ratifying nations to prosecute the hostage takers or to return them to their countries for trial. On the other hand, the success with which the Iranians used hostages to render a superpower impotent inspired terrorists in other nations, especially in the Middle East, to do the same. The unprecedented media coverage that the hostage crisis received also opened up a country that had previously been shrouded in mystery. Both during and after the hostage crisis, the United States and many other nations made a serious effort to understand the Iranian position.

From the point of view of the revolutionary factions in Iran, the seizure of the U.S. embassy in Teheran was fortuitous because it helped to radicalize politics in Iran. Once the embassy was taken, the militants set about the task of piecing together shredded State Department documents they found, with the intention of proving their contention that the American embassy was a "nest of spies." The documents that the militants recovered supported their claim that the United States and the Soviet Union had joined forces to back the shah and oppose the revolution. As a result, the extremist factions had the proof that they needed to gain ascendancy over the moderates. By taking retribution against a superpower that had been perceived for years as an external threat, the extremists rallied the masses behind their cause. Most important, though, the taking of hostages effectively thwarted any attempt that the United States may have been considering to reverse the revolution.

From the vantage point of the United States, the hostage crisis had dire political consequences. The inability of the Carter administration fully to appreciate the strength of the Islamic revival in Iran did irreparable harm to Carter's presidency. Further damage was done when a rescue mission had to be aborted in April, 1980. The failure of the operation known as Eagle Claw angered military and civilian leaders in the United States. The economic sanctions that President Carter set in place against Iran served only to increase the determination of the hostage takers. President Carter's unflagging support of the shah and his inability to resolve the hostage crisis probably contributed to Ronald Reagan's landslide presidential victory in 1980.

The effects of the hostage crisis in Iran extended far beyond the Carter administration. The hard feelings that were created by the episode went a long way toward shaping U.S. foreign policy in the Middle East. During the Iran-Iraq War, for example, the United States was unofficially on Iraq's side and even engaged in sporadic firefights with Iran in 1988. During the 1987 Iran-Contra hearings, officials of the National Security Commission stated that it was the embarrassment from the ill-fated rescue operation in 1980 that provided the incentive for the exchange of arms for hostages. The hostage crisis left behind a legacy of resentment that crippled Iranian-American relations for years.

Bibliography

Bill, James A. *The Shah, the Ayatollah, and the United States.* New York: Foreign Policy Association, 1988. This text is the most complete account now available of the events that led up to the taking of the American hostages in Teheran. A major drawback is the omission of any facts regarding the treatment of the hostages during their 444-day ordeal.

Daugherty, William J. *In the Shadow of the Ayatollah: A CIA Hostage in Iran.* Annapolis, Md.: Naval Institute Press, 2001. Written by a CIA agent who was taken hostage during the crisis, this book provides an examination of U.S.-Iranian relations during the Cold War and a detailed report of his confinement.

Houghton, David Patrick. *US Foreign Policy and the Iran Hostage Crisis.* New York: Cambridge University Press, 2001. Presents an analysis of the events, using information obtained from interviews with key personal from both sides of the crisis.

Jordan, Hamilton. *Crisis.* New York: G. P. Putnam's Sons, 1982. This story of the last year of Jimmy Carter's presidency draws from official documents and interviews to illustrate Jordan's role in relocating the shah to Panama and his secret negotiations with the Khomeini government during the hostage crisis. The book benefits greatly from Jordan's firsthand involvement in the secret negotiations.

Kennedy, Moorhead. *The Ayatollah in the Cathedral: Reflections of a Hostage.* New York: Hill & Wang, 1986. The author, the most widely known of the hostages, attacks not only the sadistic cruelty of the Iranian captors but also the arrogance of the U.S. government in Washington and in its embassies.

Kreisberg, Paul H., ed. *American Hostages in Iran: The Conduct of a Crisis.* New Haven, Conn.: Yale University Press, 1985. This insightful book tells the story of the delicate negotiations in the words of the key Americans, both inside and outside of government, who were intimately involved in the process of freeing the hostages.

Salinger, Pierre. *America Held Hostage: The Secret Negotiations.* Garden City, N.Y.: Doubleday, 1981. Although the book lacks the authority of Jordan's first-person narrative, it is more objective in its reporting of the delicate diplomatic procedures that resulted in the release of the hostages. Salinger was a news correspondent reporting on the hostage crisis.

Alan Brown

United Nations Convention Condemns Discrimination Against Women

Category of event: International norms; women's rights
Time: December 18, 1979
Locale: United Nations, New York City

> *The adoption of the U.N. resolution to eliminate all forms of discrimination against women served notice that the United Nations system had formally incorporated the principles of women's rights and gender equality*

Principal personages:

ESMERALDA ARBOLEDA CUEVAS, the special rapporteur of the United Nations Commission on the Status of Women

JOHANNA DOHNAL, the secretary of state of Austria, instrumental in changing attitudes toward the role of women in the United Nations decision-making process

DEVAKI JAIN (1933-), the Indian representative to the United Nations and initiator and first convener of the Development Alternatives for Women for a New Era

HERTTA KUUSINEN (1904-1974), a Finnish parliamentarian and official of the United Nations Commission on the Status of Women

LUCILLE MAIR (1935-), a Jamaican deputy permanent representative to the United Nations

INGRID PALMER (1938-), the chief researcher in the United Nations Department of International and Social Affairs, whose study helped to bring about the United Nations Decade for Women

HELVI SIPILA (1915-), a Finnish lawyer and a key figure in organizing the convention

Summary of Event

For most of history women have shared the experience of inequality. The cause given for this revolves, for the most part, around the concept of the division of labor necessitated by the childbearing function of women. Division of labor caused societies to evolve with separate spheres for men and women, with women mostly relegated to performing domestic chores. This soon gave rise to a cult of domesticity. relegating women to roles of peripheral importance in all but domestic matters. Over time, such roles were institutionalized through a more formal division of labor, forcing women to be treated unequally in any role they pursued outside the home. They were given limited access to resources, which subsequently affected their involvement in daily life. Women were often left out of society's political and economic decision-making processes, leaving women relegated to supportive tasks, as the positions of lesser value were transferred to the less powerful.

In an attempt to confront this evolving inequality of gender, the United Nations in 1979 drafted the Convention on the Elimination of All Forms of Discrimination Against Women. In addition to addressing female inequality in world affairs, the convention focused on byproducts of gender inequality such as poverty, underdevelopment, and educational backwardness. The convention called upon all U.N. member states to contribute to the cause of female rights by incorporating the principles of women's rights and equality between the sexes into the provisions of international law. The convention also provided for follow-up means to measure the progress and results of the resolution, obliging member states to present to the United Nations Commission on the Status of Women every five years a detailed report on major socioeconomic policies and programs initiated for the elimination of discrimination against women.

In other sections, the convention noted that women were not simply discriminated against in political and economic life; the rights to nationality, education, employment, and health were imperiled, and women were often subject to reproductive discrimination as well. Although women's childbearing and nurturing functions were respected in many countries, this very respect often resulted in the removal of women from potential economic contributions. The convention maintained that this was incompatible with human dignity and the welfare of all society and constituted an obstacle to the achievement of women's full potential.

The convention itself was the result of five years of political negotiations and maneuverings by various U.N. groups such as the Economic and Social Council and the General Assembly's Social, Humanitarian, and Cultural Committee. The resolution that was finally adopted reflected its origins in a broad-based coalition of previously single-issue-oriented groups addressing parochial agendas.

One such agenda was aimed at addressing the rights of rural women around the globe. Because of the successful formation of this political coalition, the inequality of rural women was confronted from a more politically powerful unified base. Subsequently, the plight of rural women was recognized. The resolution's preamble emphasized that, because of the interference in the domestic affairs of states by foreign occupation and domination of indigenous economies, rural women had been even more severely discriminated against than their urban counterparts. Directly addressing this concern, article 14 of the resolution called for member states to recognize this and ensure that rural women received access to adequate health-care facilities, counseling, and family-planning education. To secure the full enjoyment of the rights of all men and women, the article further stated that women should have equal access to agricultural loans and technology, equal sharing of land reforms, and equal opportunities for agricultural training and education.

In article 9 of the resolution, particular emphasis was placed on the idea that neither marriage to an alien nor change of nationality by husbands during marriage should automatically change the nationality of wives. The adopted resolution stressed that such policies in essence render wives stateless by tying a women's nationality to that of her husband. Expanding upon this topic, the resolution also declared that member states should grant women equal rights with men with respect to the nationality of their children.

Calling on member states to ensure the prevention of discrimination against women, articles 10 and 11 of the resolution emphasized educational and employment measures. Women must be assured access to the same educational conditions (curricula, examinations, teaching staff, equipment, and methodology) as men. In the area of employment, the resolution called for equal employment opportunities, including application of the same criteria and employment standards to both genders, the right of free selection of career opportunities, the right to equal advancement and all other benefits, the awarding of equal training programs and remuneration, and the adoption of effective right-to-work initiatives. Furthermore, member states were urged to take steps to prevent dismissals or the imposition of sanctions against pregnant workers and to initiate maternity leaves-of-absence without any loss of previous position and salary.

Article 12 of the resolution called upon member states to effect for women the same rights enjoyed by men in the area of family benefits, the right to bank loans and other forms of financial credit, and the right to participate in sports and other recreational activities on an equal basis with men. Family concerns were pursued further in article 16, which encouraged all member states to provide legal guarantees for egalitarian measures to eliminate all forms of discrimination in all matters of marriage and family relations.

Under article 17, the convention set up a committee to evaluate the progress toward its goals. This committee, known as the Committee on the Elimination of Discrimination Against Women, consisted of eighteen members responsible for overseeing the resolution's implementation.

The resolution was passed by a vote of 130 in favor to none against, with 10 abstentions. Explanation for the voting was varied; many of those abstaining claimed that traditional laws of their nations were at odds with certain provisions of the resolution, while the United Kingdom, for example, voted for the resolution but voiced a concern that its immigration laws might be at odds with articles 15 and 16.

Impact of Event

The convention rekindled an interest in women's rights, accomplishments, and identity. Traditional views of feminine and masculine roles in society were called into question as the convention initiated measures to be taken by various states to eliminate discrimination against women. Principal topics emerging from the convention included women's development of an independent identity, women's interdependence with other women, and women as participants in society. Acting on the convention's recommendations, the United Nations invited the world to recognize that women must have a more active role in the policy-making decisions of their governments. To ensure international participation in this regard, the United Nations called for a resolution establishing a formal decade for women. On December 17, 1979, acting on the recommendation of the Social, Humanitarian, and Cultural Committee, the General Assembly adopted eight resolutions relating to a U.N. supported initiative to describe the varying principles establishing women's place in the world community, understanding their links to social problems, and exploring these problems and their consequences. The United Nations also formally adopted the "Decade for Women," which called upon member states to ensure women's access to the world's economic and political decision-making processes and to establish a formal equality between men and women. The United Nations had officially prescribed for the world a plan to address the female concerns of humanity.

Programs were formally established to improve the status, nutrition, health, and education of women. The goal of the Decade for Women was to view women as equals in the developmental process, a goal which included recognizing women for their contribution to the family, to themselves, to their work, to their institutional constraints, and to their own liberation movement.

Although the means at the disposal of the United Nations to enforce the implementation of such a program remained limited, the process establishing the program was nevertheless potentially beneficial to the understanding of women's significance. The Committee on the Elimination of All Forms of

Discrimination Against Women played a key role in the process. Thanks to the convention, international pressure could be put on governments to rectify gender injustices and inequalities. The convention encouraged national governments to involve women in their political and economic decision-making processes, to provide periodic reviews of policies on gender inequality, and to integrate women into strategies for national development.

Bibliography

Kemp, Tom. *Industrialization in the Non-Western World*. London: Longman, 1990. Focuses on industrial growth in Japan, the Soviet Union, India, China, Brazil, and Nigeria, examining the range of political experience, the role of women, and the ideological outlook of each country. Bibliography and index.

Larsson-Bergson, Maria. *Women and Technology in the Industrialized Countries*. New York: UNITAR, 1979. Analyzes the problems created for women through technological development in the industrialized countries. Specifically addresses the issue of the consequences of technological development coming into the hands of men.

Lynn, Naomi, ed. *United Nations Decade for Women World Conference*. New York: Haworth Press, 1984. A compilation of articles reflecting the diversity that results from the different levels of socioeconomic and political development of nations and how that diversity influences the role of women. Bibliography and index.

Pietila, Hilkka, and Jeanne Vickers. *Making Women Matter: The Role of the United Nations*. London: Zed Books, 1990. Highlights the achievements of the United Nations system with regard to the advancement of women's issues. Bibliography and index.

Rodda, Annabel. *Women and the Environment*. London: Zed Books, 1991. Shows how women are affected by environmental health problems caused by industrial development, by migration from rural to urban areas, and by other problems that arise from deterioration in the social, economic, and natural environment. Bibliography and index.

United Nations. *Report of the World Conference of the United Nations Decade for Women: Equality, Development and Peace*. New York: United Nations Press, 1980. A review of the United Nations' mandates for programs designed for the enhancement of the recognition of women's rights in the world.

Winslow, Anne, ed. *Women, Politics, and the United Nations*. Westport, Conn.: Greenwood, 1995. This text addresses the role of the United Nations in eliminating all forms of discrimination against women.

Thomas Jay Edward Walker